Marfa, Marfa

Marfa, Marfa

Rasquachismo and Minimalism in Far West Texas

Josh T Franco

DUKE UNIVERSITY PRESS
Durham and London 2026

Printed in the United States of America on acid-free paper ∞
Project Editor: Lisa Lawley
Designed by Dave Rainey
Typeset in Adobe Jenson Pro by Copperline Book Services

Library of Congress Cataloging-in-Publication Data
Names: Franco, Josh T. author
Title: Marfa, Marfa : rasquachismo and minimalism in far West Texas / Josh T Franco.
Other titles: Rasquachismo and minimalism in far West Texas
Description: Durham : Duke University Press, 2026. | Includes bibliographical references and index.
Identifiers: LCCN 2026003892 (print)
LCCN 2026003893 (ebook)
ISBN 9781478039211 paperback
ISBN 9781478034179 hardcover
ISBN 9781478062745 ebook
Subjects: LCSH: Judd, Donald, 1928–1994—Criticism and interpretation | Art—Texas—Marfa | Mexican American art—Texas—Marfa | Minimal art—Texas—Marfa | Minimal art | Decolonization in art | Biculturalism—Texas—Marfa | Marfa (Tex.)
Classification: LCC N6535.M38 F73 2026 (print) |
LCC N6535.M38 (ebook) | DDC 709.764—dc23/eng/20260603
LC record available at https://lccn.loc.gov/2026003892
LC ebook record available at https://lccn.loc.gov/2026003893

Cover art: Josh T Franco, *Watercolor Study (Donald Judd, 15 untitled works in concrete, 1980–84)*, 2021. Courtesy of the artist.

TERRA
FOUNDATION FOR AMERICAN ART

CAA
Advancing Art&Design

This publication has been made possible through support from the Terra Foundation for American Art International Publication Program of CAA.

Dedicated to West Texans

. . . all of us.

Contents

Illustrations

Invocation

The following words are intended to be spoken. They were prompted by an invitation to The Ends of American Art Conference hosted by the Terra Foundation for American Art and the Art History Department at Stanford University in November 2014.

One senior art historian—not a conference participant—has since identified my performance as prosopopoeia. I hear him, *con respeto*, while I disagree. Prosopopoeia names the ancient Greek concept of speaking as an object, a *thing*. Here, the thing is not the central action, not the locus from which the voice emanates. For communicability among materialists and art historians (all people who need and love our things), I do offer the being of a plaster construction crafted in an attitude of utter devotion by a man and continuously sweated over by a family and pilgrims. But this is not the thing speaking. It is the transcribed voice of a goddess of the Americas. Not prosopopoeia, but inhabitation, presence, blessing. It is appropriate to light a candle (preferably red) before reading aloud and to blow out the candle following the last word.

⋆

Yo soy Guadalupe.
I am Guadalupe.

In one legend of my birth—my transformation five hundred years ago into a goddess of the Americas—I spoke to a bishop through Juan Diego, a dark-skinned poor man.[1]

Here I also speak in partnership with a brown-skinned boy, un hijo mio.

But we do not address a bishop today. Today, we speak to guardians of faith in something else, something called art. Their faith is in crisis.

From where I live in this plaster form, sheltered by this altered bathtub—this altar-ed bathtub—mounted on rocks, I have come to know something of the art you guard.[2] *(This speaking boy loves it too.)*

How did I come to know?

Porque yo soy La Guadalupe de Marfa, Tejas.
I am the Guadalupe of Marfa, Texas.

I first heard this place in the prayers of la familia Sanchez, appearing first to the father, Hector.[3] *(Why am I always revealing myself to men?) The Sanchez family lives in this house. They take care of me.*

This boy who speaks has a grandfather. The grandfather was himself a boy in this yard. I called this speaking boy back to this dirt-grass patch of ancestral land. I called him because I want to know more about this vecino, my neighbor.

First: What is his name? The boy gives two syllables:
"Don" y "Judd."
I cannot believe that is all.

My own name goes on forever in comparison: Coatlicue–Cihuacoatl–Tlazolteotl–Tonantzin–Coatlalopeuh–Morena–Guadalupe . . .

"But he's not exactly your neighbor," says the boy. "He died. About three years before you showed up here. But those are his things you look at all day. And all the people coming in and out of those gates are here because of him."

"Oh," I sound. I know what it's like to have pilgrims. Mine come less often now. I was more popular when I was new in town and living as a flicker in the trunk of this tree here. I was in the newspaper and everything.

El Vecino Judd's pilgrims come every day. I watch them walk around his things. Those blocks are so tall. It must hurt their necks to look up. Some pilgrims fit inside them standing. The blocks are made of concrete, so similar to what makes me in this form.

I watch the blocks change from almost white to dark gray every day. Sometimes red, when the sun is red, but then everything is red, even the yellow grass.

The blocks sit so still. They make shadows that split the light around them sharply.
Every edge a sundial.

At night they are lit by the moon. The sky is clear most nights in this desert. The boy tells me El Vecino Judd loved natural light. He would never flip a switch if he didn't have to. Did he know that the natural light at night comes from my daughter Coyolxuaqui? I don't look upward so much (the prayers at my feet keep me busy), but I know she's there because of her light.

People leave my neighbor's place with all kinds of faces. Some are so happy! Like they've never seen such things with their eyes, but they already had in their hearts. Plenty leave angry, muttering under their breath, "That is not art . . ." They all leave different than when they entered.

I wonder if people think I am art? People are led to me by their spirit, not necessarily their eyes (though much effort was given to make me beautiful, and for that I thank the Sanchez family). The boy read me a passage once, some words of El Vecino Judd's, all about things like the blocks and the spirit world. I remember a little bit:

"All forms are spiritual . . . Art must . . . be general, but at the same time out of the ordinary."[4]

I don't think I am very ordinary, so does that mean I must be art? But perhaps I am not "general" enough. Maybe you can tell me, guardians. I am curious, if not terribly concerned. Let's let some nights pass. I am here for a while, cemented and sunbaked in place.

I notice something: The other pilgrims leave no ofrendas! No talismans for mi vecino. No food. No little tin drawings. Not even a little pile of rocks. They do take. They take pictures.

Are they pilgrims if they leave nothing? Ofrendas remind me what people pray for: the little girl leaves a flower for her lost cat; the old man a cigarette's worth of tobacco for a job. What kind of blessings do El Vecino Judd's pilgrims ask?

But I guess he's not there to receive prayers. The boy says he didn't really believe like that, he thinks not anyway. But who really knows? Mi vecino's body resides in a simple pine box farther out in the desert. Like the furniture in his casitas, the pine box was made by those who knew him well. Putting things together like this—with materials from nearby and all by hand and learning as you go . . . El Vecino Judd's daughter calls it "DIY." I call it "rasquache." Rasquachismo built my own little bathtub-house.

So my neighbor is gone, and we will never meet. In town are just his things. Not "just" . . . they are interesting things. They give me a lot to think about every day.

Introduction

Rasquachismo, Minimalism

In many respects, the rasquache defiance of Chicano art production has served as an anecdotal history for a community repudiated and denied in institutional history within the nation as a whole.

—Amalia Mesa-Bains, "Domesticana"

In the context of Minimalism and Modern art, rasquachismo is more than an oppositional form; it is a militant praxis of resistance to hegemonic standards in the art world.

—Alicia Gaspar de Alba, *Chicano Art Inside/Outside the Master's House*

Minimalist sculpture is a badgering, unavoidable presence, waiting to be acknowledged.

—Pamela M. Lee, *Chronophobia*

Why Minimalism and rasquachismo should be considered side-by-side, or "cara a cara," is a driving question of this book.[1] This question is answered by citing and site-ing the town of Marfa, Texas. Responding to this question also results in queering art-historical practice. It does so not by identifying queer iconographies or hidden queer histories—though such uncovering is welcome—but by disrupting "the very means of locating stable meaning, let alone identity, at any given work's root."[2] In Marfa, what is an object of pilgrimage to some is invisible to others; what is art to a few is an alien form to audiences who never sought it; what looks like mere survival from the outside expresses a communal and creative sensibility for those who practice it; and what is high Minimalism to some is DIY to still others. Of course, time shifts and blurs all first impressions. By the end of this book, I hope the reader's vision is blurred, "rasquachified," so that they can perceive fuller, more complex pictures of the town "pulled through" studies of the artworks in question.[3]

GETTING TO MARFA

My own history with Marfa begins before I was born. In the 1940s and 1950s my grandfather, Hipolito "Polé" Hernandez, and his immediate family were farmworkers. Marfa was home base between seasonal migrations west as cotton- and fruit-picking seasons dictated. As a young adult, Hernandez moved to nearby Odessa, Texas, where he worked for thirty-five years as a forklift operator at General Tire & Rubber Co. All four of my grandparents moved from smaller towns in the area to Odessa, where they raised their children. My own childhood in Odessa was punctuated with trips to Fort Stockton, Alpine, and Marfa to visit family who still resided in those towns. During these many excursions in my first twenty or so years of life, I became familiar with Marfa as a somewhat boring, nostalgic, almost silent place.[4] I was sometimes engaged, sometimes irritated as my Caló ears struggled to converse with exclusively Spanish-speaking relatives. We ate excellent homemade Mexican food. My parents, aunts, uncles, cousins, and grandparents sat around discussing a great-grandmother and other long-ago relatives whom I would never know. (I was made keenly aware on which side of the border each was born.) Some of these relatives are buried in Marfa's cemeteries. One of my cousins married into a ranching family for whom Marfa provides the nearest civic services and social life. As older connections between our family and Marfa pass on, new ones form.

For those not familiar with Marfa, none of this is remarkable. The initiated, those who have made this journey, are likely awaiting my acknowledgment of the town's behemoths: Donald Judd, Minimalism, and contemporary art. The delay echoes my experience. Often written up in publications like *Vanity Fair*, *W Magazine*, and *New York Times Travel*, Marfa is popularly perceived as an outpost of Manhattan in Far West Texas.[5] It is a node in a global network of post-1945 art destinations that has achieved pilgrimage status. Pilgrims are initially drawn by the significant collections of Minimalist works at the Judd Foundation and the Chinati Foundation/La Fundación Chinati (hereafter referred to as Chinati). Judd moved to Marfa around 1972, and subsequent years have witnessed a significant increase in tourism and relocation there by other artists.[6] According to then–Associate Director Rob Weiner,

Chinati alone received more than ten thousand visitors between 2011 and 2012, more than quadruple the number of residents who call Marfa home.[7] If "during the sixties, the relationship of the avant-garde and commerce was as reciprocal and sustaining as it had ever been," this commerce now includes auspicious travel (and generating documentation in the form of social media) to such anointed destinations as Marfa.[8]

While my route to Marfa typically involves driving south and slightly west from Odessa in a car with parents, siblings, and often cousins, aunts, uncles, and grandparents as well, people drawn by Judd and contemporary art most often drive into town from the opposite direction. They fly into El Paso, where they rent a car. Those with friends in town might be fortunate enough to have someone pick them up at the airport. In either case, they depart the airport and drive east, leaving behind the mountains that surround El Paso for a flatter desert landscape that becomes slightly mountainous again three hours later as they near Marfa. Passing Elmgreen & Dragset's *Prada Marfa* (discussed in chapter 2) on their right signals that they will arrive in Marfa within the next half hour. When they encounter the first intersection with traffic lights, their host might inform them that this is in fact the only traffic light. From this intersection, the heart of town, they'll note the picturesque Presidio County Courthouse to their left and US Route 67 unfurling into the southern horizon to their right.

Marfa's population oscillates from census to census around the two thousand mark. A drive from one end of town to the other takes a matter of minutes. Everything is "close," physically, but a geography of social consciousness pictures different experiences of proximity and distance in Marfa. My grandfather's childhood home shares a small traffic circle with three landmarks: Marfa's public housing complex, a US Border Patrol headquarters, and the first entrance to Judd's public collection, Chinati. Yet I grew up completely unaware of Judd's presence. It was an unacknowledged layer, a tourist and art world concern, or so I might have conceived it if I had even realized that many of the white people, los gringos, we encountered were tourists and art folk. Marfa did not mean Minimalism for me until I undertook an art history major in college. Marfa, for my family, was never avant-garde. It was and is rasquache through and through (though I would also not learn of this word until much later, undertaking my own process of "Chicanization").[9] Thus, Minimalism and rasquachismo constitute the dual site, the palimpsest, from which I begin.

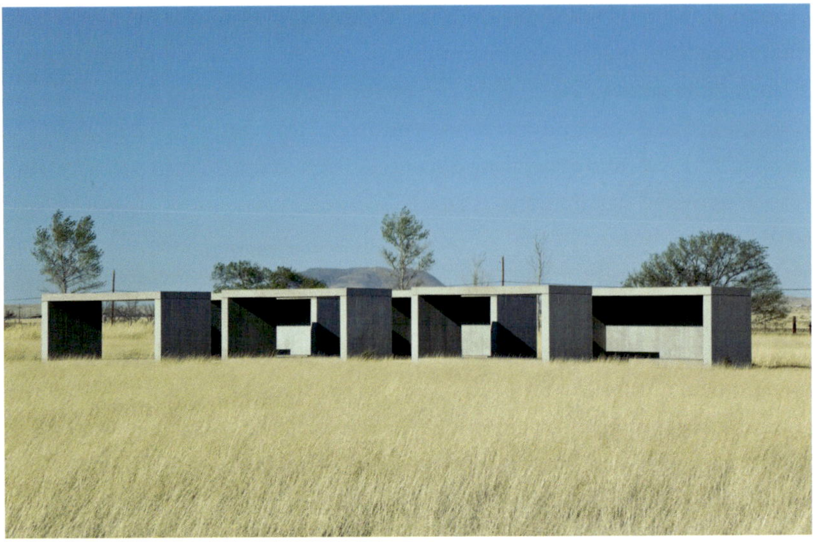

FIGURE I.1 Detail of Donald Judd's *15 untitled works in concrete*, 1980–84, one of fifteen groupings arranged in a line over approximately one mile. Photo: Florian Holzherr and Douglas Tuck. Donald Judd Art © 2025 Judd Foundation/Artists Rights Society (ARS), New York.

In this book, I sketch some of Marfa's histories and the encounters they make possible today in order to articulate the spatializations and aestheticizations that produce the town socially, both on the actual streets of Marfa and in the social realms in which it is inscribed elsewhere. As an art historian, I begin from analyses of artworks and arts-based institutions' roles in producing the town. However, other key institutions are addressed, including the US military, the US Border Patrol, the railroad and ranching industries, and the Catholic Church.

I do not have only theoretical "sites" in mind. My thinking began from direct observation of sculptural proximity. Judd's *15 untitled works in concrete* (1980–84) are situated outdoors less than a third of a mile from an altar in the backyard of my grandfather's childhood home (figures I.1 and I.2). The altar was built by Hector Sanchez, whose family still resides in the house. It comprises a hand-painted statue of the Virgin of Guadalupe, a stone-encrusted, upturned bathtub housing her, and a shallow, cemented grotto at her feet.[10] Sanchez constructed the shrine to honor an apparition of Guadalupe that ap-

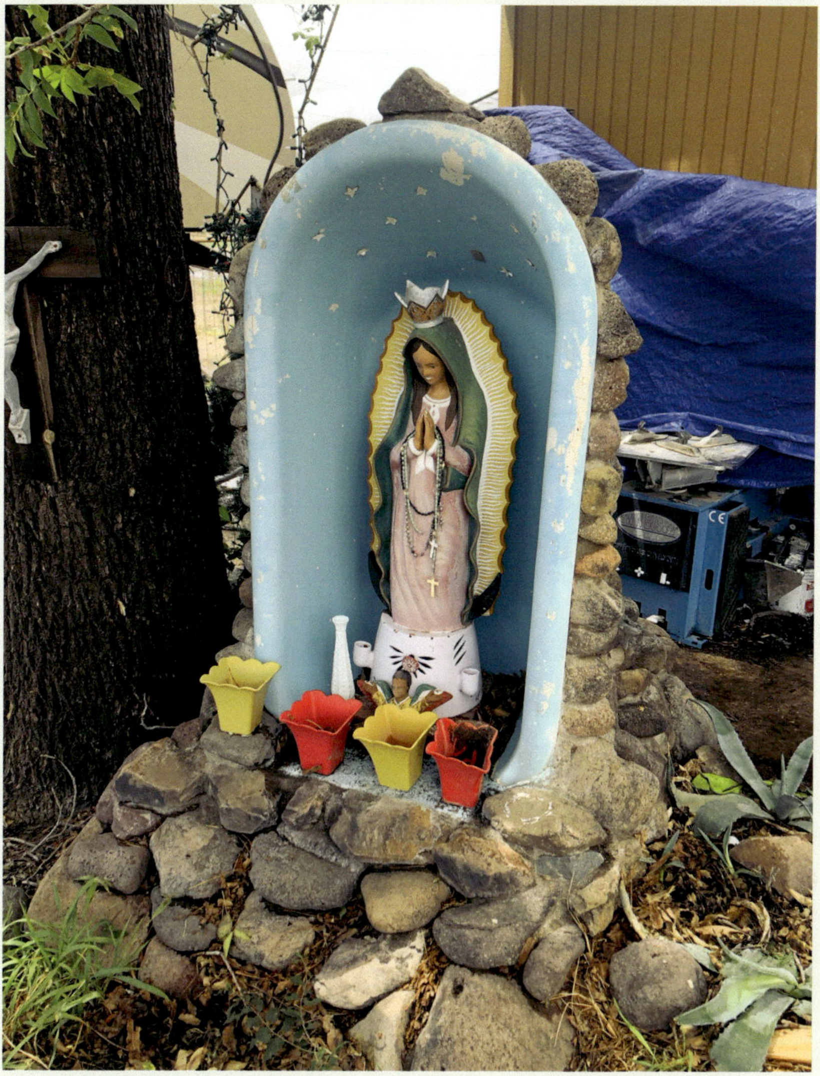

FIGURE I.2 Hector Sanchez, altar for the Virgin of Guadalupe, Marfa, Texas, 1997.

peared to him and a companion in the fall of 1997.[11] She appeared nocturnally as a white, slowly moving figure embedded in the trunk of the tree that now presides over her less ephemeral sculptural form. Were it not for her downcast eyes and the wall around Chinati (evidence of its former purpose as a US military base), Judd's untitled works in concrete would be directly in her sight. They remain locked in this configuration today.

While at the outset of this work the analytic coupling of Minimalism and rasquachismo seemed a novelty relevant to Marfa alone, other historical moments and contemporary sites continue to reveal themselves as already having addressed the same or similar concerns, if only obliquely in some instances.[12] Together, they are a slowly revealing constellation that shifts the established bearings by which Minimalist art and work called Chicanx art are navigated. A recent additional complication in nomenclature is the spreading use of the *x* in *Chicanx* and *Latinx*. I use *Chicanx* in this book for both its welcomed disruption of gender legibility and its graphic cleanness relative to the alternative, *Chicana/o*. Readers may consider the *x* an expanded container that includes the *o* and the *a* rather than outright rejecting them, especially in instances where the word is used to refer to art in historical contexts where it was not an option at the time. This allows me to deploy the *x* asynchronously, but not ahistorically. *Chicana* and *Chicano* do remain in direct quotations; proper names of institutions, movements, publications, and so on; and where the preference of a described individual is known. Finally, the *x* forces reflection on the linguistic border zone in which many Latinxs in the United States live; if read in Spanish, one would pronounce *x* as "ch," and in English it is inherently awkward. Welcome to the experience of living between languages, a feature shared by much Chicanx artistic production discussed here. There is no easy resolution.

But there is little Chicanx art in Marfa. That is, one does not think of Marfa's galleries and institutions when one thinks of the typical locales where such work incubates: Los Angeles, San Antonio, Albuquerque, Santa Fe, San Francisco, San Diego, and so on.[13] Chicanx artists have occasionally exhibited work in Marfa, and one of these uncharacteristic and particularly auspicious instances is addressed in chapter 3.[14] *Art* here signals the production of works sponsored, collected, or otherwise sanctioned by curatorial intention and located in self-identified galleries, arts residencies, or museums. Few artists who identify as Chicanx maintain studios in Marfa, and none of the institutions there explicitly serve Chicanx or Latinx aesthetic concerns.[15] So the question must be asked again, slightly reworked: If there is (almost) no Chicanx art in Marfa, how does it demonstrate the need for thinking about the histories of Minimalism and Chicanx art together?

While decreasing, the majority of Marfa's population remains identified as "Hispanic," presumably most of whom are Chicanx, Mexican Americans, or Mexican immigrants (50.8 percent).[16] Many Marfa residents, including my own relatives, speak norteño Spanish or a Tejano mix of Spanish and English at home. It is this population's production of objects for public display, domestic observations, Spanish-English Caló, and various daily habits that lay the grounds on which I make my argument for Marfa's key position as a site for considering Minimalism and Chicanx art alongside one another. This heterogeneous "compendium of all the movidas [roughly, 'tactics'] deployed in immediate, day-to-day living" was first formally brought under the rubric of "rasquachismo" by Tomás Ybarra-Frausto.[17] In these everyday practices, he locates the origin of formal and conceptual characteristics that would later be recontextualized as components of Chicanx art upon the latter's entry into academia, museums, and galleries.

Ybarra-Frausto was not the first to deploy rasquachismo, but he was the first to theorize it on paper for an art world readership.[18] He calls it "one form of a Chicano vernacular, the verbal-visual code we use to speak to each other among ourselves."[19] Beginning with literature in the 1920s such as Daniel Venegas's novel *Las aventuras de Don Chipote, o, cuando los pericos mamen* (1928), Ybarra-Frausto shows us the working-class, immigrant roots of rasquachismo. What readers take away from his description is that a rasquache attitude confronts the everyday with more than is needed to survive it. This is done through an innovative approach to the materials provided by circumstance, "tenacity and adaptability," and a certain valued locura, madness.

In the 1930s and 1940s carpas (tent shows) and tandas de variedad (vaudeville shows) traveled across the Southwest United States, further spreading a rasquache aesthetic. Rasquachismo here was deployed by the peladitas and peladitos. According to Ybarra-Frausto, for these characters—the Chicanx "everyman" and "everywoman" of their time—rasquachismo was a way to reconceive the everyday, presented first as a struggle for survival, then as a site of vitality and sustenance. On the ground, this reconception takes the form of movidas, which are "the coping strategies you use to gain time, to make options, to retain hope."[20] When did the relationship begin between these lived quotidian movidas and what gets sanctioned, institutionalized, as art?

In the 1960s and 1970s, as Chicanxs turned "inward to explore, decipher, and interpret elements from the Chicano cultural matrix, artists and intellectuals found strength and recovered meaning in the layers of everyday practices."[21] Artists, including myself, continue turning inward in the extant, in flux "cultural matrix" of Chicanismo. In a note, Ybarra-Frausto identifies some artists by name, providing examples of rasquachismo that inspired his foundational essay. David Ávalos's *Hubcap Milagro #3* is included in the list.[22]

Ávalos's wall-mounted mixed-media work comprises an amputated trunk of a gutted male figure, a hubcap, two flanking shot glasses serving as votive candleholders containing upright, erect lipsticks, and a stainless-steel rotary saw blade positioned as the figure's halo (figure I.3). Beneath the void left by the eviscerated core, sculptural testicles adorned with a carved, flaccid penis in low relief protrude between muscular thighs. A heart is carved into his torso, pierced by crude nails. Ávalos's piece strikes me as an allegory of the project of this book. Imagine a figure: She is educated in the United States as an art historian in the early twenty-first century, familiar with the canonical works of the previous century and armed with knowledge of historical precedents and formal vocabulary to aptly analyze unfamiliar works of the present. Were this scholar to come across *Hubcap Milagro #3* without title or curatorial context, she might easily locate it within the histories of avant-garde assemblage, kitsch, and queer art. Jasper Johns and Joseph Cornell might be immediate references for the combinatory forms. The upright lipstick would hearken in her mind to Claes Oldenburg's 1969 *Lipstick (Ascending) on Caterpillar Tracks*.

Nothing is necessarily wrongheaded about our fictional art historian's interpretation. For one, records show that Ávalos was impressed by Oldenburg well before he created *Hubcap Milagro #3*.[23] It is quite possible he was aware of Oldenburg's much publicized installation at Yale, in which a monumental pneumatic lipstick component is central.[24] Similar to the relationship between lipstick and the masculine-coded military vehicle on which Oldenburg's work sits, the lipstick in *Hubcap Milagro #3* complicates the gender codes by which one might read the piece. It contrasts almost comically with the bald head and robust torso of the masculine figure supported by the macho signifiers of hubcaps and rotary saws. Furthermore, as an assemblage of found objects and obscure signifiers produced in 1980s Southern California, it certainly locates itself comfortably within well-established North American art practices. Aptly enough, then, our viewer situates *Hubcap Milagro #3*

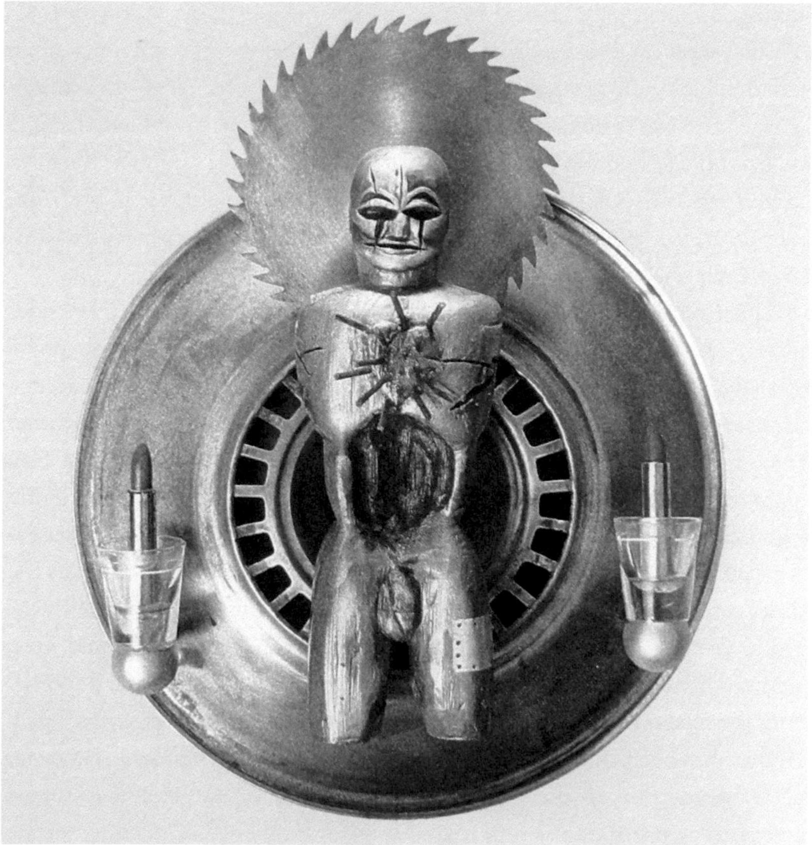

FIGURE I.3 David Ávalos, *Hubcap Milagro #3*, 1985.

within the canon with which she is familiar. Yet this reading does not precisely identify the fuller, conflicting historical conditions that might also account for Ávalos's work.

Ybarra-Frausto identifies *Hubcap Milagro #3* as an auspiciously rasquache work. Why? Not all of Ávalos's assembled objects are as "found," or arbitrarily selected, as our viewer might assume. In the world of vernacular Mexican American Catholicism, a milagro is a small devotional object, often hammered out of tin or other cheap metals into the shape of an animal or an image representing the devotee's object of prayer. In that context, the rotary saw blade takes on new significance: *Formed of* metal and useful *for forming* metal, it both demonstrates and short-circuits the practice of milagro-making. The raunchy, critical humor of the uncapped, deployed lipsticks standing erect on either side of the unnervingly barely there presence of an etched penis—above which the saw blade glintingly menaces—reads as a comment on the constructedness of gender through socially coded genitalia and maquillage, but also more than that.[25] In the context of popular Mexican Catholicism, they also stand as potential critiques of homophobia and colonially imported organizations of the social through racialized gender disseminated and policed by the Church.

This irreverence is further grounded in the hubcap's allusion to lowrider culture. The practice of lowriding sets US Chicanxs apart from la gente por el otro lado, that is, from Mexican national identity present south of the border. To conservative Mexicans, as well as assimilationist and conservative Mexican Americans, lowriding demonstrates the deterioration of traditional Mexican values resulting from the ongoing Americanization of migrant Mexican youth. Together, the eviscerated gut, nearly absent phallus, discharged lipsticks, rotary saw, and hubcap circle the Catholic symbol of the sacred heart at the work's center. Menacingly and comically, they cloud the object's legibility: sacred or profane? Earnest or ironic? Rasquachismo suspends these questions.

But our not-wrongheaded novice art historian would miss the opportunities presented by such suspensions. Beyond indicting art history yet again for what has been continually devalued by omission, this fictional encounter raises the question of whether it would be possible, or even desirable, for art history to incorporate the differential ways of knowing and seeing that are necessary to understand a rasquache aesthetic. Canonical terms art historians receive in training are most often Eurocentric ones delivered as universals. These terms can cross borders freely, their fluidity sanctioned by dominant histories. This occurs, for instance, when an art critic calls the activity of neo-Indigenous Nahuatl-speaking danzantes in Texas "performance art" and few bat an eye. In contrast, if the work of an artist like Thomas Hirschhorn were described as "rasquache," most readers would be curious at best while, at worst, the critic would be accused of producing nonsense. The operation, in other words, is firmly unidirectional. In a rasquache spirit, the various "incorporations" of the differential modes of seeing that enliven Chicanx art (and perhaps a Chicanx art history) are deployed here as movidas geared toward thriving beyond survival in the discipline, and beyond a desire for inclusion within institutions of art and higher education. In this book, these movidas are equally applied to Minimalism.

So, what of Minimalism in this conversation? Pamela M. Lee characterizes Minimalism's presence as "badgering."[26] She makes her argument within a well-known lineage of those who have felt berated by Minimalist works, beginning with Michael Fried.[27] Judd himself voiced frustration and disavowal, not of the works but of the association itself. According to him, "There was in no way a group at all."[28] But Minimalism's apparently confrontational nature has ignited others outside this heavily trafficked art-historical genealogy of art historians and artists. Bringing other viewers' critical positions into art history will alter how we understand that genealogy. I want to evince the significance of doing so and the fact that I am not the first to see how Minimalism and rasquachismo are foils, though I extend this observation substantially. Further argument as to why Marfa matters for Chicanx art, even though no significant body of Chicanx art resides here, is embedded in this evidence.

THREE DEGREES OF RASQUACHISMO

Besides the canonical litany of those perturbed by the insistent presence of Minimalist works, Chicana cultural theorist Alicia Gaspar de Alba also felt badgered. Before attending to her indictment of Minimalism, I turn our attention to her elucidation of the connections between Chicanx vernacular aesthetics and their significance for community formation, keeping in mind the communities of Marfa. In a significant structural expansion of rasquachismo, Gaspar de Alba identified works like Ávalos's as "third-degree rasquache," following Celeste Olalquiaga's formulation of three degrees of kitsch:

> "Third-degree kitsch" includes icons and paraphernalia that have been recycled by the art world in the makings of "happenings," assemblages, and mixed-media installations. In Chicano/a and Latino/a art, this takes the form of *altares*. . . . This artistic installation differs from home altars of the first-degree kind, says Olalquiaga. "As a recent exhibition title suggests, the recasting of altars is often meant as a 'ceremony' that invests them with a new political signification and awareness." . . . Third-degree rasquachismo . . . informs the work of Chicano and Chicana artists—writers, musicians, filmmakers, and other producers of culture.[29]

Here, via Olalquiaga, Gaspar de Alba presents a description of rasquachismo that honors its origins while reflecting the multilevel experiences of it relevant when she was writing in the 1990s. Those origins are in the "everyday" movidas theorized by Ybarra-Frausto a few years before. While he looked back to a set of references from the first half of the twentieth century, Gaspar de Alba addresses the situation from the perspective of her own time, when for an increasing (if still relatively low) number of Chicanxs, subjectivity was less likely to be formed through farmwork and other rural and working-class experiences than through popular culture and formal education. In her address she does not leave behind Ybarra-Frausto's references but links them indelibly with her own through the reorganization of the category into degrees. Her words continue to inform rasquache practices today, continually reaffirming the productive value of her renovation.

Particularly valuable in Gaspar de Alba's restructuring of rasquachismo is its opening up of possibilities for relation between Chicanxs who have had, and chosen to remain involved in, the experience of higher education and adjacent intellectual cultures and those who have not. These are often prominent intrafamilial distinctions, and thus Gaspar de Alba's framework becomes *intimately* valuable and not merely structurally, academically interesting. Her work provides a tool for avoiding the bankrupt understanding of such situations as standoffs between cultural/familial "traitors" and those who uncritically reproduce Chicanx cultures, exacerbating their ossification into heteronormative, multicultural ornament. I do not discount the vernacular Guadalupe of Marfa who appeared at the site of my grandfather's childhood home because I have a PhD in art history. Rather, working within the structures established by Ybarra-Frausto and Gaspar de Alba, I embrace this loaded, site-specific sculpture using the tools from all my realms of experience: my Chicanx upbringing and higher education. Theorist Gloria E. Anzaldúa writes about an analogous position in the context of feminisms of white women and women of color: "I can write . . . and yet I realize that many of us women of color who have strung [academic] degrees, credentials and published books around our necks like pearls that we hang onto for dear life are in danger of contributing to the invisibility of our sister-writers. '*La Vendida*,' the sell-out."[30] First- and third-degree rasquachismo provide richer starting points for speaking across these distinctions than the framework of "sell-outs" and "real" Chicanxs, even if the trope of selling out cannot be completely denied. Having three degrees of rasquachismo allows one to stand outside this trope to revise it creatively and communally or simply to reject it.

Returning to the terms in an art context, the breakdown of rasquachismo into three degrees is key for clarifying the communal connection between what might otherwise seem politically and aesthetically disparate productions. For example, on one hand, there are third-degree works like Ávalos's, exhibited in contemporary art spaces, while on the other, there are first-degree private milagros and milagro-bearing altars in homes, yards, cemeteries, and churches throughout Latin America and the United States, including in West Texas. It is not that the third degree demonstrates a higher level of self-consciousness or artfulness than the first, despite the implication of a graduated scaling. Rather, the degrees are distinguished by different sites and intended audiences; they are shaped by different but closely related experiences of coloniality that manifest along a spectrum of identity constructions understood, if often contradictorily, as Chicanx.[31] Often the material results appear dramatically different. If they do share morphological vocabularies, as in the case of altars, which have a growing art-world audience, they are physically and/or contextually *sited* at radical distances from one another (a white cube rather than a yard, for instance). However, first- and third-degree rasquachismo share a commonality in resisting and creatively exceeding ongoing processes of subjugation and other lasting colonial traumas. Gaspar de Alba began the project of articulating a rasquachismo relevant to Chicanx artists and scholars at the end of the twentieth century, finding words for negotiations of the everyday that are *not* marked by certain experiences of labor, religion, and rural life that fueled, for instance, the Chicano Movement.[32] As noted, they are often instead inflected by experiences of urban environments, higher education, and increasingly globalized information traffic. As is the case in my family, first-degree practitioners are often the parents and grandparents of those who express themselves in the third. The degrees are felt and lived cyclically rather than linearly, as elders witness and the young remember our elders' accounts, fantastically and politically interpreting them through our own daily living situations and creative practices.

FACING MINIMALISM

Gaspar de Alba directly pits rasquachismo against Minimalism: "In the context of Minimalism and Modern art, rasquachismo is more than an oppositional form; it is a militant praxis of resistance to hegemonic standards in the art world."[33] Why, among the myriad other labels for postwar and contemporary art in the 1990s, does she single out Minimalism, along with "Modern art," as the aesthetic against which rasquachismo is cast as a "militant" defiance? For one, many art historians have demonstrated that Minimalism and Modernism were never very friendly, even among themselves.[34] The line in the sand drawn by Michael Fried's "Art and Objecthood" article in 1967 was precisely between these two camps (in many ways, it distinguished them as distinct camps in the first place), and Judd is indeed a named enemy in his writing. I choose to examine Gaspar de Alba's reading at length, however, due to her position in American and Chicanx studies and in order to bring those fields in contact with the trajectories of these ideas in art history. These are important border crossings to undertake to create conditions in which these fields inform rather than ignore one another.

Taking the statement as it is given, then, Gaspar de Alba interprets Minimalism as the most exemplary form of a discriminatory Modernism.[35] If we give ourselves over momentarily to the most popular characterizations of Minimalism's forms she may have had in mind, her reasons become clearer: By the 1990s when Gaspar de Alba wrote, Minimalism had become a referent for multiple design fields from fashion to furniture, its formal qualities codified in terms of pristine materials, an austere approach to color, rectilinear profiles, hard surfaces, and a visual echo of architectural surrounds. In rasquachismo, on the other hand, "Aesthetic expression comes from discards, fragments, even recycled everyday materials such as tires, broken plates, plastic containers recombined with elaborate and bold display . . . and even embellishment of the car. The capacity to hold life together with bits of string, old coffee cans, and broken mirrors in a dazzling gesture of aesthetic bravado is at the heart of rasquachismo."[36] It is clear why, to Gaspar de Alba, Minimalism *appeared* diametrically opposite to rasquachismo. Their contrasting approaches to space and materials—and the cultural meanings ascribed to them—constituted some of the stakes of battles being waged in the 1980s and 1990s across institutions of art and higher education, battles in which she participated. The 1992 exhibition CARA: *Chicano Art: Resistance and Affirmation*, Gaspar de Alba's case study, was itself a prominent negotiation between a "mainstream" art institution—in this case the Wight Art Gallery—and the creative production of "a community repudiated and denied in institutional history within the nation as a whole"; that is, Chicanxs.[37]

Yet within the catalogue of the exhibition the grounds of this opposition are already questioned:

> There is an irony here—if you are in a position to enjoy it: those who never made it till now arrive to find the Museum in ruins. . . . But it gets

> worse. They arrive to find their identity already gone, their Culture in fragments, their Nationhood dispersed, and their Monuments reduced to canonical rubble. The site they were to occupy is nothing but a razed discursive plane. Welcome to the New Art History. There is room for everyone and a place for none.[38]

Penned jointly by Marcos Sanchez-Tranquilino and John Tagg, the essay that opens with these words is ultimately about the futility of capturing or curating identity within the context of the museum. It is not necessarily mired throughout in the glib nihilism suggested by this pithy first paragraph. It does, however, contend with the solidity that Gaspar de Alba's statement assumes. If the museum is in ruins, the canon reduced to rubble, casting rasquachismo as "a militant praxis of resistance to hegemonic standards in the art world" rings quixotic. Yet Tagg's and Sanchez-Tranquilino's earnest participation in CARA and continued investment in Chicanx art does evince some faith in the category (to match that of Gaspar de Alba) or better said, in projects that continue to struggle against and with the grain of Chicanx identity formation through visual presentation.

More than a decade after CARA and Gaspar de Alba's study, film and Chicanx art scholar Chon A. Noriega writes, "History is a palimpsest and not just the story of the victors; and one does not undo the victor's history as much as weave one's writing into and around the other stories."[39] This comes from his introductory essay for an anthology of key texts from the Chicanx studies journal *Aztlán*, in whose pages Chicanx artists have been a major presence alongside debates around Chicanx aesthetic sensibilities. Throughout the essay, the mechanics of wrenching concessions from power (and acknowledging what power requires in return for conceding) are reconsidered. Noriega cites Emma Pérez's concluding line in *The Decolonial Imaginary: Writing Chicanas into History*: "Forget the Alamo," Pérez closes in serious jest. Many of the spaces Chicanxs now hold, especially in higher education, were ceded due to the militant spirit of scholar–activists. In citing this line here, Noriega complements that militancy with "laughter."[40] He also points out that forgetting is its own kind of memory. Both moves demonstrate the central role paradox plays in the history, analysis, and production of Chicanx thought and art—be it "popular," "contemporary," "vernacular," or "fine."

In Marfa, it is crucial to note that there are social and physical walls around fine art and that many, both locals and visitors, are intimidated. I have felt it. My family has felt it. Sometimes harsh, *militant* statements drawing lines in the sand feel necessary. I refuse to disavow the capacity of these stances to make it possible for one to survive, to shore up a sense of self in the presence of objects that seem alien and threatening at times, especially when one finds them in spaces considered utterly familiar—home—prior to the strange encounter. Is it possible to "forget" Marfa? It is clear that, in recent history, Judd's story has been the dominant story of Marfa outside the town. Forgetting, as Pérez deploys it, is a historical method that makes weaving one's stories "into and around" the dominant one an act of complexly relating to power without conceding to it and without uncritically turning a blind eye to its badgering presence. The chapters of this book are such acts of weaving.

DIFRASISMO, DOMESTICANA, AND DECOLONIALITY

The title of my book, *Marfa, Marfa,* and the chapter titles demonstrate the unique Nahua literary trope of difrasismo. I deploy this trope as a titling device following Laura E. Pérez's example. She describes difrasismo's function as maintaining "the sometimes culturally untranslatable coexistence of . . . noncanonized aesthetic systems and the philosophies and larger social imaginaries in which these are embedded."[41] Thus, difrasismo is one way in which I attempt to articulate my insistence on the uneven multiplicity of Marfa. This introduction positions "Minimalism, Rasquachismo" as the overarching difrasismo of the project, within which each of the following chapters has its place.

While the dialogue between third-degree rasquachismo and Minimalism is not entirely unfamiliar—it is rather well populated if one knows the signs to look for—the dialogue between first-degree work and Minimalism is seemingly nonexistent. The chapter "Pilgrim, Approach" stages one of these conversations, called for by the existence of an altar dedicated to an apparition of the Virgin of Guadalupe neighboring Judd's public collection of his own and his contemporaries' permanently installed works at Chinati.

Chapter 2, "Marfa, Aztlán," begins from a recognition that Marfa is socially, commercially, and aesthetically inscribed in spaces far beyond West Texas. This reterritorialization is one of the primary mechanisms through which the town has become associated with certain art worlds and social realms also associated with art destinations like New York City; Beacon, New York; Joshua Tree, California; Santa Fe, New Mexico; and other sites that currently hold some status for contemporary art goers. This chapter does not deny those associations but recognizes that Marfa is also sited in Aztlán. This is the name mythically given to the Southwest of the United States by Nahuatl-speaking peoples who migrated through the area, ultimately settling in what is now Mexico City. Chicanxs in the United States have appropriated the notion of this territory through political action, literature, performance, and visual art since the 1970s. In this chapter I present the tools and language needed to reinterpret art produced in Marfa as produced in Aztlán.

The third chapter, "Making, Aesthesis," takes cues from a community of scholars and artists engaged in the project of decolonizing aesthetics. This chapter dissolves a distinction between so-called natural processes of making and making as undertaken by artists in Marfa, specifically Donald Judd. Tim Ingold's theorizing of making provides language for articulating this particular project and connecting it with the concerns of those attempting to decolonize aesthetics.

The conclusion reflects the increasing role of yards and yard art. Consciously reinterpreting West Texas as a network of yards—sites of idiosyncratic and personal creativity that are almost always on view for the wider world—produced surprising new visions and modes of thinking. The conclusion of this chapter and the book is a demonstration of "hanging out" in these sites. Through conversations with two fellow travelers, art historians Jana La Brasca and Max Tolleson, readers are given a glimpse of what it means not only to write about and historicize Marfa but actually to be there, lovingly and in great company.

In her project of distinguishing kitsch from rasquachismo (a response to Ybarra-Frausto's essay), artist and scholar Amalia Mesa-Bains is led to invent a neologism: domesticana. Like Gaspar de Alba, she is also responding critically to Olalquiaga, particularly countering the latter's framing of religious iconography in some women artists' work. Unlike in Olalquiaga's formulation, "For Mesa-Bains, the use of religious figures and motifs is not purely ironic, not entirely a question of opportunistic *détournement*. Rather the work connotes the sacred *and* the secular, the political *and* the transcendental, the feminist *and* the pious."[42] For femme-spectrum Chicanx artists, practicing domesticana, a feminist rasquachismo, means inhabiting a tense space between affirmation of women's typical domestic activity and "resistance to the subjugation of women in the [same] domestic sphere."[43] There is an emphasis on "ephemeral, site-specific works," and most of the work "elaborates on traditional forms such as the reliquary, capilla [small, outdoor chapel], domestic memories of bedroom altars, vanity dressers, ofrendas . . . , and everyday reflections of femininity and glamour."[44] Paradox is crucial to successfully practicing this simultaneous reverence for and resistance to aspects of women's roles in domestic life. Mesa-Bains looks to her own work and that of Patricia Rodriguez and Patssi Valdez for examples of such paradoxical work that, "unlike kitsch, seeks not an appropriation of low over high but in fact a state from within Chicanx culture."[45] The attitude with which I write and the methods in which I work are aligned with this "new domesticana defiance." I do not promote appropriation, translation, or revolution in Marfa. Instead, I articulate an inhabitation of "fractured loci of enunciation" within and significantly constituted by the multiplicity of a town.[46] The voice of the book is reverent *and* resistant. Functioning as a difrasismo comprising many difrasismos, this work addresses the fields of Minimalism, rasquachismo, Chicanx studies, American studies, and art history broadly not in the name of synthesis or mutual transparency but for something else: the possible expression of a "decolonial aestheTic/aestheSis." This notion is reintroduced in the penultimate chapter, where the book is situated within the context of the Modernity/Coloniality/Decoloniality (MCD) collective.

Thinkers and concepts associated with MCD recur throughout this book, particularly when considering the relationships between art, aesthetics, and radically different purposes for making and displaying objects. One advantage of turning to MCD is access to thought that provides a different, complementary sense of the paradoxes offered by Chicanx art scholars such as Mesa-Bains, Sanchez-Tranquilino, Tagg, Noriega, and Pérez. In particular, I have in mind MCD scholar María Lugones's essay "Playfulness, 'World'-Traveling, and Loving Perception." Lugones speaks to and within an audience of women of color yearning for coalition among themselves. Forming this coalition is difficult, however. A central difficulty is unlearning to perceive one another from "arrogant" perspectives of domination; that is, as beings who can be and are "grafted" to one's own existence as abuse-able, servile, ignore-able, and available without qualification. Lugones tells us she learned this lesson first as a child growing up with a domestically bound mother (including her own active role in this binding) and observing the treatment of servants in Argentina's upper classes. She writes,

> It was not possible for me to love my mother while I retained a sense that it was fine for me and others to see her arrogantly. Loving my mother also required that I see with her eyes, that I go into my mother's "world,"

> that I see both of us as we are constructed in her "world," that I witness her own sense of herself from within her "world." Only through this traveling to her "world" could I identify with her because only then could I cease to ignore her and to be excluded and separate from her. Only then could I see her as a subject, even if one subjected, and only then could I see at all how meaning could arise fully between us. We are fully dependent on each other for the possibility of being understood and without this understanding we are not intelligible, we do not make sense, we are not solid, visible, integrated; we are lacking. So traveling to each other's "worlds" would enable us to be through loving each other.[47]

These lessons echo with behavior Lugones observes among women of color in the United States, even as these very women proclaim desires to love one another. Arrogant perception can be horizontal as well as vertical in her schema. The "world-traveling" she demonstrates here is key to how I propose Marfa might be considered differently than it has been.

Many Marfans live preoccupied with their own struggles around arrogant perception. I write from my own ongoing negotiation, with a knowing suspicion that it resonates with many. This preoccupation has much to do with a strong desire to love and be loved, to be neighborly, to enter conversation together in Marfa's unique visual and sculptural field with an ease that does not always come readily. Does this lack of ease have something to do with the isolation of Marfa? Does this isolation and the smallness of the town emphasize the difference of cultures, value systems, language backgrounds, class statuses, ethnic identities, and understandings of art and beauty held by its constituents? Furthermore, what if, for some of us (perhaps all, it might turn out), multiple positions—understood as constitutive of our positions in the worlds from which we see and are seen—have been internalized? Lugones understands a multiplicity of positions as central to the experience of women of color. What she also illustrates is that these positions are also located in *multiple worlds*. As I reread her essay, I am struck by the experiences by which she comes to this formulation. They are remarkably close to how I see my selves in Marfa. Of "worlds" Lugones writes, "I will lead you to see what I mean by a 'world' the way I came to propose the concept to myself: through the kind of ontological confusion about myself that we, women of color, refer to half-jokingly as 'schizophrenia' (we feel schizophrenic in our goings back and forth between different 'communities') and through my effort to make some sense of this ontological confusion."[48]

Accents, ways of eating, cultural references, aesthetic judgments, physical boundaries, language: My enactments of all of these can shift dramatically almost from block to block in Marfa. With the Sanchez family in the kitchen of my grandfather's former home, in the public library, in the galleries or the bookstore, an ontological confusion betrays itself in the ways I take up these aspects of my selves anew at each site. This is a different inhabitation of Marfa from the culinary consumption of the locale bolstered by features in glossy lifestyle magazines, on travel websites for the middle and upper classes, or for artists who inhabit the town for longer but still temporary residencies. My footing inevitably trips down Marfa streets, socially cobbled as they are under many of our feet. To enjoy leisure in Marfa is an elusive state, as anxiety about being the appropriate self in the appropriate setting rarely ebbs.

Because I write as many selves, I realize that some possible tropes must be discounted here. I am not writing about performativity. Nor is this an argument for multiple sites of authenticity, which presumes the value of essential natures. I do not perform. I am not "more authentic" here rather than there. (If I do perform, then I am also performing right now, always.) Rather than performances, I understand my running around Marfa(s) as many acts of traveling, following Lugones:

> The shift from being one person to being a different person is what I call traveling. This shift may not be willful or even conscious, and one may be completely unaware of being different in a different "world," and may not recognize that one is in a different "world." Even though the shift can be done willfully, it is not a matter of acting. One does not pose as someone else; one does not pretend to be, for example, someone of a different personality or character or someone who uses space or language differently from the other person. Rather, one is someone who has that personality or character or uses space and language in that particular way. The "one" here does not refer to some underlying "I." One does not experience any underlying I.[49]

This makes all the difference in an attempt to discuss issues of competing notions of art, ethnicities, language formations, and modes of perceiving others in the name of constructing tools for conviviality, if we are not to argue according to bankrupted notions of inclusion/exclusion and margins-and-centers. Lugones wrestles with the question of how women of color love one another, understanding that to love in the sense she desires requires the difficult work of unlearning to perceive one another arrogantly. Who do I love in Marfa? My family members who live and have lived there; my colleagues whose ongoing willingness to think with me about art and life marks me; my friends with whom I share spaces and meals and drinks (not mutually exclusive categories, though frequently the demarcations instantiate themselves clearly and unsettlingly); even the tourists I invariably share a few beers and meals with during any given visit. To demonstrate a love that comes from a recognition and learned undoing of arrogant perceptions, Minimalism and rasquachismo are two worlds I propose to travel.

BIENVENIDOS A MARFA, MARFA

Pilgrim, Approach

1

"Son patrañas del demonio," . . . said Ida Prieto of Marfa. "The Virgin is not a novelty, she does not appear on a tortilla or a wheat field. When she does appear she appears in human form." . . . In the meantime, people keep making their way to Hector and Ester Sanchez's house every night to see the image of the Virgin Mary on the tree trunk.

—Rosario Salgado Halpern, "Virgin Mary Image Appears in Marfa"

The cover of the October 13, 1980, issue of the *New Yorker* features illustrator Arthur Getz's rendering of 101 Spring Street, a virtuosic five-story cast-iron construction designed by architect Nicholas Whyte and built in 1870 (figure 1.1). At the time, the building had already served as artist Donald Judd's New York City home and studio for twelve years. In Getz's picture, its Mercer Street façade is in shadow, while its narrower Spring Street face is illuminated by bright sunlight. Below on the sidewalk stands a group of people who look upward, their gaze guided by a figure nearest the Spring Street entrance. The guide's hand rests high on a slender column while he faces the crowd. The concentrated focus of the group indicates the specialness of this site and their intentional presence. Whether they have come to appreciate the architectural landmark dating back to the nineteenth century or the presence

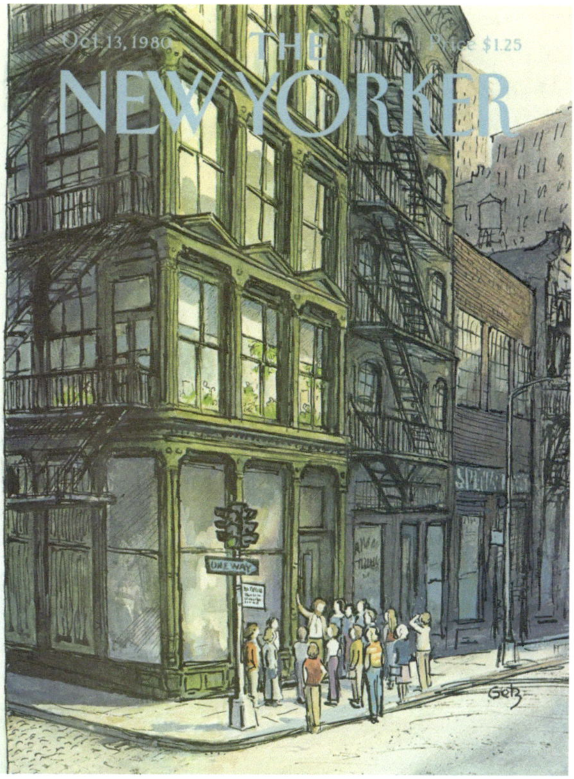

FIGURE 1.1 Arthur Getz, illustration of 101 Spring Street, New York, featured on the cover of the *New Yorker*, October 13, 1980.

of the already famous artist living and working inside it since 1968 is unclear. Getz's own awareness of the artist's presence is clearer, if one looks carefully enough: Judd's beloved cacti collection is prominently featured through the second-floor windows.[1] This is the only clue we are given to the building's internal activity. While the subject of the group's conversation is indeterminable, their desire to be there is evident.

Whatever the group's discussion, their physical presence and attentive postures evince the trouble and time they took to be there. In light of the aura they clearly sense radiating from the building (illustrated by Getz's fulgid rendering of its Spring Street face), *could we call such figures "pilgrims"?* Understanding and deploying this term through sites constructed and neighbored by Judd's activities are the objectives of this chapter. The cacti hint at the location of the two pilgrimage sites in the Southwest that are my focus: Chinati and the nearby backyard of my grandfather's childhood home, now occupied by Ester Sanchez—longtime director of the Marfa Public Library—and her family. The latter is far less known, so I give that account before bringing Judd's Marfa fully back into the story. My unpacking of this question, then, largely occurs through a discussion of the latter's public collection in Marfa, though 101 Spring Street remains a part of the story, as Judd developed these sites contemporaneously and with equal care and attention. First, however, I turn to the understandings of pilgrimage I have in mind.

MAPPING PILGRIMAGE THROUGH *MARFITA*

In the summer of 2011, artists Alison Kuo, Joshua Saunders, and I undertook a "double pilgrimage" to Marfa. That is, we conceived of the journey—from New York City to Austin, Texas, where Kuo and I met Saunders, and then on to Marfa—with the altar dedicated to the Virgin of Guadalupe *and* Chinati, the overlapping Minimalist and rasquache fields, as our explicit destinations. To our knowledge, we were the first to have made our way to Marfa with Minimalist and rasquache sites in mind from the outset. We were not sure what exactly "double pilgrimage" would mean after we passed from the center of the state to its western region. Perhaps we would erase the rich worlds of both in our attempt to avoid subrogating one to the other. Were we after sharp critique or aesthetic promiscuity? Are the two ever cooperative? Would we feel at home in either? Our passage had to raise these questions. It was "necessarily ambiguous" and in that space over time we shifted to becoming "liminal *personae*," as anthropologist Victor Turner puts it.[2]

This journey was one step in the two-year development of our collaborative installation MARFITA (teatrista Natalie Goodnow was also a collaborator, though she could not join us for the pilgrimage).[3] It was the first time Kuo and Saunders had visited Marfa, though as contemporary artists educated in Texas, they already keenly felt Judd's and Marfa's presence: "A pilgrimage to Marfa is a must for any contemporary art aficionado," as one review of MARFITA would later note.[4] Flesh-to-flesh and flesh-to-object encounters occurred. Their impact on our respective artistic practices is worth thinking about within the framework of world-traveling proposed in the introduction, which provides a basis for the discussion of pilgrimage. Turner's understanding of liminality and *communitas* illuminates many of the turns.

As fate would have it, in the days before our departure, I received a call from Ester Sanchez. She let me know two things that at first caused anxiety: Due to medical circumstances, she and her family would not be there when we arrived; and the Guadalupe statue itself would be out for cleaning and repainting during the time we would be in Marfa, so Saunders and Kuo would not encounter it before the culmination of our project in October. Ester did let us know that we were still welcome to make ourselves at home in her backyard. The drive to Marfa then became a restrategizing session. Eventually, we took the absence of the sculpture itself as an opportunity. Its bathtub housing and raised concrete foundation remained in place. The echo of our own liminality on arriving in the yard (Chinati's first gates just over our shoulder) resounded in the ambiguous emptiness of the rasquachified bathtub's vertical oblong cavity. In response, we three inhabited the yard as a field for play, imagining the offerings we might have placed at Guadalupe's feet. In her absence, we gathered materials into an assemblage that filled the structural space where her plaster presence regularly stood (figure 1.2). The disappearance of the object from the site, the shrine architecture, and our pilgrimage were part of a process of "being reduced or ground down to be fashioned anew and endowed with additional powers to enable [us] to cope."[5] Our fashioning anew took place within a sculptural void, built up by tongue-like maguey leaves and plastic toy guns, where our unexpected situation enabled us to create meaningful object-centric ritual.

Kuo filmed this process. In reflection, we wondered whether the act was rasquache (or even Minimalist, in the detritus-collided vein of John Chamberlain, whose work is permanently installed just a few blocks away). As a white man and a woman with a Chinese father and an Anglo mother, both artists much more familiar with the aesthetic vocabularies related to and generated by Judd, what did it mean for Saunders and Kuo to consider their roles in our collaborative act as demonstrations of rasquachismo? Is it more "authentic" when I, a Chicano, undertake the same production? As Lugones writes, and as I will demonstrate, world-traveling cannot rely on reading events through such a rubric. "*One does not experience any underlying* [authentic, essential] *I*."[6] Neither can Saunders nor Kuo—nor I for that matter—consider our rasquache exercises as unmediated by specific social, historical (modern colonial) constitutions.

Turner's distinction between "communitas" and "community" serves to generate much more complex readings than debates over authenticity. How

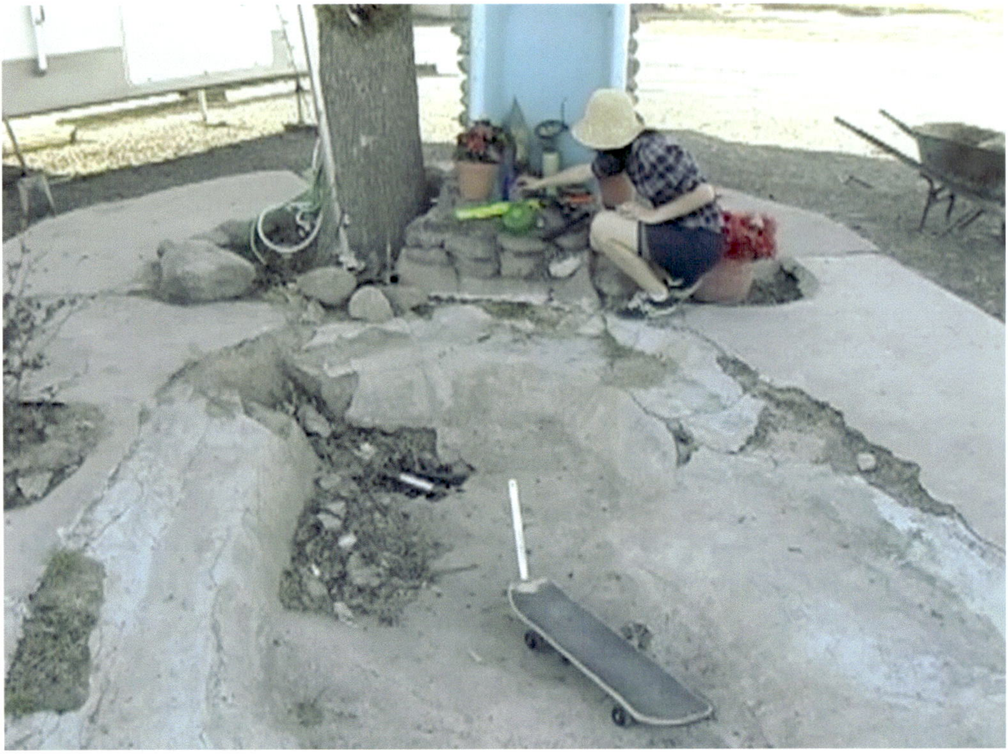

FIGURE 1.2 Alison Kuo, still from *MARFITA* altar film, July 2011. Kuo, pictured here, created this film as part of the installation project *MARFITA*, a collaboration between Kuo, Natalie Goodnow, Joshua Saunders, and me. The film documents experimentation with found objects as offerings and sculptural assemblage in the empty housing of the Sanchez altar. The absence of the Guadalupe statue created an opportunity for investigating objects as sculpture, sculptural absence, sacred place production, and ritual performance.

can Marfa be imagined not as the latter, a mere "area of common living" populated coincidentally by Minimalist and rasquache knowledge holders, but as an experiment in the former? That is, communitas as an experiment in what "emerges recognizably in the liminal period, . . . [a] society as an unstructured or rudimentarily structured and relatively undifferentiated *comitatus*, community, or even communion of equal individuals who submit together to the general authority of the ritual elders."[7] Marfa acutely poses the questions of whose rituals and whose elders. Along with our audience, in *MARFITA* we attempted to address these questions while experimenting on a micro scale

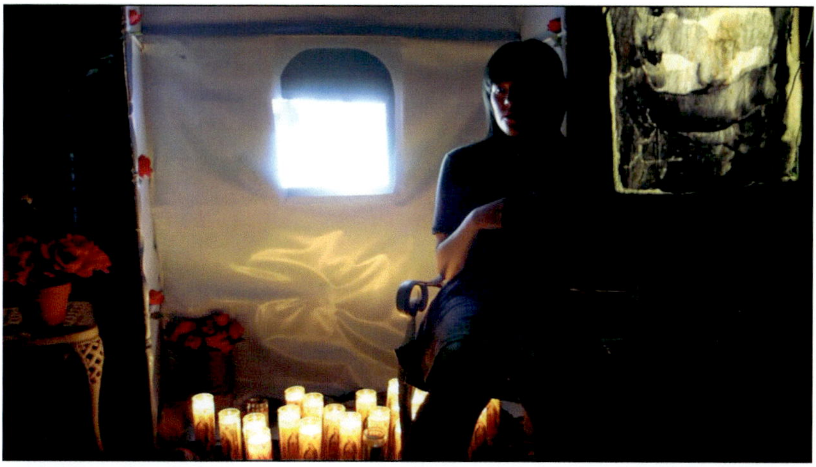

FIGURE 1.3 Alison Kuo with her altar and film *MARFITA*, October 2011. Co-Lab, Austin, Texas.

with this "undifferentiated *comitatus*." We learned that to do so requires a differentiated vision. Like rasquachismo, communitas gambols between the sacred and the profane, the high and the low. "Liminality implies that the high could not be experienced unless the low existed, and he who is high must experience what it is like to be low," Turner writes.[8]

Kuo's decisions in her final contribution to *MARFITA* attempt to capture the loss of a core "I." She constructed an altar from plastic sheeting, PVC pipe, zip ties, and fabric roses that stood nearly three times the height of the Sanchez altar. I had suggested that Kuo fabricate an equally enlarged plush Guadalupe to fill the altar, plush being a medium she had previously utilized. Kuo ultimately resisted, however. For one, she was at a point in her practice where plush creations no longer held her interest as much as a foray into the then-unfamiliar medium of film. Additionally, her pilgrimage to Marfa confirmed her unease at taking up the image of Guadalupe with little personal experience of her power and meaning. This was driven home by the fateful absence of the actual Guadalupe image in the altar. Guadalupe would not appear to Kuo. Thus, her work in *MARFITA* also eschewed the Virgin's image within the flimsy plastic nicho (figure 1.3). Instead, the video documentation of our fumbling activity (making offerings or assembling sculpture?) is projected from behind through a translucent sheet of Plexiglas set in the nicho space, recalling Guadalupe's absence that week in Marfa.

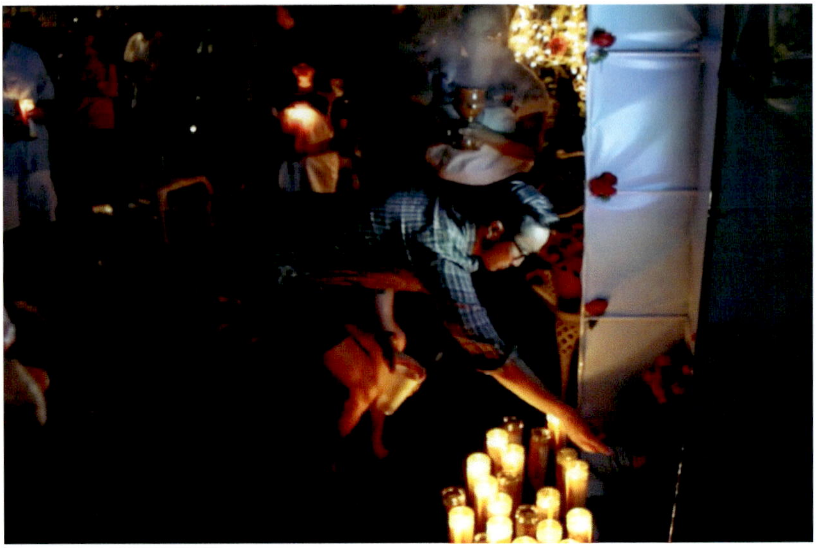

FIGURE 1.4 Audience participant making an offering in the nicho created by Alison Kuo on opening night of *MARFITA*.

At *MARFITA*'s opening, Goodnow and a team of danzantes invited the audience to join in procession and prayers dedicated to Guadalupe. More than one hundred participants joined the slow, drumbeat-driven march around the East Austin block where the gallery was located. The sacred function of the altar space dedicated to Guadalupe was performed by offering her image back to the absence in Kuo's construction, in the form of candles bearing her likeness, much as pilgrims did on that earlier night of her Marfa apparition (figures 1.4 and 1.5). Thus, Kuo's sensitivity to the responsibility of world-traveling was enacted in her not handling images central to that travel. This sensitivity laid the grounds for others' pilgrimages that night. While Kuo's production combined with Goodnow's and the danzantes' performance resulted in a warm if—for many—unfamiliar invitational setting, an image by Saunders proved more troublesome. I will return to this trouble at the close.

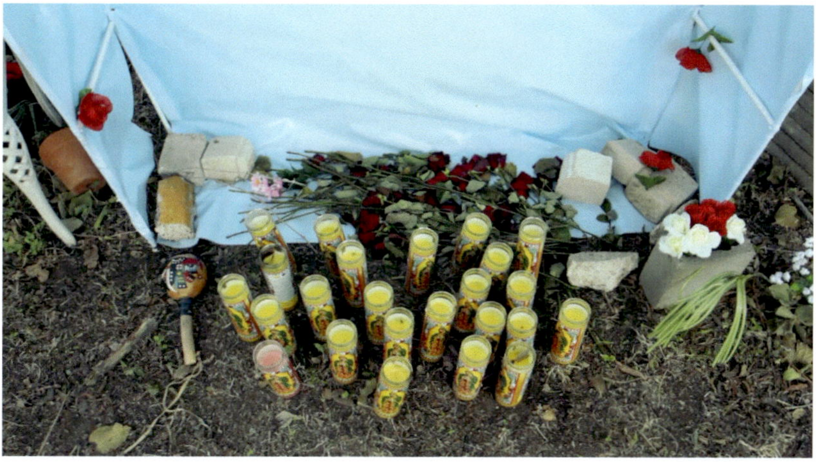

FIGURE I.5 Votive candles, roses, and various offerings left in Alison Kuo's nicho by *MARFITA* participants.

LA GUADALUPE APPEARS

Ask amateurs of art who are not from West Texas but have visited Marfa about their journey and you will likely be met with an exasperated, but elated sigh: "What a trek!" And with such phrases they flash a badge of honor. "I made that journey," they are telling you. "I earned the rank of pilgrim." And *pilgrim* is indeed the prevailing term, encountered frequently in Marfa-related travel and lifestyle sites and blog entries throughout the Internet and in personal accounts. Rather than defer without question to their newfound credentials, I want to put pressure on this identification as "pilgrim" by referencing Lugones's taking up of the term alongside Turner's rubric for communitas. This provides a central site through which to map multiple Marfas. Lugones writes, "Indeed, this pilgrimage is a walking against and away from that hushing of the manyness of the past in the present by both dominators and those resisting domination. But sometimes the history is of me and you, life history in the flesh, moods, tendencies, and dispositions to live big or small, to tame and trash someone's spirit or to live side by side in the task of overcoming incomprehension—all levels of the political."[9]

I imagine in spatial terms what Lugones sets up for her reader philosophically: The "incomprehension" to be overcome is that between those whose

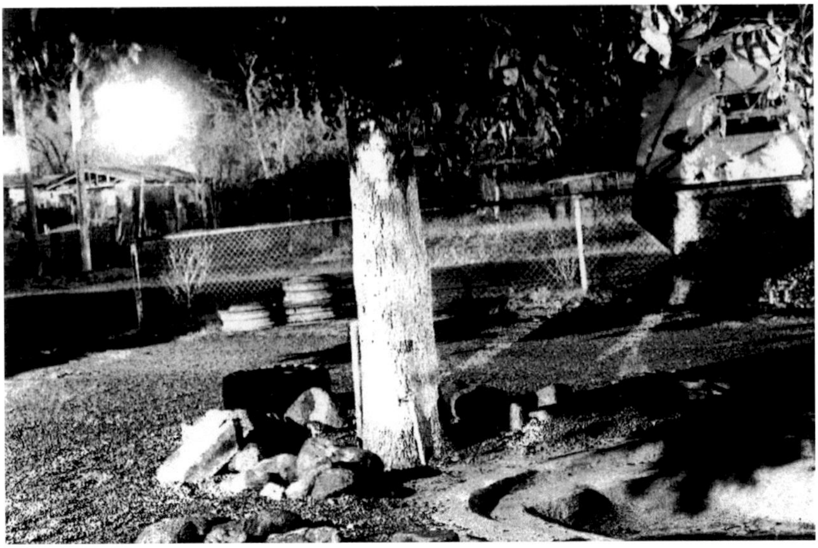

FIGURE 1.6 La Virgen de Guadalupe apparition in Sanchez yard, Marfa, Texas, November 1997.

daily realities are constructed and lived, if unconsciously, through rasquachismo and those for whom Marfa embodies Judd's "platinum-iridium" standard of art installation.[10] While I examine others' pilgrimages in this chapter, I am also undergoing my own. Through this writing, I return to a place I long took as utterly familiar but whose familiarity was seismically disturbed in 2009 upon my discovering the presence of Judd and the Marfas his presence unintentionally brought into being, interwoven among mine, my family's, and those who inhabit Marfa as we have—immigrants and longtime residents of Mexican and Indigenous origin, working class, Spanish- and Caló-speaking and, until my generation, mostly uninitiated into higher education and its adjacent art worlds. Rather than choosing between a nostalgia-fueled rejection of the former or a forgetting of the latter in a demonstration of a certain kind of social, cultural, and aesthetic "upward" mobility, the pilgrimage I undertake in the following pages is my own walking *into* Marfa's manyness. It is a refusal to comply with the hushing of this manyness. And like Lugones, I see this hushing happening not unidirectionally, exclusively from top down or vice versa, but from both "dominators and those resisting domination." I attempt and encourage being open to *all* that vies for attention in Marfa, disregarding the closures constructed between nostalgic local accounts, the com-

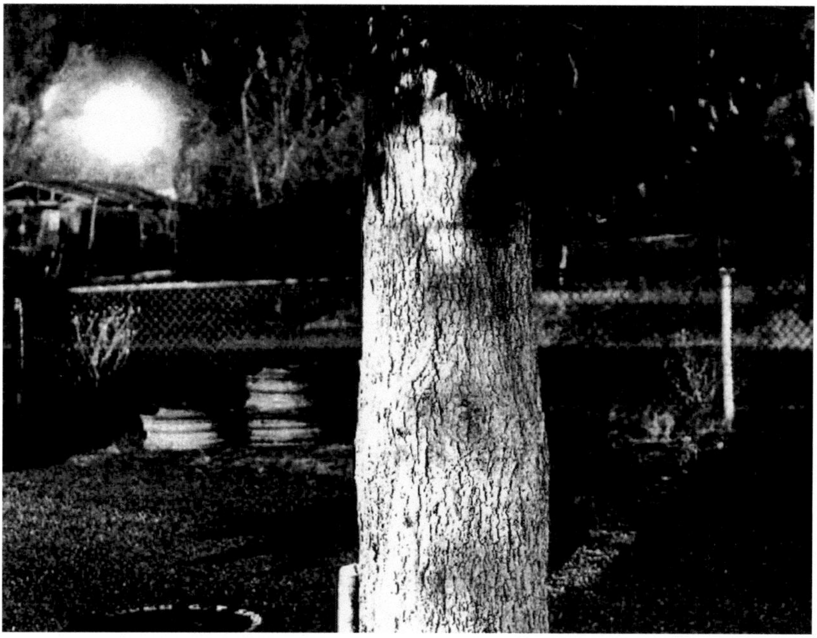

FIGURE 1.7 Detail of La Virgen de Guadalupe apparition in Sanchez yard, Marfa, Texas, November 1997.

mercially motivated popular press, and the inevitable disciplining performed by art history. My first opening appeared in the yard where my grandfather played as a child.

Thursday, October 30, 1997. Hector Sanchez sits in his backyard in Marfa, Texas, with his compadre Esteban Alvarez. The sun is setting on the Chihuahuan Desert while they lounge, drinking beers, digesting dinner, presiding over Sanchez's children. The sun sets, and shortly afterward, a figure of nearly human scale and shape made of light and embedded in a tree reveals itself. Shortly, the figure becomes legible as a rebozo-clad feminine body standing with hands clasped in prayer, eyes downcast (figures 1.6 and 1.7). Sanchez reads this image as a visitation from La Virgen de Guadalupe. He is not the only one. Beginning with his own family, the curious and devoted come regularly for weeks to witness the nocturnal apparition.

Ralph Acosta was among those who came. Journalist Miriam Halpern photographed him for the article in the local paper featuring the apparition (figure 1.8). Acosta's gaze settles on a distinct point, presumably the appari-

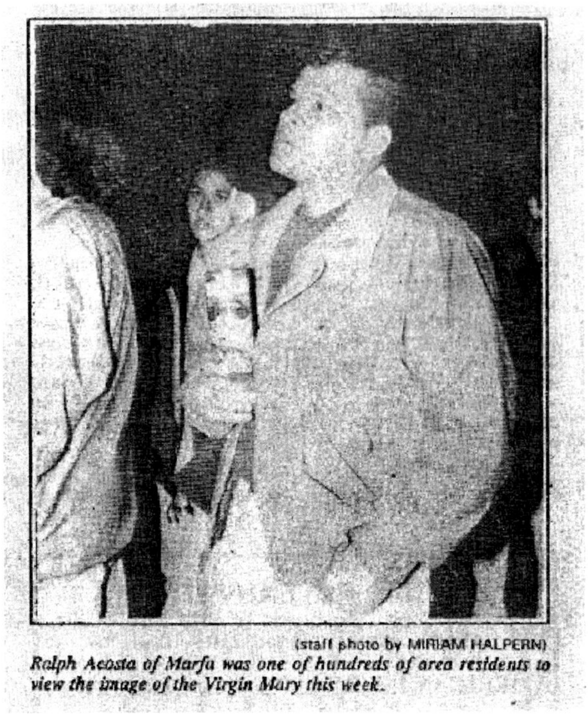

FIGURE 1.8 "Ralph Acosta of Marfa was one of hundreds of area residents to view the image of the Virgin Mary this week." *Big Bend Sentinel*, November 11, 1997. Photo: Miriam Halpern.

tion, and finds an echo in the focus of a woman standing behind him, looking in the same direction. One hand slouches in his left hip pocket while the other holds a devotional candle. Based on the occasion, it is likely that the candle bears the image of the Virgin of Guadalupe, though it may also bear one of the Virgin's other personae typically depicted on such items. Another possibility is that Acosta has brought along a candle bearing the image of a non-Marian saint with whom he identifies, either by choice or by date of birth. In any case, it is important to note that he, undoubtedly like many that night and for the subsequent two weeks of the nocturnal apparition's recurrence, came prepared to witness a sacred image *with and through* other sacrosanct images borne on candles, wallet-sized cards, metal pendants, and so on. This is one everyday exchange—image and contemplation in return for image and divine attention—to add to what Serge Gruzinski identifies in his analysis of Guadalupan images as "indications [that] are enough to reveal the extreme complexity of a continuous creation that was never reduced to a simple, concrete translation of an aesthetic, political, and religious discourse, and that requires the ceaseless interweaving of the threads of art history and institutional history, of social history and cultural history."[11] The images invoked by the photographic account of Acosta at the apparition site truck in a shared Mexican American Catholic iconography. In this chapter, I undertake an "interweaving," as Gruzinksi calls it, in order to make sense of image encounters across visual vocabularies *without* a shared source of meaning. I map their "world-traveling" as it plays out among Marfa's social complexities. I present this world-traveling through the trope of pilgrimage that, as has been noted, is already a term through which many frequently describe theirs and others' inhabitations of the town. The social complexes focused on—the worlds to be traveled—are differing histories and ruptures of the definition of *sculpture*. In the traveling, I demonstrate the significance of a map of Marfa drawn with traversals of both the Minimalist and the rasquache in mind.

Hector Sanchez's wife, Ester, is a faithful skeptic. Alongside her husband she honored the Guadalupe image as a devout Catholic, while also acknowledging the explicable play of light: "I see the shape of a woman wearing blue, I see the Rosary and the crown. I'm sure it's a shadow from something, but why is it in that shape? . . . I'm sure there's an explanation, but it's amazing."[12] Reporting on the event for the *Big Bend Sentinel*, journalist Rosario Salgado Halpern extends this logic: "The image appears to be created from a yard light and/or a light from the nearby [US] Border Patrol headquarters filtering through tree limbs onto the whitewashed tree trunk."[13] In our conversations Sanchez reaffirms this observation along with her continuous faith in the event's sacredness.

The faithful and curious peregrinate mostly from the local area, though Ester's recordkeeping hints at the far-reaching touch of the Mexican mother of God.[14] The yellow spiral notebook in which Ester invited pilgrims to sign their names and places of origin includes the West Texas, New Mexican, and Mexican towns of Shafter, Alpine, Fort Davis, Odessa, Hobbs, Ojinaga, and other regional hamlets (figure 1.9). Then there are less frequent, far-flung inclusions like, simply, "ITALY" (figure 1.10). The latter highlights the distance between the Roman seat of papal power and the vernacular Catholi-

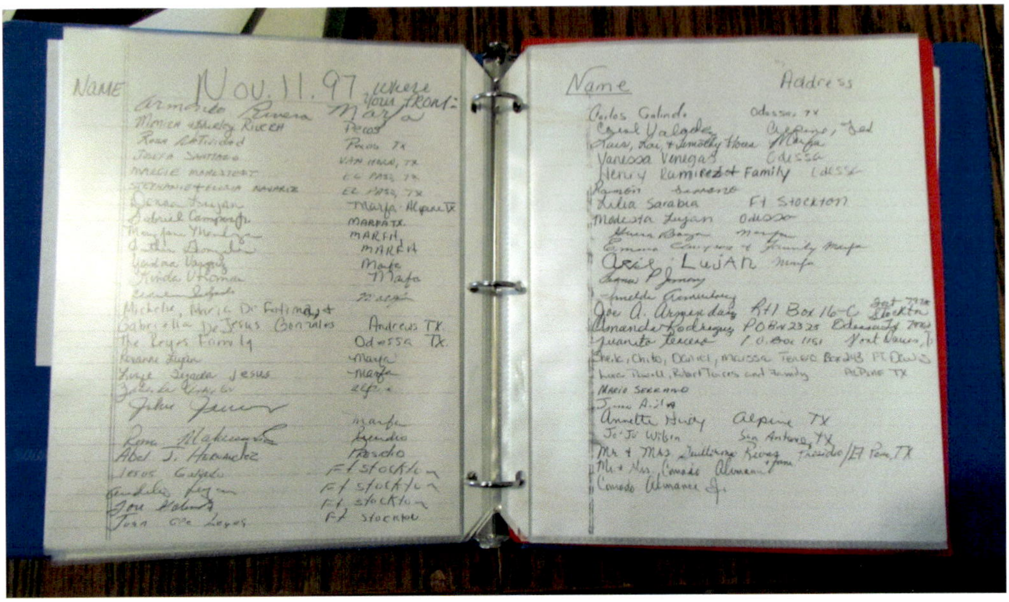

FIGURE I.9 Pages from Ester Sanchez's pilgrimage log, originally written in a yellow spiral notebook. Sanchez placed photocopies of the pages in protective plastic sheets in a three-ring binder.

cism tinged with pre-Columbian iconology that has fermented in the "New World" since the early sixteenth century.[15]

Following Mexican and US Latinx Catholic traditions, Hector Sanchez responded to the apparition by constructing a site-specific altar beneath the host tree (figure I.2). Approximately three feet tall, the plaster statue of Guadalupe was purchased from a factory on the Mexican side of the border where her sculptural form is mass-produced. The statue was then hand-painted by Sanchez and Alvarez before being set in an upturned bathtub now serving as a nicho. This rasquache repurposing from bathroom fixture to sacred niche is emphasized by affixing stones to the tub's exterior. This entire composition—statue and housing—is elevated on a bed of rocks cemented into place. Complementing the natural arboreal awning above, the Sanchez yard already contained a dug and cement-coated shallow grotto to which the altar's base is oriented. The grotto was later filled in to prevent standing water (figure I.11). It also often ended up catching toys, windblown debris, and some of the fallen offerings left by pilgrims to mark their visits and materialize their requests

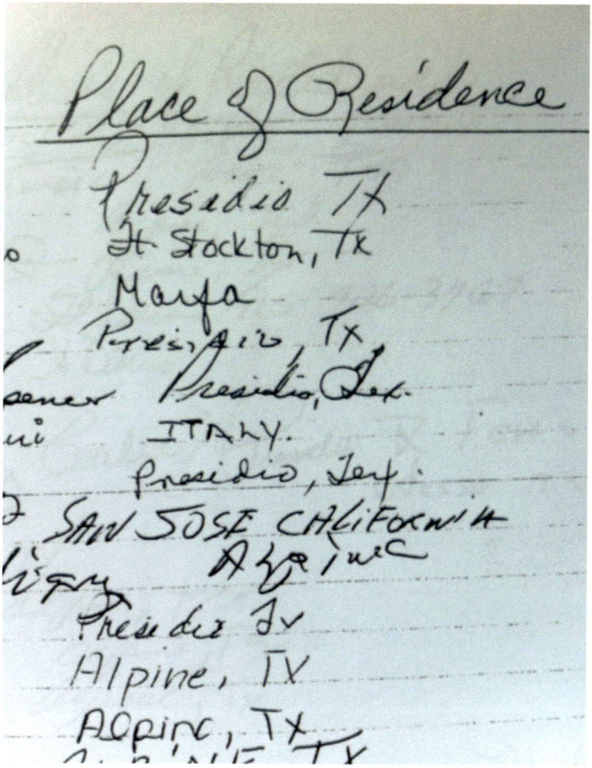

FIGURE 1.10 Detail of Ester Sanchez's pilgrimage log, showing Italy as place of residence for one of the visitors.

to Guadalupe. The altar was completed one month before Hector Sanchez passed away. Roger Garcia, another Marfan and family friend, has repainted the statue at least twice since its installation.[16] The Sanchez family maintains the altar as a whole, cleaning and redecorating it periodically.

Such sculptural works—and the images generated by them—play key roles in the world-traveling occurring here. They provide the physical markers at which the pilgrimages I examine culminate. In part, this examination joins others in taking up the vexing task of defining *sculpture* in postwar art history. My aim in this chapter is to aggravate the history of postwar American art, so long as *aggravate* is understood in its original Latin sense, *aggravāre,* to make heavier (not necessarily in the sense of an irritant). This aggravation began by calling Sanchez's work "site-specific," opening it up to readings much

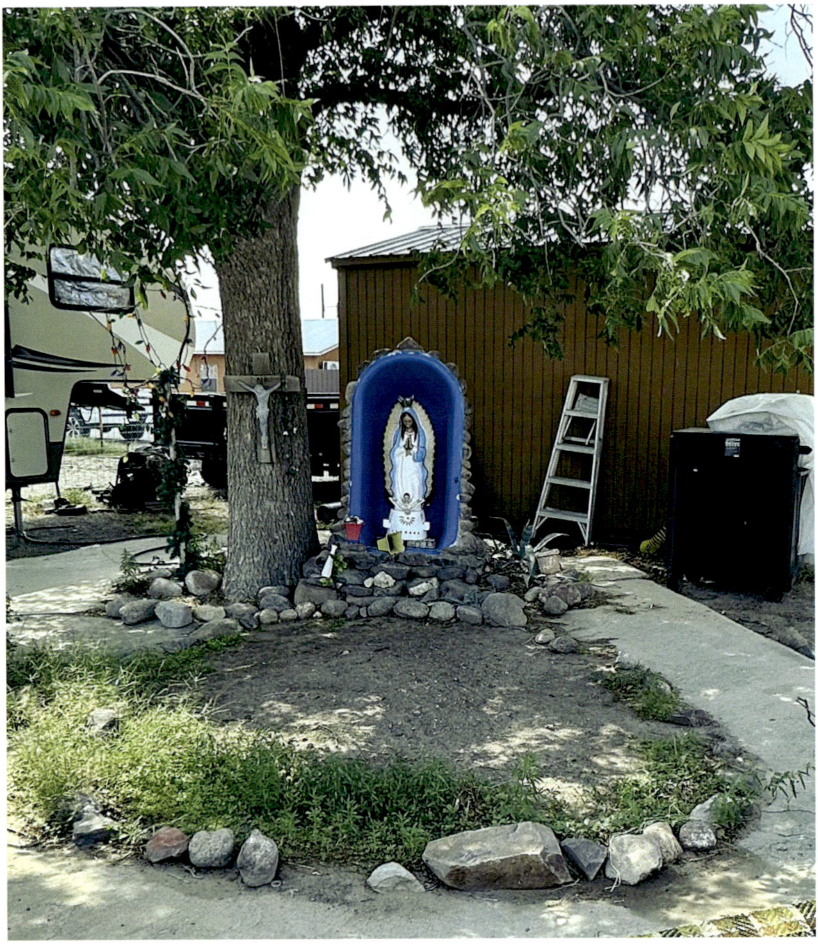

FIGURE 1.11 Grotto and Guadalupe altar, Sanchez yard, Marfa, Texas.

more familiar in connection with other Marfa sites. Thus, it serves to further fill out the sculptural population of Marfa, then to investigate this expanded, coinhabited field. Where and why else do people flock pilgrim-like to Marfa and around what objects do they congregate (encouraged by what circulating *images* of said objects)? To answer this, we must briefly return to New York City to get us back to Marfa, by now a well-worn itinerary.

MANHATTAN TO MARFA

By 1968, Donald Judd's career had hit its stride, marked by his first major retrospective at the Whitney Museum of American Art in New York. That year, in another part of Manhattan, in a place not quite yet known as SoHo, he purchased a five-story (plus basement and sub-basement) cast-iron building at the corner of Spring and Mercer Streets. He had recently been awarded a fellowship of seven thousand dollars from the John Simon Guggenheim Memorial Foundation, which may have helped underwrite this purchase. Also helpful, if obliquely, was an advance from gallery owner Leo Castelli in the same year for gathering materials and constructing the pieces for Judd's Whitney retrospective.[17] For many artists at the time, the Cast Iron District of New York, which played host mainly to light industrial and textile manufactories throughout the nineteenth century, was an advantageous location. For Judd it was a site both embedded in the urban network of galleries, universities, and museums that brought attention to his work and located at a psychological and infrastructural distance from the middle-class values, uncritical patriotism, or suburban settings he rejected on a variety of principles.[18] Combined with the available industrial spaces that allowed for the production of work on a significantly larger scale than traditional studio spaces, the Cast Iron District was ideal for Judd as he developed the visual and spatial vocabularies with which he is most associated.

Judd and Julie Finch, his wife at the time, were even more fortunate than most in acquiring an entire building. That building, 101 Spring Street, was designed to showcase the virtues of cast-iron architecture (figure 1.12). The boldest feature of this new building material was the possibility for greatly increasing the ratio of glass to load-bearing building materials. Because the building is situated on a corner, two façades are almost entirely glass, allowing natural light to flood the interior on two fronts. This light had a particularly striking texture as well, due to the original nineteenth-century dripped-glass windowpanes having aged almost one hundred years at the time of sale. For Judd and Finch, this irresistible feature overtook any concerns for the immense amount of work the building required to transition from a site used for a century for the fabrication and sale of textiles and other dry goods to a suitable location for their artistic practices (Finch had a dance studio on the second floor) and the raising of their young family. The couple purchased the entire factory building for $68,000. There were significant costs beyond this

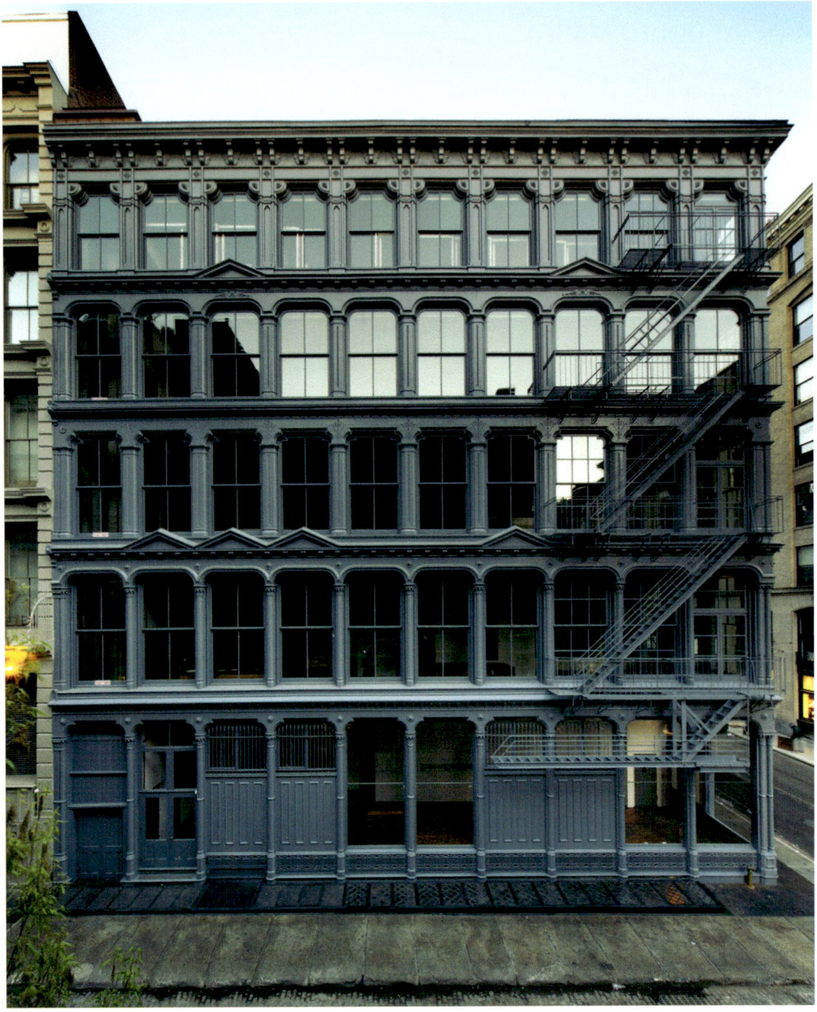

FIGURE I.12 Donald Judd's home and studio at 101 Spring Street, in New York City. Nicholas Whyte (architect), built 1870. Photo: Joshua White. Courtesy Judd Foundation Archives.

price, including various immediately necessary renovations, from replacing a faulty boiler to clearing out a century's worth of industrial detritus.[19]

Not all the detritus that littered Manhattan was mere trash to Judd, however, and it is worth pausing on this fact to note that Miminalism and rasquachismo are not as diametrically opposed as Chicanx art scholar Alicia Gaspar de Alba's framework would have it.[20] Scrapping, salvaging, and repurposing are as much features of Judd's emergent Minimalism as they are hallmarks of rasquachismo. Writing of the transition from brick-and-cast-iron loft buildings to steel-and-glass office towers in New York City, art historian Joshua Shannon observes that "as both aspects of this architectural transition proceeded, printing pallets, iron pipes, and sheet-metal cornices cropped up as loose things, the rejects of an ever-more-ethereal urban environment. It was in this uncertain terrain that Judd's sculpture operated, picking up these objects and half-integrating them into incomplete patterns."[21] Judd was incorporating found industrial components into his three-dimensional experiments before he acquired the cast-iron building he would make his home and studio. However, the same conditions that made 101 Spring Street available to Judd and Finch—remnants of industrial manufacturing as it migrated from the city to the suburbs—were also the conditions of possibility that allowed Judd to make those first objects. Writer and curator John Coplans once asked Judd about the components of his earliest three-dimensional work, specifically an asphalt pipe that was the central component of a wall-mounted work: "All your materials of this kind were just what you could find lying around?" Judd responded, "Yes. A lot of it was primarily because it was cheap, and also I didn't care about it being precise."[22] This exchange demonstrates a scrappy sensibility akin to that inherent in rasquachismo, profoundly troubling the distinction between Chicanx art and Minimalism constructed by Gaspar de Alba.

The idealness of the situation on Spring Street—in regard to the neighborhood, not the building itself—was short-lived. Within just a couple of years of Judd and Finch's purchase of 101 Spring Street, the area once designated "Hell's Hundred Acres" was rapidly transforming into SoHo.[23] The presence of artists, gradually made known through gallery owners, collectors, and the artists themselves, chipped away at the reticence many New Yorkers and real estate developers had once maintained regarding the area south of Houston Street. Soon, there were organized Saturday art fairs, where open studios and street festivities invited art enthusiasts to fill the streets and loft spaces transformed by the artists' presence. The walking tour pictured by Arthur Getz for the *New Yorker* in 1980, for instance, was unimaginable in 1968, when Judd first moved to the area. Judd, critical of the direction the neighborhood was taking (a welcome condition for other artists), as well as of the related consumer-minded commercialization of its storefronts, and concerned for his pottery and cactus collections, began looking for real estate elsewhere.[24] By 1972, following a visit in 1971, he settled on Marfa, Texas.[25]

How did Judd come to find Marfa, much less inhabit it so fully? The first response is made clear by Judd himself:

> In late 1946 I and four other soldiers went by bus from Fort McClellan, Alabama, to Los Angeles, where we inveigled a ride from the Army Air Force to San Francisco in order to be shipped to Korea to pester the world. This was the first time I saw the Southwest, unfortunately according to the days and nights of the bus. Since everyone knows that nothing is accidental and that everything is fully planned, it's not surprising that I sent a telegram saying: DEAR MOM VAN HORN TEXAS. 1260 POPULATION. NICE TOWN BEAUTIFUL COUNTRY MOUNTAINS-LOVE DON 1946 DEC 17 PM 5 45.[26]

From at least 1969, Judd road-tripped frequently from New York to the region of Baja California and other parts of Mexico. This was another way he became familiar with the Southwest United States. Having the means and the motivation to get out of New York by the early 1970s, Judd settled on Marfa as an appropriate area for the fullest expression of his ideas about architecture and the permanent installation of art. In his words, "I chose the town of Marfa (pop. 2,466) because it was the best looking and the most practical, and rented a small house, thanks to the help of Mae Adams, now Firstbrook, who worked at the motel."[27] That small first house would expand over the subsequent decades into multiple residential, commercial, and land properties in and around town.

The Judd Foundation oversees the properties left by the artist, save one. My focus here is that separate entity, Chinati, founded by Judd as a museum on the grounds of the former US Army Fort D. A. Russell. Dia Art Foundation lent its financial and institutional support to this effort until 1986. Judd continued to develop the site throughout his lifetime. Chinati continues to grow its collection according to his vision. This growth takes place through extending the collection itself, running educational programming for Marfa residents, and coordinating a highly selective artist's residency. The heart of Chinati, the permanent installation of works selected by Judd, includes work by the artist himself, Claes Oldenburg and Coosje van Bruggen, Ilya Kabakov, Carl Andre, Ingólfur Arnarsson, Roni Horn, David Rabinowitch, Richard Long, John Wesley, Dan Flavin, and Robert Irwin.

Chinati is located on Marfa's southern edge. Visitors must pass through two thresholds to enter: The first is perpendicular to the Sanchez family's yard

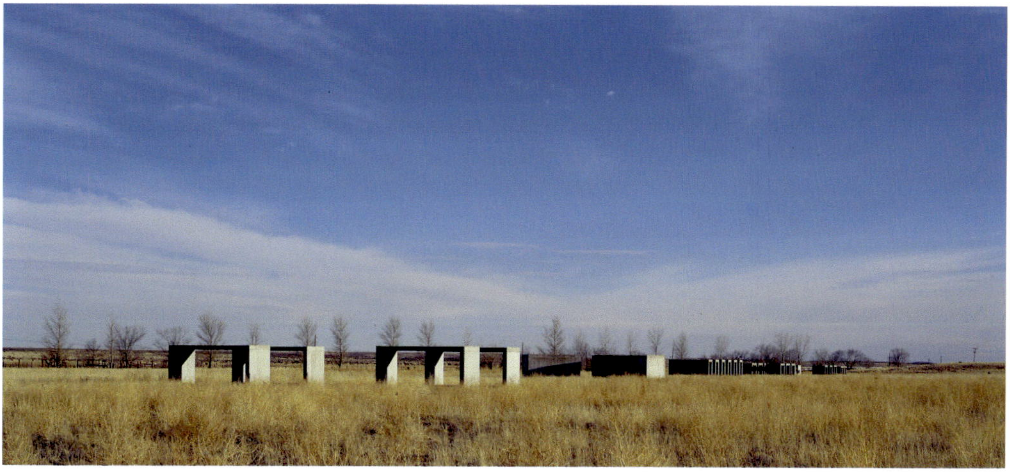

FIGURE 1.13 Donald Judd, *15 untitled works in concrete* (detail), 1980–84. Permanent collection, Chinati Foundation, Marfa, Texas. Photo: Florian Holzherr. Donald Judd Art © 2025 Judd Foundation/Artists Rights Society (ARS), New York.

and composed of a chain-link fence visually reinforced by two sloping, white stucco walls; the second is a swinging wooden gate where one enters the parking lot adjacent to the welcome center. Director Emeritus Marianne Stockebrand wrote of another Judd property—La Mansana de Chinati, also known as The Block, located in Marfa's downtown—that it "is a complete microcosm in its own right, which—like a monastery—has all of life's essentials, from an excellent library to a chicken coop."[28] (An adobe wall acts as the physical boundary for this space.) Stockebrand's words—particularly "microcosm"—also describe my sense of entering and exiting Chinati through its two thresholds, reinforcing the aptness of conceptualizing Marfa through world-travel and pilgrimage. The Sanchezes' yard, formerly my grandfather's—which shares a traffic circle with Chinati's lower entrance—might be considered its own cosmos. The site and installation of Guadalupe's image is at its center, with domestic activities and slow residential traffic—that is, everyday life—inscribing their own paths next to those initiated by Judd. Next to Hector Sanchez's altar, I will focus on one of Judd's orbiting bodies in this chapter, fifteen multi-unit concrete works, arranged linearly in an open field on Chinati's grounds (figure 1.13). This returns us to the primary tasks of this chapter: world-traveling in order to understand how images mobilize and are mobilized by two neighboring pilgrimage sites; clarifying the differences in the terms of each pilgrimage to unlearn "arrogant perceptions"; and examining the role of sculptural objects in these processes.

Peter Reading, the first poet to hold the Lannan Foundation's highly regarded one-year residency in Marfa, memorialized the fifteen concrete works as follows:

> Across the windswept, Pronghorn-browsed brown grass
> Judd's row of concrete, seven-foot-high boxes
> stretches a mile north-south, signifies zilch.
>
> Some days I've seen Antilocapras shelter
> from noon sun of a hundred-and-some degrees
> in those cute sculptures—yes, and shit in'm too.[29]

The "concrete, seven-foot-high boxes" do provide uncanny shelter for the antelope. It is easy for them to find relief from the West Texas sun, wind, and dust at any time of day among the boxes' various orientations and arrangements of sides (solid concrete or open air). A visitor-beaten trail runs the "mile north-south" along which "those cute sculptures" are arranged. To call them cute and to recall the shitting of antelope are certainly deliberate moves by which Reading characterizes his own approach to an object of many art enthusiasts' pilgrimages. This cheeky and localizing approach diminishes the prestige held by the group and the artist in many art-historical narratives. Recalling that antelope occasionally shit in them disturbs the "microcosmic" sense one might have of the site; antelope flow freely between the Chinati Foundation grounds and elsewhere, unlike visitors who must check in first. (But this sense is only disturbed if one takes *microcosmic* to necessarily imply insularity.) That the group "signifies zilch" in Reading's estimation leads into the long-standing debates around Judd's works' (non)allusive nature. Reading's position is ultimately ambiguous. Is this line an endorsement from his own experience that, as the artist wanted, the work succeeds at *not representing* but *being*? Or is the poet asserting the irrelevance of their art-historical status to most people, echoing the antelopes' indifference? Put another way, is Reading supporting and validating the artist's vision of an art that breaks with (European) traditions of representation? Or is he questioning why people (pilgrims) go so far out of their way to encounter objects that to him seem insignificant and not worth the trouble?

Locals have grappled with this question since the early 1980s, when installation of the works began. It is difficult to ignore them even if one never sets foot inside the foundation. They are prominent in the landscape, particularly from the nearby, heavily used US Highway 67. For some Marfans, they have transitioned from meaningless objects to exemplars of "art." Their capability to signify can transform over time (an effect of permanent installation). And one's approach—down to the direction from which, at what time, and for how long one looks—matters. Jack Brunson, a retired border patrolman, gives his account of this transition:

> You have to stop and look at those [fifteen concrete works] and wonder what in the heck they are. But then I understand later.... I guess it's the old thing of "art's in the eye of the beholder." You sat up there on the hill on the Southwest side sorta' and look back down there and watch that in the afternoon.... You could see that you're looking at something that you never saw before ... take your time and watch, and you see art.[30]

This begs the question: On what terms does Brunson sense this transformation when looking at the concrete works? Judging from his first impression, when he "wonder[s] what in the heck they are," it is doubtful that the transformation has anything to do with resemblance. That he notes the specificity of cardinal direction and time of day as integral signals that their placement in the landscape and relationship to shifting natural light are key. Thus, he locates their artfulness in their behavior *as objects*, rather than in any representational qualities. While Brunson is a refreshing and novel source, this observation is old hat in art history and has been troubled, reaffirmed, and troubled again since Judd began creating three-dimensional works. By 1966, art historian Rosalind Krauss had already articulated the whole of this oscillation.

ALTAR-ING THE "EXPANDED FIELD"

Krauss cites Judd himself in identifying successful work as that which "asserts its own existence, form and power. It becomes an object in its own right." As Krauss understands it, this object-ness relies on a "presumptive reduction of art from the realm of illusion—and through illusionism, of meaning—to the sphere of transparently real objects." Against this abstract model, she then describes her own experience: "Approaching Judd's latest work from within this frame of reference, one is totally unprepared for the extraordinary beauty of the sculptures themselves, a beauty and authority which is nowhere described or accounted for in the polemics of object art and which leads one to feel all the more acutely the inadequacy of the theoretical line, its failure to measure up (at least in Judd's case) to the power of the sculptural statement."[31] Perhaps it is this unaccounted-for power that catalyzes Brunson's ultimate characterization of the concrete works. In any case, for both the Krauss of "Allusion and Illusion in Donald Judd" and Brunson, Judd's works are not conventionally allusive or illusive, but neither are they *mere* objects. Both of their approaches—from the gallery and the hilltop, respectively—result in identifying the works' proprioceptive force as not sufficiently captured in that term. While this one statement is all we will get from Brunson, Krauss's subsequent work over the years as an art critic and historian grapples with the vexing "power of the sculptural statement." I now turn to a later instance of her grappling to understand this power as it operates between the neighboring pair of Minimalist and rasquache works in Marfa.

Later, in her 1979 essay "Sculpture in the Expanded Field," Krauss took stock of the moment and recent history in which she found herself, when the category of sculpture had "expanded" to "become almost infinitely malleable." Though her essay is not concerned with Judd, the problematic it takes on remains relevant for Marfa, a landscape laden with so-called sculptures. Because the project of modernist sculpture in the preceding era was frequently linked with the refining and reducing of the medium to its inherent qualities, it was unable to account for the sheer multifariousness of techniques and materials artists began taking up in the 1960s. Her observations—of earthworks, of the absorption of the pedestal in Minimalist sculpture, of the use of industrial materials and techniques, and of the inclusion of new media like television—attest to this. Looking to other areas of criticism for a logic that might begin to account for this novel variety, Krauss turns to the then-growing notion of postmodernism "in order to name this historical rupture and the structural transformation of the cultural field that characterizes it."[32]

In three increasingly dense diagrams, Krauss schematizes the fate of the sculptural category (figure 1.14). Modernist sculpture is suspended between two negative statements: it is "not landscape"; it is "not architecture." Three-dimensional work of the 1960s and 1970s confronted this logic with so many experimental spatial and material interventions that this ease of definition collapsed, yet the term *sculpture* was still being applied to such pieces. Krauss's

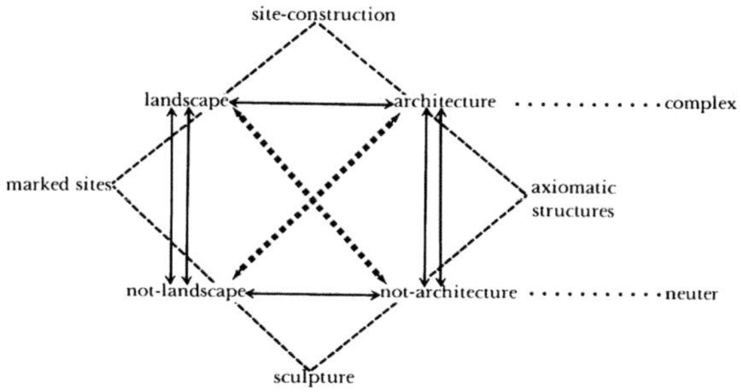

FIGURE 1.14 Rosalind Krauss, final diagram for "Sculpture in the Expanded Field," 1979.

essay and accompanying diagrams aim at redeeming the term through articulating a structural expansion of its underpinning logic to match what she observed happening around her. *Sculpture* is no longer the middle term between two things it is not, but "rather only one term on the periphery of a field in which there are other, differently structured possibilities."[33] New terms emerge: *site-construction, marked sites,* and *axiomatic structures.* Thus, the category of sculpture was protected from a postmodernist implosion in which it would lack any meaning at all and could still prove useful in accounting for works like those of Carl Andre, Mary Miss, Bruce Nauman, Richard Serra, Robert Smithson—and, of course, Judd. Shortly, I will introduce *altar* and *altar-installation* to reconfigure these markers yet again.

But if a more fixed sense of the term *sculpture* is not an objective of my writing or of most subsequent scholarship, why is Krauss's writing on the subject of such interest? The answer lies in her observation of a frequent move performed by many of her contemporaries in their attempts to make sense of these emerging works: the overly eager placement of artists' practices in a long genealogy, including "Stonehenge, the Nazca lines, the Toltec ballcourts, [and] Indian burial mounds."[34] Her colleagues reached back millennia when reaching back merely to Naum Gabo or Kasimir Malevich no longer sufficed, she notes. While they aimed to deepen the definition of sculpture through this tactic, the result of historicizing sculpture in the *longue durée* was, contrary to all good intentions, an "obscuring" of the term. To this claim I offer little contention. But Krauss's rigorous attempt to define the historical bounds of the term *sculpture*—against such heterogeneity-inducing moves as reading *Spiral Jetty* alongside the Nazca Lines—results in the *invisibility* of certain manipulations of material and space to the disciplinary eyes of art history and in her own writing, work that now comprises a substantial part of the central theoretical canon of the discipline. My concern lies precisely in the obscuring of sculpture as an identifiable artistic category, exemplified by its most advanced practices, when it is equated with the constructions of historically "primitive" cultures from the druids to the Aztecs. Where Krauss goes on to reestablish sculpture's terms and particular history, I pick up this thread and carry it across worlds, continuing the travel between vying fields in Marfa.

Krauss, true to the task she sets out for herself, exposes the tokenizing of ancient cultures enacted by the thinking she critiques. In doing so, she aims to pull sculpture from the wreckage. Revisiting this exposure with different aims—to address and rectify the *peopled* aftermath—matters because in Marfa, but not only in Marfa, works like those of such great concern to Krauss and her peers neighbor creative productions that also manipulate space, concrete, dirt, plaster, paint, and various ephemera but that are not called "installation," "sculpture," or "earthworks." Rasquachismo, as Gaspar de Alba and others have deployed it, enacts its own rupture with Modernism on its own terms. Krauss recognizes the oft-cited pre-Columbian inspirations for rasquache works—Aztec and Toltec cultures—only in order to demonstrate the fallacy of identifying them with the postwar artworks in her field. I recognize them for their capacity to illuminate works in the field of Chicanx cultural production that was burgeoning at the time of Krauss's essay but was outside her field of vision.

A 1986 editorial decision during Krauss's time at the helm of *October* further nuances this observation of her perception of pre-Columbian American cultures (and their role in contemporary cultural productions). I am thinking of the inclusion of Georges Bataille's essay "Extinct America" in an issue of that year devoted to his work. My interest rises immediately in reading his first lines: "The life of civilized peoples in pre-Columbian America is a source of wonder to us, not only in its discovery and instantaneous disappearance, but also because of its bloody eccentricity, surely the most extreme ever conceived by an aberrant mind. . . . This observation applies, it is true, mostly to Mexico."[35]

In the US borderlands with Mexico where Marfa squarely sits, this "bloody eccentricity" costumes itself as the decolonizing compendium of attitude, style, and approach to materials I am calling rasquachismo. It decolonizes by disidentifying with Bataille's fantasizing and exoticizing eye. Our transmuted inheritance of that "aberrant mind" is only illegible if one is unwilling or unable to travel worlds, to take up multiple modes of perceiving, ranging back and forth among the historically reified and the repudiated vernacular.

The "source of wonder" that is pre-Columbian America is not as distant in time and space as Bataille has it.[36] Many people of Mexican descent still explicitly consider the Aztecs a part of their constitution, however fantastic the connection may seem (to say nothing of the actual Nahuatl-speaking peoples still living in parts of southern Mexico, whose connection requires far less fantasy). I offer a familial demonstration in a letter from my grandmother Esperanza Hernandez, wife of my Marfa-raised grandfather, herself born in nearby Shafter, Texas. I wrote to her, curious whether she could provide any information about our family's Indigenous heritage. She responded:

> Querid Joshua, No le avia contestada por la razon que queriamos preguntarle a algen de los Indios Indigenás, pero creo que nadie de nuestra familia saven. Lo siento mijo. Lo unico que yo se es que creo nosotros los mexicanos benemos de los Astecas y Spañoles. [*sic*][37]

Lives imagined so—descended from "Aztecs and Spaniards"—are undertaken in particular places, places occasionally shared with some of Krauss's objects of concern. Marfa is one such site. I consider disparate "sculptural" traditions side by side not because they share a genealogy to be neatly traced and elaborated (I fully agree with Krauss on this) but because the people who made and care for them currently produce their civic space and aesthetic environment side by side. Whereas Krauss's primary concern is sculpture, in this writing I use sculpture as a means by which to address and reimagine such lived coproduction of a place. So alongside terms like those debated by Krauss in the 1960s and 1970s, Marfa calls for the acknowledgment of additional relevant terms active in rasquache object-making, terms like *capilla*, *nicho*, and most encompassing, *altar*.

Judd's architectural projects, furniture, and art constitute distinct practices.[38] However, echoes between proportions, shapes, and relations of panels (or floors, walls, and ceilings) do exist. At 101 Spring Street, for instance, the fifth-floor bedroom includes a baseboard around its perimeter, creating a recessed plane (the floor) which resonates with the recessed plane of an anodized aluminum work located in the third-floor studio (untitled, 1966). Some

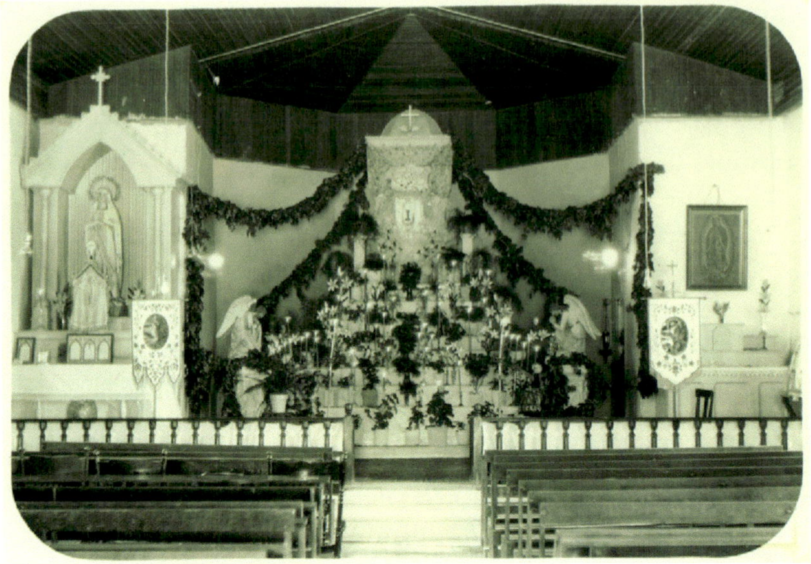

FIGURE 1.15 Interior of Sacred Heart of Jesus Catholic Church in Shafter, Texas, ca. 1920s. Junior Historian Files, Marfa Public Library, Marfa, Texas.

of the one hundred works in mill aluminum at Chinati also feature such recessed surfaces.[39] The structures and objects known by the two terms I introduce below demonstrate a similar play of scale and interrelating parts across art and architecture. For this analogy, it is instructive to consider Hector Sanchez's altar alongside the Sacred Heart of Jesus Catholic Church in nearby Shafter attended by my grandmother as a child (figure 1.15).

I also turn to the work of artist Marie Romero Cash and altar historian and theorist Kay Turner, with a focus on two especially relevant architectural terms, *capilla* and *nicho*.

CAPILLA/CAPILLITA—CHAPEL/LITTLE CHAPEL: Architecturally, *capilla* can be applied to an independent, inhabitable structure *and* to internal features of a larger building (such as a cathedral) meant for housing and displaying objects rather than sheltering human bodies (even if size would permit). Regarding the Shafter church, it is small enough that the entire building could be referred to as a capilla. Inside, the clearest example is to the viewer's left (to the right of the large central recess housing the church's main altar).

The simulated architecture, attached to the wall but visually independent of its surround, is distinguished by the Gothic-style arch with its shallow recess housing a Marian sculpture. This complements the framed picture of the Virgin of Guadalupe on the opposite flank of the main altar. At the sculpture's feet there is a still smaller architectural model, with the same peaked roof and perhaps a miniature Gothic arch as well (a curtain blocks this from view). At this scale, *capillita* becomes the more appropriate term. The diminutive signals a shift in purpose premised on portability. This particular capillita appears to be permanently situated, but it may not be. It may function as do some New Mexican capillitas that Marie Romero Cash describes in her study: "A capillita (little shrine) consists of a statue of the Holy Family (Jesus, Mary, and Joseph) enclosed in a wooden niche. The custodian prepares a schedule by which each family in the coro ['core' of a church's social organization] is allowed to keep the capillita one day of the month. The niche is placed in the family's devotional area, in which flowers have been placed and candles lit, and special prayers are recited by members."[40] Where devotees move to capillas, capillitas are moved between devotees. This movement is fluid between corporate and domestic sacred spaces. Scale plays a significant role in this movement.

NICHO—NICHE: This refers to the space in which statuary is placed. In the Shafter capilla, this is the space defined by the Gothic arch and slender relief-carved columns. Romero Cash identifies nichos in other structures as well: shallow spaces of just a few square inches built into almost wall-sized wooden altar screens, or the pictorial space created by handmade tin frames hung on a wall.[41] The last strikingly demonstrates the elasticity of the term. There is no room in this particular nicho for three-dimensional representation (an example pointed to by Romero Cash is crayon on paper), putting it at the furthest possible distance from the term's more architectural meanings.

These meanings can collide in a single work like the Sanchez altar. Unlike the capilla in Shafter, the Sanchez altar stands independently outdoors, rather than being attached to an interior wall. The result is that, particularly from the back, its sheltering function is more apparent than its displaying function (figure 1.16). From the front, it prominently serves as a display space for the statue of Guadalupe. Whether the installation reads as capilla or nicho depends on the direction from which one approaches this upturned and altered bathtub. The Sanchez altar is also situated in the same functional

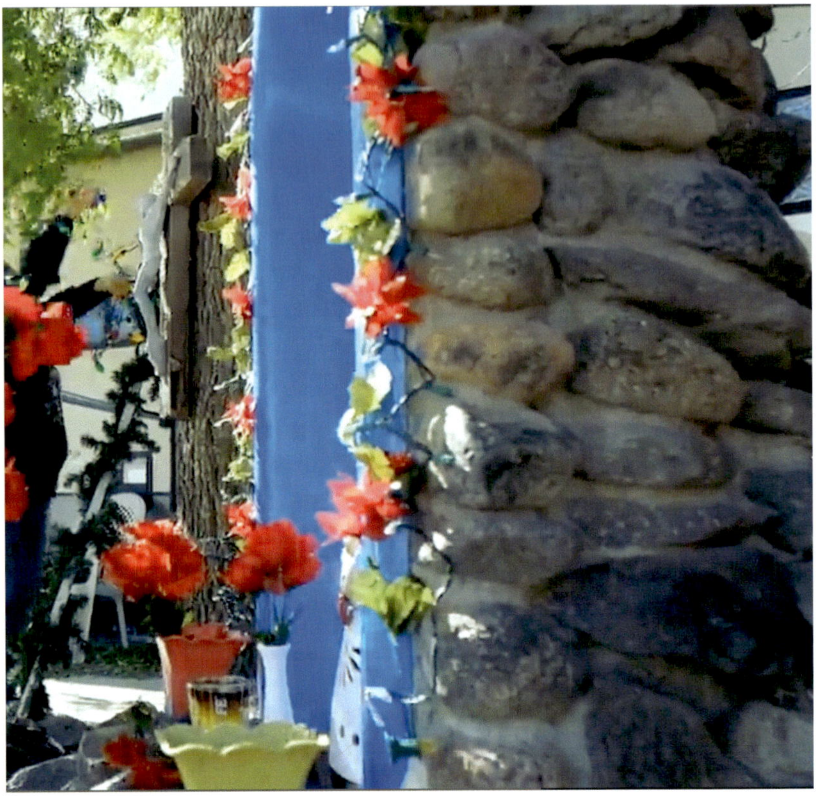

FIGURE 1.16 Guadalupe altar, Marfa, Texas (detail). Video still, December 3, 2023. Videographer: Sarah M. Vasquez.

middle ground as the capilla in Shafter. It is too small to function as a chapel one might physically enter, but it is too large (and cemented to its base) to serve as a portable capillita. In any case, portability would contradict its reason for being, to mark the site of Guadalupe's apparition in the yard. The importance of site specificity resonates with much of Judd's motivation for making art and architecture and moves us closer toward what distinguishes altars from capillas/capillitas and nichos (though these remain viable descriptions of altars' components).

The production of specific and sacred space is integral to Kay Turner's description of domestic altars:

> The age-old task of religious art has been to bridge the division between the sacred and mundane, the spiritual and the material, the Self and the Other. We now live in a time when this division is at its most extreme, but, from the very beginnings of human consciousness, a particular religious art form has assuaged the terror of separation by creating a special site to serve the human desire for relationship with unseen gods and spirits. We call that place an altar, a place set apart to house the images of powerful sacred beings, who by their presence can be called upon for help and comfort.[42]

I propose adding Minimalism and rasquachismo to the list of "divisions" to be "bridged," though I am proposing different languages and conceptions for such inclinations "of human consciousness" that do not so quickly reinstantiate inside/outside dichotomies. Here, this proposal is anchored in Judd's concrete works and Sanchez's altar for the Virgin of Guadalupe. I place Krauss's diagrams in contact with terms relevant to altar-making and other rasquache productions to offer language for this "bridging" activity.

From various trajectories, the building and forms of altars have already cross-contaminated the realms of art production and theorizing in which Krauss and Judd consciously operate(d). Amalia Mesa-Bains's installation work is a frequently cited example of this contamination, which Pérez has termed "altarity." Of Mesa-Bains and other contemporary Chicanx artists, she writes:

> I see their work as sacrificial ofrenda, as transmutation of social or personal suffering into penetrating visions of the present and brave sightings of hopeful, better futures. The pun in the subtitle of this book, *The Politics of Spiritual and Aesthetic Altarities*, thus refers to these works as offerings on the altar where the material and the still disembodied are invoked, and where the embodied is reminded of its ultimate identity with the socially or culturally disincarnate that it would "other" or relegate to the realm of seeming nonexistence. The Chicana art in the chapters that follow extends itself, offering what to many are still "foreign" and suspect, and thus unintelligible, knowledges: the cultural "differences" of the non-Western, the female, the queer, and the poor.[43]

To reiterate: Altars and the spaces they provide for making ofrendas are "where the embodied is reminded of its ultimate identity with the socially or culturally disincarnate that it would 'other' or relegate to the realm of seeming nonexistence." For one, this helps keep in focus that rasquachismo is first and foremost an intangible sensibility and an attitude, though it has clear implications for material form. Secondly, Pérez's spatializing of the altar's function is invitational, "offering what to many are still 'foreign' and suspect, and thus unintelligible, knowledges."

Precisely to counteract this threat of unintelligibility, I find it crucial to begin from an altar in Marfa as a site where objects and neighboring places may be transformed into a site of conviviality. What is gained by simultaneously invoking Krauss's expanded field of sculpture (with its Minimalist and post-Minimalist constituents) and a body of works and terms demonstrative of rasquachismo in the context of Marfa? The feedback between first-degree rasquache altars and art-historical diagrams defining sculpture leads to an increased mutual visibility based not on a politics of inclusion but on the fostering of a genuine interest in those with whom one produces place, and to suggestions as to how we might proceed to act on this interest and build a new language for its expression.

Third-degree rasquachismo like Mesa-Bains's work intentionally contaminates, relying on the "suspect, and thus unintelligible" knowledge of women's domestic altars performed and displayed in spaces dedicated to contemporary art. Mesa-Bains terms her hybrid works "altar-installations." Of such third-degree rasquachismo, art historian Jennifer A. González writes, "At a time when temporary and site-specific installation art had gained mainstream acceptance as a legitimate art form, Mesa-Bains worked within and across this framework by incorporating traditionally ephemeral and impermanent practices from Mexican popular culture in her gallery installations. Linking these two social and artistic practices, the artist recognized and emphasized the parallels between genres of display from two distinct cultural domains."[44] Frictions inevitably accompany such "parallels." González read Mesa-Bains's work as energized by this friction, an expression located between Mexican and Mexican American altar building and art-historical site specificity. It carries on "both as a continuation of ancient and ongoing Mexican devotional traditions, and as contemporary art."[45] But the first-degree rasquache altar in the backyard of the Sanchez home has no such concern. Its purpose is to site and shelter Guadalupe so that she may comfortably receive her children and the curious. It is Chicanx artists' and art historians' task, if we choose it, to invite her and associated rituals into third-degree work that traffics in contemporary art. It is a blessing—ofrendas honored—when she accepts.

THE TROUBLE WITH JOSHUA SAUNDERS

The responsibilities inherent in coproducing place out of space can be attended to through the visual and the sculptural so that Marfa may be better protected from typical effects of cultural tourism, so that its rasquachismo avoids the trap of becoming culinary and second-degree (cynically commercialized). This responsibility—key to world-traveling—is enacted in the flesh-to-flesh and flesh-to-material encounters of pilgrims with one another and with their site-specific destinations. While Marfa in some ways demonstrates very clearly the exhaustion of the traditional category of sculpture, it raises "pilgrimage" as a new site of inquiry in which to revisit our understandings of objects and audiences in the "expanded field." Things that *might be* called sculptures happen to be at the culmination of such pilgrimages. The expanded field has a proven allure, one I investigated along with the conceptual means by which people make their way to and through the Minimalist and rasquache fields. In conclusion, I return to the 2011 installation MARFITA to consider images and sculptures produced by pilgrims conscious of both fields.

For MARFITA, Joshua Saunders reconstructed a stylized version of the Sanchezes' kitchen inside the gallery (figure 1.17). At first glance, it recalled a number of Mesa-Bains's installations: a domestic room demarcated by a rough-hewn dining table, mass-produced artworks prosaically framed, a popped beer can, and an open Bible, all daring the viewer to decide whether they are in an intimate familial space or a contemporary art gallery. But Saunders's particular style of walking this line asserts itself soon enough. While the reconstruction as a whole held visitors' visual interest and clearly conveyed the domestic setting in which Sanchez likely sat contemplating the gravity of Guadalupe's apparition, one image in particular acted as a lightning rod for accusations of misappropriation, sacrilege, and ethnic stereotyping. Hung on the wall, in the kitchen/gallery, *Disco Face Mary w/ Neon Native Shank* is based upon a found image of Mary (one progenitor of Guadalupe) gazing up at her son Jesus on the cross (figure 1.18), her hands uplifted in a gesture of grief. The image is cropped tight so that only Christ's bloody ankles and feet are visible just above Mary's head. Saunders makes two further interventions: Over Mary's face he pastes a cut piece of shimmering, multicolored metallic paper, displacing the flattening gold leaf that has a long history in Marian representation directly onto her face, now in the form of fractured

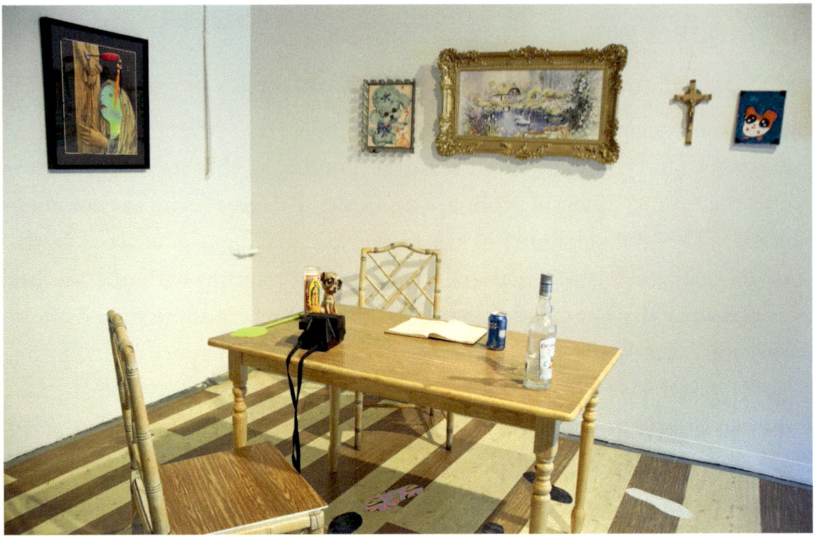

FIGURE 1.17 Joshua Saunders, detail of untitled Sanchez family kitchen reproduction, *MARFITA*, 2011.

and silvery contact paper; and at the point where blood flows out of Christ's right foot, a "shank" adorned with Day-Glo plastic beads, artificial feathers, and string protrudes.

Saunders's collage raises the question of approach anew. Is *Disco Face Mary* another iteration of contemporary art that can be loved but cannot love back (like Judd's)? Or is it a divine image, understood to love in return for offerings and prayers, as is the Guadalupan statue residing in Marfa? (Saunders cites research into Guadalupe for *MARFITA* as inspiration for this piece, which he considers otherwise uncharacteristic of his practice.) The glittery face Saunders puts on Mary both mocks and reveres. Ultimately, she is fickle: In conversations where I have had occasion to present this image, it proves incendiary to a wide range of listeners, including conservative Mexican American Catholics, leftist Chicanxs, Indigenous people, and their progressive, white self-proclaimed allies.

This is all to assert that comfort and ease are not endemic to world-traveling (this is not a call to politeness). Often, images generated by pilgrimage become the sites, the intersections, from which one decides to resist the "hushing of the manyness" or to comply with it (be it politely, derisively, or otherwise). Whatever one's approach in response to the image—pilgrimage

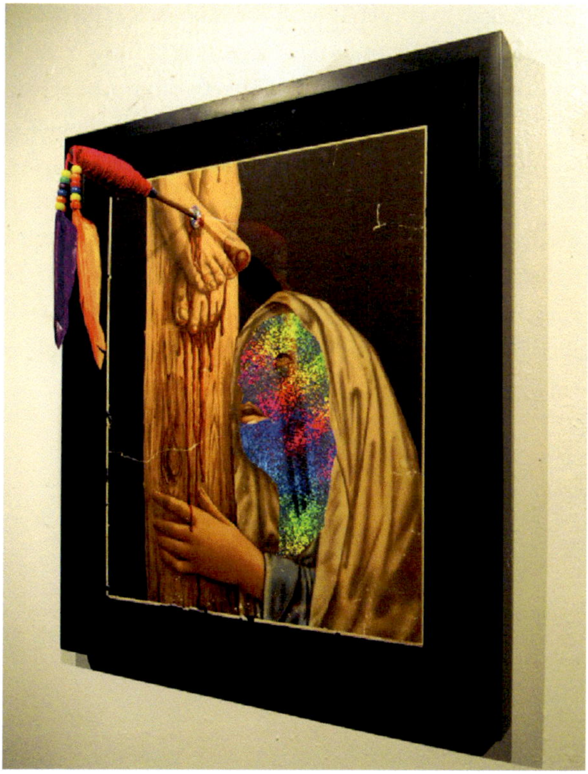

FIGURE 1.18 Joshua Saunders, *Disco Face Mary w/ Neon Native Shank*, MARFITA, 2011.

or hushing—Saunders, as well as Kuo, has certainly contributed to the complex, seemingly incessant unfolding of Guadalupan images.

My own contributions to *MARFITA* were miniature versions of Judd's *15 untitled works in concrete* and *100 untitled works in mill aluminum* (including their housing, two repurposed artillery sheds). These remained in the gallery's yard, barely lit on the night of the opening, disappearing in favor of the lighting and performative focus on Kuo's altar and Guadalupe's present absence. Re-creating these in miniature and neighboring them with the enlarged altar was the central component of our experimental question: How could we decentralize Judd's work and Minimalism characteristic of the art world's focus on Marfa in order to question that focus—in a sustainable and transformative way—through a symbol of creative works by its Mexican American inhabitants? In this chapter, I addressed this question through the concepts of world-traveling and pilgrimage, elaborating from them a framework for reconceiving inhabitations of Marfa often understood and performed as merely or delightfully incongruous. In her review of *MARFITA* for the *Austin American-Statesman*, titled "A Little Take on Marfa's Culture Clash," critic Jeanne Claire van Ryzin writes that *MARFITA* "troubles the boundary between two distinct groups that treasure Marfa with the same depth of reverence."[46] In the spirit of being both troublesome and reverent, I have reimagined (certainly not alone) the "clash" as an opportunity for world-traveling and conviviality, with Marfa as the apex and passage of multiple pilgrimages.

Marfa, Aztlán

2

We, the Chicano inhabitants and civilizers of the Northern land of Aztlán, from whence came our [Aztec] forefathers, reclaiming the land of their birth and consecrating the determination of our people of the sun, declare that the call of our blood is our power, our response and our inevitable destiny.

—Alurista, "Preamble to the Plan Espiritual de Aztlán"

To reoccupy Aztlán, the oppressed hallucinate—and that practice has no borders.

—Laura E. Pérez, "El Desorden, Nationalism, and Chicana/o Aesthetics"

"We are in different fields of vision and knowing even when we stand together in the same physical space."[1] In an open letter written in 2012, I addressed these words to an artist who saw many aspirations for his practice fulfilled in West Texas, where I grew up. He was deceased at the time. Regardless, I imagine us walking through town in the letter. We visit sites significant to either or both of us. I contemplate with him a quotation painted as a mural on the old elementary school façade. I inquire about the varieties of Mexican food he had or had not consumed here. I address him one artist to another, across generations, across physical space (I wrote from the Netherlands), and across the open wound between incarnate and disincarnate life. The town we amble through is Marfa, Texas; the artist, Donald Judd. Presently, *this* writing extends descriptions, mappings, of these fields of vision, constituted as they were and are by our distinct positions within Marfa's social fabric. These include but are not limited to Judd's and my own, ultimately placing them all in relation to Aztlán, the grounded and mythical, historical and fantasized Chicanx homeland.

While the appropriation of Aztlán has a long history in the broader Chicano Movement, it has also been taken up in art terms before. Here, I bring Marfa into this effort. Curator Howard N. Fox has written about the distance from Aztlán as a helpful concept demonstrated by artists such as the collective ASCO, Christina Fernandez, Alejandro Diaz, and others; in doing so he reinscribes its legacy in their work and provides an apt definition useful here: "If *Chicanismo* ... stressed a distinctive cultural identity and the reclamation of a suppressed and all-but-forgotten history, Aztlán gave palpable form and a geographic locus to a vague and ancient past.... Indeed, the shopworn but pointed protest of Chicano culture that 'We didn't cross the border; the border crossed us' is an evocation, sometimes unwitting, of the place and the civilization that is imagined to be Aztlán."[2] Marfa sits squarely in this geographic zone where many of us were crossed by the moving border. Aztlán names the territory according to our view of history, and in this chapter I practice looking at art in Marfa from the same view of art history. How place is understood directly relates to the tools with which one looks. Railroad surveyors establishing the rail lines in the nineteenth century looked on the West Texas landscape quite differently than, say, artists looking to make a new home in Marfa today. What readings of the land and the art here result when we imagine standing on and before that land and art conceived as components of Aztlán?

MARFA'S MANY PROMISES

Marfa offers a variety of promises to different seekers. To Judd, Marfa promised what his close colleague and curator Rudi Fuchs calls the "ideal museum." This museum is one in which art can be produced and permanently installed in harmonious partnership with its surroundings. Fuchs writes, "Now an artist has created one of these ideal museums himself—far from the inhabited world, as it is called."[3] For me, Marfa holds out the promise of a focused laboratory in which it is possible to refurbish and forge new rasquache tools for looking back on and significantly revising postwar art history. These revisions are particularly aimed at existing views of postwar art's many nonurban sites as uninhabited, a view expressed by Fuchs in regard to Marfa.

People, my people, were and remain there, rigorously *inhabiting*, if invisibly to many.

To frontiersmen of the late nineteenth and early twentieth centuries, Marfa was open range for making one's fortune, in adventurous experiences if not also in mineral wealth. This spirit of intrepid exploration and rollicking cowboy danger among "Indians" is well documented by the maverick, beloved Texas historian J. Frank Dobie. In the opening chapter of one of many books, his reflection on the promises of adventure in the Southwest illuminates a fantasy enjoyed by many Texans. He writes, "It is a world of illimitable vistas, of geological inscrutabilities, and of things both animate and inanimate deeply hidden."[4] Tom Lea's illustrations for the book picture this sense of unlimited potential through images like that of two square-jawed cowboys in profile surveying the distance from the edge of a sharply dropping cliff face (figure 2.1). It is my contention here that these vistas are not, in fact, "illimitable." However, I do not aim to close off the capacity to see them as such; rather, the argument I present here delimits a multiplicity of views to ultimately produce a much richer view of Marfa, to make manifold our perceptive capacities. In owning up to the limits, myriad points for crossing—"world-traveling" in María Lugones's sense discussed in the previous chapters—are also established.

For ranchers, Marfa and the larger Chihuahuan Desert promise nourishing grasslands and ample roaming space. Kerr Mitchell, whose great-grandfather drove cattle into West Texas in 1884, details the advantages: "Out in this part of the world, we don't get very much rain. Consequently, the grass is a lot stronger and you grow animals a lot better and you don't have to feed them a lot of minerals and stuff. . . . Out in the hill country, east Texas, where you get 50 to 60 inches of rain a year, you get no minerals at all in the soil."[5] The animals too, buffalo in this case, find their own promised land of plenty here.

In Marfa, small but vividly salient within a largely unbuilt expanse, there is also the promise of cover in an otherwise easily and heavily surveilled landscape for undocumented border crossers coming from Mexico, a hundred miles south. Their transient and endangered occupations are known through ephemera like those documented in photographer Delilah Montoya's large-format pictures of migrant campsites. Montoya has also photographed salient resources installed in the desert to aid migrants in distress (figure 2.2). Discarded backpacks, abandoned shoes, and emptied food and water con-

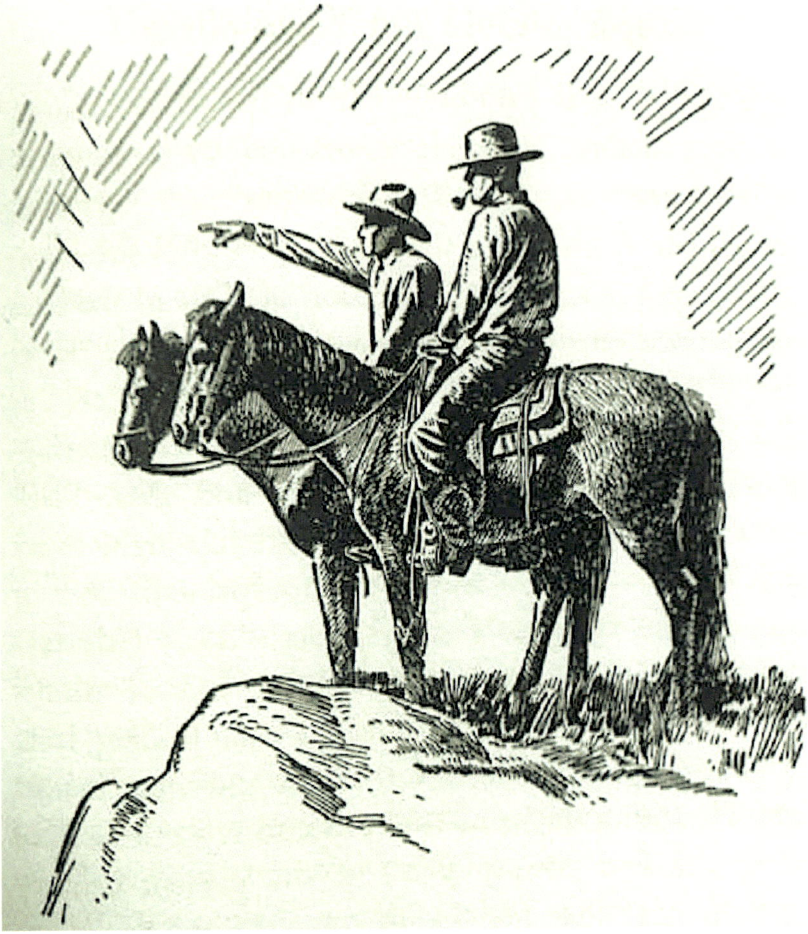

FIGURE 2.1 Tom Lea, illustration for J. Frank Dobie's *Apache Gold and Yaqui Silver*, 1939.

tainers are often found in Marfa as well, at spots known to some locals but kept secret in solidarity with crossers. To those undertaking the surveillance, the US Border Patrol, Marfa strategically locates a headquarters for the area between larger city-anchored checkpoints like the one near El Paso, almost two hours away. For migrant farmworkers like my grandfather, who did hold citizenship in the United States, Marfa provided a place to establish roots and receive schooling amid an otherwise mobile life determined by crop cycles from Texas to California.

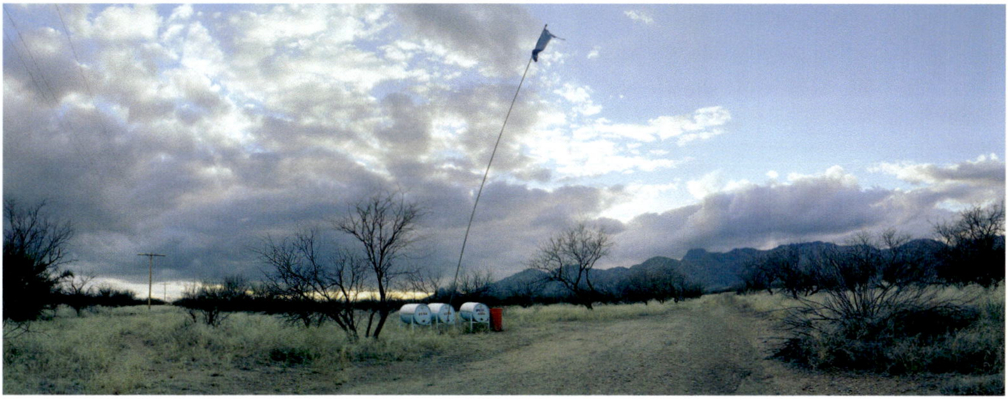

FIGURE 2.2 Delilah Montoya, *Humane Borders Water Station*, 2004. Ink jet on eSatin, 49 × 18 in. Print date 2008, diebond mount, edition of 2.

Increasingly, Marfa is embraced as prime real estate by designers, contemporary artists, and the institutions that support them. For some of them, Marfa provides a getaway and backdrop, as described in an interview with designer Emily Jerome on the website Shoplatitude. The transcript is interspersed with an archival photograph of Judd (Jerome's godfather, it is noted in the interview), shots of town, and images from Jerome's lookbook created in Marfa in 2010. The interviewer Julia Chaplin's introduction puts the point I reiterate here succinctly: "Marfa has taken over as the new destination muse for art-inspired fashion designers. Prada keeps its conceptual road side boutique there and Proenza Schouler pit stop in from NYC for visual refreshing."[6] Artists who take up permanent residence find residing there on a daily basis not a refreshing escape, but still a rewarding experience. In the PBS *Art in Context* documentary *Marfa: The Land and the Light*, Ann Marie Nafziger notes that Marfa "still feels like you're kind of on the edge. It's really attractive psychologically to be here." Michael Camacho, identified as a "green builder" in the film, voices reflectively: "The people who come to Marfa, the people on a whim, the people like me, the transplants . . . there's just something about it. It's kind of a young city. It's kind of a fun city." Beyond the edginess and youthful fun, there is, according to some, a psychic cost paid in return for Marfa's inspiring setting. Jeff Elrod identifies "a pathology to everybody that lives here" which he vaguely links to its remoteness.[7] Keep in mind that "remoteness" is relative to one's existing fields of vision, from where one starts out.

In conjunction with the ongoing articulation of Marfa's novelty, a parallel discourse paradoxically roots the town firmly in well-established geography. If New York stole the idea of modern art some seventy years ago, it has now also subsumed the idea of Marfa. Institutional developments undergird the ever-increasing itineraries of individuals traveling back and forth between Marfa and Manhattan. Since the public opening of 101 Spring Street in June 2013, the increased visibility of the Judd Foundation's New York and Texas bases now plays a prominent role in this circuit. Likewise, the development of Ballroom Marfa's programming sustains a robust roster of events in both locales. At the individual level, there are a number of New York–based artists who, like Emily Jerome and the designers known as Proenza Schouler, repeatedly return to Marfa on retreat. Eventually, some buy property and take up semipermanent residence there. Such is the case with artist Andrea Claire, once an artist-in-residence at Chinati Foundation, whose primary studio is in Brooklyn. She owns land outside Marfa as well.[8] This is an increasingly frequent phenomenon.

Some artists are situated between Marfa and New York through more idiosyncratic circumstances. Filmmaker Rainer Judd is such a figure. Brought to Marfa by her artist father in the mid-1970s, Judd attended Marfa Elementary as a child. As an adult, the town provided the setting of her short film *Remember Back, Remember When*. Sitting in the sub-basement conference room at 101 Spring Street, Judd discussed the three significant geographies in her life—Marfa, New York, and Los Angeles—through astrological assessment. She recounted, "Some astrologer told me that New York is healing for me, Marfa is mental clarity, and California is rewards. I was like, 'yes.' There is a lot of mental clarity possible for me personally in Marfa. But it's also just got a change of pace that comes through the air and the change of altitude. It's very ethereal. I don't know how to pinpoint that change."[9] Judd does, however, have clear ideas about framing its cinematic, if not psychic, landscape. When asked how she meets the challenge of taming the "wild" West Texas vistas, Judd quickly drafted a simple sketch: Within a rectangle, a straight line crosses the bottom of the frame. A tree and a stick person stand atop the line in the bottom right corner. Negative space, the sky, fills most of the frame otherwise, effectively conveying the feeling of inhabiting and filming in West Texas. Indeed, it is difficult to imagine anything other than a still frame and wide shot doing justice to the immense West Texas sky, demarcated only by the flat horizon line, a single tree, and a solitary body to drive home a sense of scale.

Throughout popular online and print media, carefully curated features of Marfa's social, environmental, aesthetic, and intellectual topography are published to situate the town within international circuits of desirable locations. Marfa's relative isolation, its flora, fauna, physical topography, and climate are deployed to locate it within visions of the desert along a spectrum between brief unsustainable fantasy and actual lived experience. In 2010, photographer Mario Sorrenti produced the spread "Field of Dreams" for *W Magazine*. The shoot, located in Marfa, was documented in a short film, *Made in Marfa*, for *W*'s website. According to the narrator, *W* dispatched Sorrenti, model Raquel Zimmermann, and crew to Marfa for the unique light, the flat terrain, and the domineering sky. Curiously, after all the trouble of getting to Far West Texas, icons of Marfa are mostly ignored or distanced to the point of anonymity: not just contemporary artworks and their spaces, but the Paisano Hotel and French Baroque–inspired courthouse associated with the film *Giant*; the then floridly mural-covered Blackwell School; the Crowley Theater and Ballroom Marfa, host to some of the most avant-garde contemporary film and music artists; and the kitschy, picturesque adobe viewing station constructed to aid in catching a glimpse of the haunting Marfa lights, to name a few. Whence, then, comes the impulse to title the film *Made in Marfa*? Why not *In the Chihuahuan Desert*? Or *In Far West Texas*? Or simply *In the Desert*? Clearly, notable cultural capital has accrued to Marfa that any fashion editor would be remiss to squander. Accessing this resource no longer requires its particular hallmarks, but merely its name. The town's name itself is now the only requisite icon.

The *W* shoot represents the most fantasized end of the spectrum of Marfa's allure. Less unabashedly luxurious images of Marfa are offered by writer Rubén Martínez and other artists discussed here. Martínez's journalistic collection of essays contains a chapter devoted entirely to Marfa, where the author held a Lannan Foundation residency in 2002. Sensitive to the "disregard for native populations," much of the chapter functions as exposé, uncovering the century-long occlusion of Mexican life in Marfa, of which the arts are only the most recent agent. He writes, "The problem was simple: although they are a large majority, Mexicans are largely invisible in Marfa—invisible, that is, mostly north of San Antonio Street, where the government buildings and most local businesses are located, and where the galleries and restaurants of the boom alighted. This erasure was so absolute and reflexive as to be unnoticeable to those who performed it."[10]

Martínez's reportage is punctuated with lovely descriptions of the desert, as he succumbs to the same allure that eventually motivated the boomers' erasure of Marfa's Mexicans. But even these passages contain more than hints at the overall critique on offer:

> The landscape was perfect: the town sat on an immense grassy plain. There was oil several dozen miles north, around Balmorhea, but Marfa had been cattle country, and the waning of the industry tantalized the imagination of liberal Texas millionaires (there are a few) with the possibility of buying up hundreds of thousands of acres to create huge swaths of land that could be reclaimed to a "pristine" state. The Davis Mountains, painterly with their combination of lyrical and violent features—notches and domes, faces of stone and bands of forest—were far enough away to shade blue with distance.[11]

What a difference from the frame offered by the fashion photographer and the supermodel. For all Marfa's promises, it also contains, as Martínez's work shows, many threats. Amid the utopic frameworks, accounts of such threats are less readily available, more difficult to coax out of the town, as Martínez recounts.[12] Occasionally, however, accounts of discrimination erupt.

In 2001, Marfan Tony Cano published his novel *The Other Side of the Tracks*. The novel was brought to my attention at my Marfan grandfather's funeral by Tony Gaspar. Gaspar is technically my grandfather's nephew, but as they are close in age, they were effectively childhood and lifelong *carnales*, a term perhaps most appropriately translated to English as "bros." Gaspar and Cano were also carnales. Cano's novel is purportedly a fictional account of life in Marfa and West Texas in the 1950s and 1960s from a young Mexican man's perspective. However, most of the names of people and places, including "Marfa," are identical with figures and locations existing outside of the fiction. The story is full of standoffs and painful retellings of blatant discriminatory moments in restaurants, on the streets, at work, in school, on basketball courts, and in the characters' love lives. Mostly those characters, the rambunctious teenage boys self-identified as "Los Chinglers," quickly brush off these slights.[13] A spirit of resignation pervades, crystallized in such lines as "He obviously understands that what has just happened to him at the cash register is all just the sad reality of life we must endure in this part of red and brown neck country of West Texas."[14] In this picture of Marfa, the line between brown and white remains firm and stark. Material for blurring the line lies dormant in the story, however, waiting to be mobilized—not least in the detail that the protagonist Tony's mother works day in and day out at the locker plant, a building now serving as an exhibition space for Chinati's rotating artists-in-residence.

Martínez closes his chapter on Marfa with a moment at a public gathering in which an activist elder and borderlands historian speaks:

> "What do you do with your neighbors?" Enrique asked. "What do you do with your neighbors?" he asked again. And once more shouting: "What do you do with your neighbors?"
>
> "You talk to them," he said, now in a gentle voice. "You love them. You marry them. You become them."[15]

Becoming one's neighbor can be an uncomfortable process. This is perhaps why so many find it easier to comply with erasure, both of oneself by others and of the other by oneself. What follows is an invitation in the form of spatial invocation. Accompanying the many visions already fixed on Marfa, it is time to picture West Texas in Aztlán. Marfa already resides in this phantom territory, but this fact is shrouded. It goes mostly unsensed even to the Mexicans and Mexican Americans, those on whose behalf Aztlán's politics and mythology has accrued over the past sixty years.

ENTER AZTLÁN

In 1969, the poet Alurista performed *El Plan Espiritual de Aztlán* at the first National Chicano Liberation Youth Conference in Denver, Colorado. It opens:

> In the spirit of a new people that is conscious not only of its proud historical heritage, but also of the brutal "Gringo" invasion of our territories, we, the Chicano inhabitants and civilizers of the Northern land of Aztlán, from whence came our [Aztec] forefathers, reclaiming the land of their birth and consecrating the determination of our people of the sun, declare that the call of our blood is our power, our response and our inevitable destiny.[16]

This aggressive stance roots itself in what philosopher Nelson Maldonado-Torres identifies as the "paradigm of war." It does so in this excerpt through terms like "invasion," "territories," "forefathers," determination of our people," and "inevitable destiny." Similar to Cano's account of brown-versus-red-neck life in Marfa, the preamble rehearses the same nationalist and territorial logic it rails against. Maldonado-Torres describes this "paradigm of war" underpinning modernity as "a way of conceiving humanity, knowledge, and social relations that privileges conflict or polemos. . . . [It] can be characterized in terms of the privilege of conflict or the celebration of the reduction of the singularity of individual entities and subjects to the generality of the concept, to Being, to an ethnos, or to a totality in philosophical reflections."[17]

In the opening of *El Plan*, it is immediately evident that the identity being galvanized, the subjects the document calls forth, are aptly characterized in such terms: Alurista initiates and celebrates the "reduction of the singularity of individual entities . . . to an ethnos"; that is, to Chicanx identity. In the same breath, Alurista, on behalf of Chicanxs, the "new people," announces consciousness of a "proud historical heritage" and calls out the "brutal 'Gringo'" against whom the Chicanx subject is to construct or "reclaim" himself. Also in the opening statement, "we" Chicanxs are described as the true and first "inhabitants and *civilizers* of the Northern land of Aztlán." That Alurista lays claim to past and presumably future capacities and intentions to "civilize" signals a self-understanding rooted in the civilized/primitive binary that was part and parcel of the colonial modern logic that the 1969 gathering sought to indict. At the gathering, these past and future true civilizers are called to unify as the "Chicano" *ethnos*. This early expression of Chicanismo squarely complies with and reimposes colonial modernity's logic onto its own origin mythology and political project. The "unity" of these subjects, as well as the individual unity of the singular Chicanx subject, is first priority in the list of "Organizational Goals" included later in the document. Nationalism is the "key" to this unity and the "common denominator" among Chicanxs to which we are, according to the program set forth in *El Plan*, all reducible and which all of "La Raza can agree upon."[18] Decades later, such universal agreement still eludes us. For many, this totality is no longer or never was a goal, though the desire still has its voices.

Alurista's spiritual claims accord with geographical (re)configurations. His Aztlán echoes with calls for Reconquista, the repatriation of lands ceded to the United States by Mexico in the 1848 Treaty of Guadalupe Hidalgo that closed the US-Mexican War. Relatively soon after the Denver gathering, muralist Emilio Aguayo installed *Somos Aztlán* at the University of Washington's

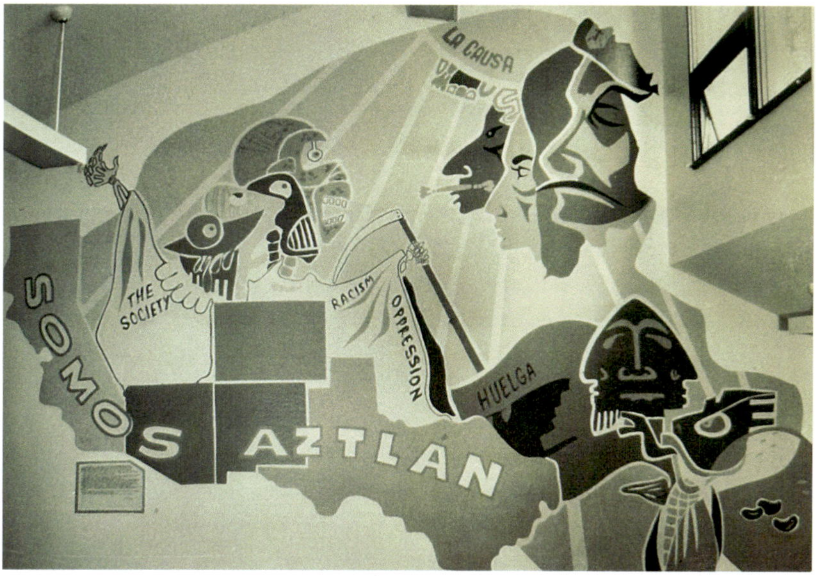

FIGURE 2.3 Emilio Aguayo, *Somos Aztlán* mural, 1971. Ethnic Cultural Center, University of Washington, Seattle.

Ethnic Cultural Center (figure 2.3). The only clearly identifiable regions in the mural are those states in the ceded areas, including a Texas-shaped form elongated and torqued through its central region just east of the Panhandle. Aguayo's artistic license with Texas' silhouette accommodates the snaking all-caps text "SOMOS AZTLÁN" ("We are Aztlán"). In this cartography, Marfa sits somewhere below the space between the Z and the T.

In this parcel of Aztlán, artist Franco Mondini-Ruiz installed the immersive environment *Giant* at Ballroom Marfa in 2004. Ballroom's description reads:

> In the North Gallery, Franco Mondini-Ruiz presents a new, large-scale installation titled "Giant." This massive, baroque assemblage of found objects dominates the Ballroom's front gallery floor, expanding Mondini-Ruiz' signature vignettes of culturally-fused visual components. Investigating the hybridization of Mexican-American identity and the culture of consumerism, Mondini-Ruiz' sculptural installation will further focus on issues surrounding border politics, racial and class interactions, and cultural tourism.[19]

The artist revisits these final points in his oral history for the Smithsonian's Archives of American Art, recorded just four days after his public opening at Ballroom. In light of the interview, the official description reads as unsettlingly euphemistic. Here is his personal analysis of "racial and class interactions" in Marfa:

> MONDINI-RUIZ: Marfa is a fascinating thing, too, showing in Marfa, because—look what's happened. The people that are sponsoring Ballroom are white, liberal, Democrat aristocrats and from some of the wealthiest, most important, historical families, and very well intentioned, but they've gotten that colonial payback.
>
> ... The Chinati Foundation is, you know, Northeastern money and society money and new money, as far as Texas is concerned, and it took over Marfa. And so they're being colonized.
>
> ... Donald Judd ... this Yankee, this white Yankee, nouveau-riche guy has colonized Marfa and the original colonizers that own all the land and got it from the Mexicans, hate it. They're being snubbed and becoming second-class citizens in their own community, so they open "Ballroom." They're going to show them. You know, so now they know how we felt hundreds of years earlier when they came and all of a sudden somehow owned all our land and all our buildings.
>
> INTERVIEWER: What a bizarre experience for you to go—to be invited to go into the Ballroom to create an installation.
>
> MONDINI-RUIZ: Well, we're being used. Because that's the only way they can win—beat Chinati at their own game, saying, "We're better than you because we show black people and Mexican people, we won," you know? They don't mean it that crassly, but it's their little way of saying—so, we've become very, very strange political bedfellows. We're still kind of being used, but at least I've got some money in my pocket and I got to express myself honestly, and we're not invisible anymore. You know, we're seen as a valuable tool to assert themselves, you know? But still, even within the Marfa Foundation [*sic*], as much as they tried to integrate, it was still the Mexicans doing all the work, and all the whites going to the party afterwards, for the most part. But they tried their best, and it's going to still take another one hundred or two hundred years for all this to finally become utopic. So I just thought that's a very interesting, fascinating post post colonial[ism]. The colonizers being colonized and fighting back.[20]

I am certain I have been similarly "used," but I am exhausted by retracing the bounds of the "game," the war paradigm, in which Mondini-Ruiz, I, and other artists of color and queerness are recruited as pawns (sometimes by ourselves). What I want to invoke now is neither Aguayo's muralized Aztlán with its clear, unyielding lines nor a reiteration of Cano's and Alurista's visions of a fixed standoff between brown and white, or Mondini-Ruiz's effectively eternally delayed utopic harmony between them. I refuse to wait one hundred years.

While I sympathize and identify with these pictures of Marfa from my own experiences, the Aztlán I propose from this point on is a site of radical desorden, or disordering, following Laura E. Pérez in her essay "El Desorden, Nationalism, and Chicana/o Aesthetics." Her hermeneutic of disorder historically accounts for experience and representation of Marfa's gentrifications but moves differently through them than the "hermeneutics of suspicion" exercised in the perspectives I just described. That is, I do not posit Aztlán as yet another counterclaim but a claim meant to disorder the grounds for making impermeable and warring territorial claims at all. In contrast to the absolutism of Alurista's preamble, Pérez's schema is as follows:

> We occupy a nation that does and doesn't exist. We practice a nationalism that we do and don't believe in. We produce art and thought from the useful scraps of norms we mock. American locos, several screws clearly loose, we Chicana/os have tenaciously dedicated ourselves, like other marginalized folk, to conversing with images that "sane" folks don't see. Our rasquache productions—garbled and annoying as Spanish to the racist's ear—still produce a knowledge whose ragged discursive edges scrape at the delicate skins of the dominating culture's claims to normality, authority, and universalism. . . . To reoccupy Aztlán, the oppressed hallucinate—and that practice has no borders.[21]

What visions does a hallucinatory occupation of Marfa, Aztlán, produce? On behalf of Chicanx art in the early nineties, Mel Casas aspired that it become "relevant to EVERYONE" (figure 2.4). He, too, hallucinated a schema. I propose desorden as the method for negotiating the fourth register from the top in Casas's diagram: the negotiation of "national," read "dominant," art criteria and "regional" Chicanx art. Through desorden, Marfa, Aztlán, might become a site like that called for by Pérez, a territory of ongoing "cannibalistic" relations between Marfa, Manhattan, Marfa-on-the-border, Marfa-in-the-desert, and Marfa International.

To hallucination, I add that Aztlán is also produced through the ongoing performance and representation of metabolism between land and body. Here

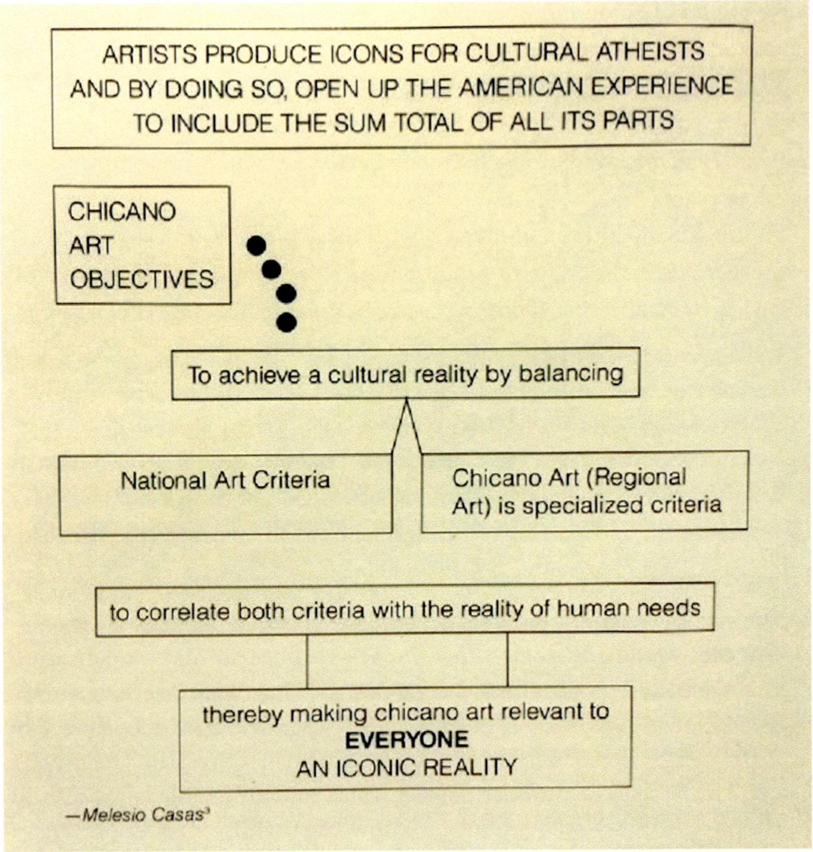

FIGURE 2.4 Mel Casas, flow chart detailing the relevance of Chicanx art, 1991. According to Casas, "Artists produce icons for cultural atheists and by doing so, open up the American experience to include the sum total of all its parts."

I focus on a small group. Their inclusion in this context does not imply that the artists discussed necessarily sense their own presence in Aztlán, though some certainly do. In addition to Judd, artists like Margarita Cabrera and the duo Elmgreen & Dragset have worked out their own heuristics for reading the Marfa landscape aesthetically, physically, socially, spiritually, and ecologically. If we are willing and attentive, they can generate novel and valuable views of Aztlán alongside the forms of legibility provided by other economies of meaning. The artists do not need to see Aztlán in order for this art historian to see their work in it. However, perhaps as Aztlán is repeatedly brought to intervene, this might shift. In any case, it is my argument that we do not need to wait: Chicanx art, and Aztlán, are already relevant to everyone. This relevance awaits activation.

WHAT TO WEAR IN AZTLÁN

In the summer of 2010, Ballroom Marfa exhibited the group show *In Lieu of Unity/En lugar de la unidad*, which aimed to bring "together artists from Mexico—citizens, residents and emigrants—who have sustained a curiosity about social relations in their art practices. . . . Through varied perspectives on what it means to be together, these artists relinquish utopian ideas of unity."[22] Aztlán is also proposed here in lieu of unity. It is another substantial conceptual borderland whose shareability is in question.

Margarita Cabrera's cacti sculptures, sewn together from discarded US Border Patrol uniforms, were included in the show (figure 2.5). Cabrera is a Mexican-born artist who has a studio in El Paso, and who is often included in Chicanx art exhibitions, catalogues, and essays. Like most fine art objects, the cacti move from the studio to galleries and museums, then on to collections all over the world. Cabrera's work regularly includes emblems of movement: vehicles that move bodies across long and short distances, insects that follow epic migratory patterns, and the millions to billions of dollars that are exchanged across the US-Mexico border in the form of manufacturing contracts and household goods. Images of people are rarely, if ever, present in the final products of her work. But people and their places, or struggles for place, are a central theme in most of them.

More than a theme, the status of those whose hands craft much of Cabrera's work, including these cacti, is itself actively at stake in debates around movement, particularly movement across the US-Mexico border, through Aztlán. The studio assistants she employs have often crossed the border from Mexico. Many are former maquiladora workers along the border, maquiladoras being sweatshops where mostly women work under harsh conditions and for little pay. Working for Cabrera, they are given fair shares in the profits made from the sale of artworks, are frequently if not always named as artists in exhibition didactics, and work in dramatically improved conditions. Studio assistants are also aided on the path to US citizenship. This all happens under the auspices of Florezca, a for-profit enterprise functioning as a multinational corporation that promotes cultural capital.[23]

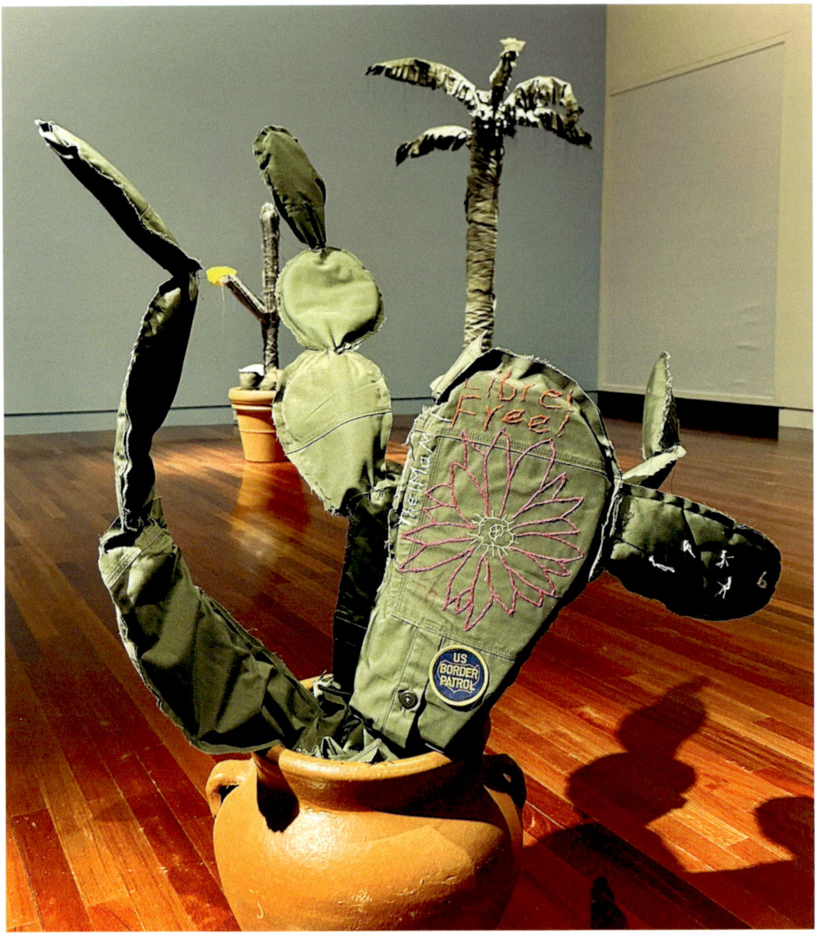

FIGURE 2.5 *Margarita Cabrera: Space in Between* installation at Colorado Springs Fine Arts Center at Colorado College, March 7, 2025–December 13, 2025. © 2026 Margarita Cabrera/Licensed by VAGA at Artists Rights Society (ARS), New York.

These sculptures replicate cacti often with nopales full of las tunas (pads full of fruit). This plant family has a long-standing and multivalent position in the cosmologies and craft economies of Indigenous peoples in the Americas. One of its recent symbolic associations is its prevalence in the landscape where the Border Patrol presents a greater danger to border crossers than the cacti's needles. Again, Delilah Montoya's photography highlights the harsh

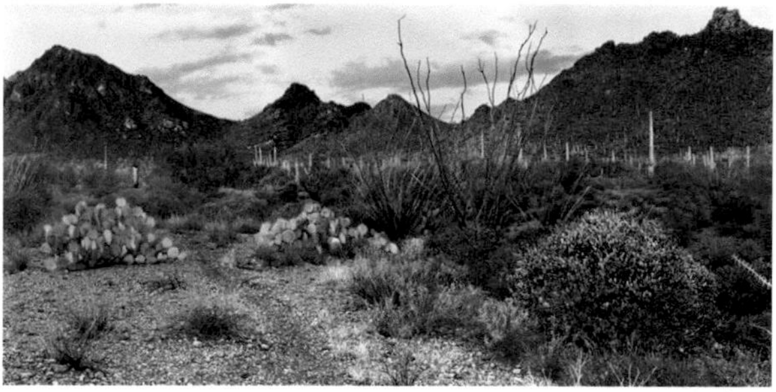

FIGURE 2.6 Delilah Montoya, *Saguaro Crossing, AZ*, 2004. Ink jet on eSatin, 49 × 18 in. Print date 2008, diebond mount, edition of 2.

conditions that must be crossed, a journey made more difficult by Border Patrol agents, who in the 2024 fiscal year reported more than one and a half million "encounters" in the Southwest, according to Customs and Border Protection self-reporting.[24] Cacti like those inspiring the forms of Cabrera's sculptures dominate the left middle ground in at least one of Montoya's large photographs (figure 2.6). In these artworks, the threats posed by the land's native flora and those posed by border agents are inseparable; traversing Aztlán is made treacherous by both.

Cabrera conflates the relatively new bodies of Border Patrol agents and the plant bodies that have populated the area for eons. Again, the materials that make up the plants are remnants of discarded Border Patrol uniforms. Not only can one now imagine their bodies interrupted in their acts of surveillance and capture, but furthermore, they are stripped of one of the sartorial symbols of the power—the distinctive green government-issued uniforms—that authorized those very acts. The swatches of forest green fabric, often still carrying their badges, are dismembered and reconfigured in the name of resistant meaning-making. In acts of irreverence for their legal right to inflict violence on bodies, their clothes, transformed into a sculptural medium, are imaged with stitched glyphs that call out their source as what has been overcome. Figures are shown preparing to cross the border successfully. The sun shines. The chillantes, bright colors, of the threads render a helicopter, a Border Patrol vehicle, and the agency's logo, emptying them of their threatening power. This act of creative resistance holds even more meaning because of the hands doing the dismantling and the stitching. Because many

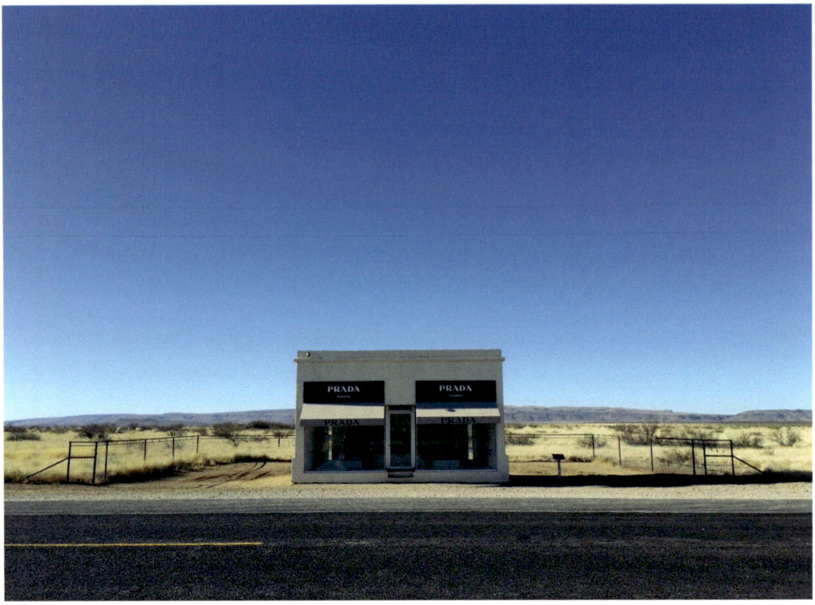

FIGURE 2.7 Elmgreen & Dragset, *Prada Marfa*, 2005. Photo: Max Tolleson.

of the makers are undocumented, the work demonstrates a Reconquista, a reclaiming, played out in sartorial territory by brown bodies.

One of many jarring experiences possible in Marfa is shopping. One can find some of the same labels and styles one might encounter in SoHo, and at similar price points. Art openings and public events are populated with stylish silhouettes that could be seen at similar venues in large cosmopolitan centers all over the globe. The internationalization of fashion and art manifests in Marfa, given its significance in a global network of contemporary art exhibition and commerce.

In Aztlán, one must also think seriously about fashion. This theme, if not this approach, is highly visible in Marfa already, embodied in *Prada Marfa*, the collaborative work of artists Michael Elmgreen and Ingar Dragset (figure 2.7). The sculpture is intriguing for the remarkable connections it forges and the economic, social, and cultural asymmetries it reproduces and lays bare. Its inspiration positions us geographically in a fashion house that has global appeal anchored significantly in its reified locale, Italy, a country long understood as a standard setter of haute couture. What *Prada Marfa* exposes is that

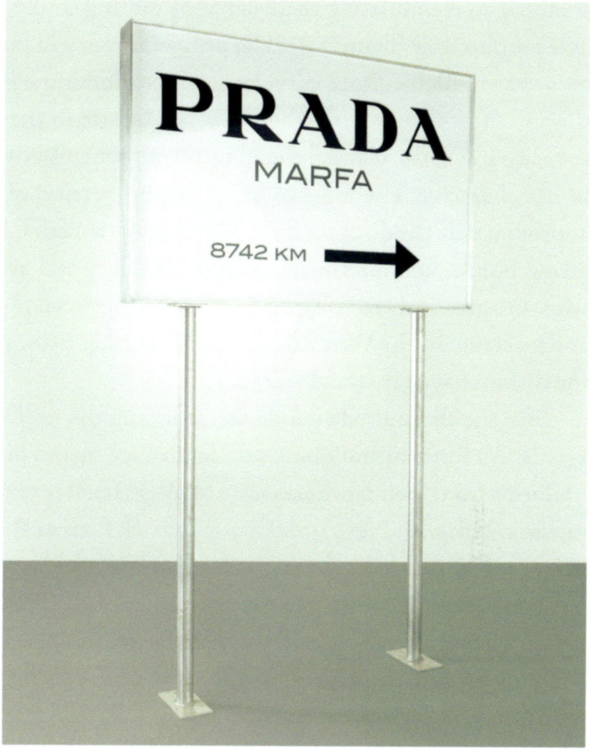

FIGURE 2.8 Elmgreen & Dragset, *Prada Marfa Sign*, 2005.

association with such "good taste" no longer requires the purchase of goods, so widespread is the understanding of its cultural meaning. The artist statement reads: "the artwork will never function as a place of commerce, since the door is always locked."[25] Yet thousands flock to it yearly. There is no object to be gained by these pilgrims. There is only the association, the selfie for social media, and the noteworthiness of travel to Marfa. It is this account that patrons "wear" to attest to their tasteful consumption, not the actual fabulous shoes or handbags that are always out of reach inside the locked sculpture. One is to be impressed by the act of pilgrimage to this Milan in Aztlán, as opposed to any sartorial acquisition.

But the object does prevail, or more specifically, consumerism's success at making salable things from less accessible experiences does. Alongside the creation of the site-specific sculpture *Prada Marfa*, large prints and a free-standing sign simulating road signage pointing to the site were made available for purchase (figure 2.8). The print's currency in popular culture's claims on access to high culture is evidenced by its longtime inclusion on the set of the TV series *Gossip Girl*, where it was a fixture in the home of the wealthy socialite Lily Bass, whose refined taste and art collecting are central features of her character. The mileage noted on this version of the sign, "1837 MI," is approximately the distance from Marfa to New York City. The clean, straight arrow, not to mention the mass reproducibility and availability of the print, work imaginatively to collapse the distance between the taste-making center and its claim on Far West Texas. The art market makes the movement across the distance appear straightforward.

Imagine those Prada goods accessorizing the uniforms of Border Patrol agents. An internal and quite mundane office memo outlining a shipment of uniforms from their fabrication site to West Texas reveals that Marfa, Aztlán's sartorial link with New York City goes back further than either Cabrera's or Elmgreen & Dragset's works, at least as far back as the 1970s (figure 2.9). This document returns us to the experience of the Border Patrol agent, from inside a banal operation in his own daily life. In the opening and concluding paragraphs, note the addresses where the uniforms for agents in Marfa were fabricated: 180 Madison Avenue and 475 Park Avenue South, New York, New York 10016. The body that stamped "RECEIVED" on November 21, 1973, likely wore a version of the uniforms now rasquachified into sculptures by Cabrera and her collaborators. Consider the fraught movement of Cabrera's undocumented coproducers. The cacti expose free trade's violent erasure of distance and difference, while *Prada Marfa* instantiates it repeatedly. Both operations are writ large on the clothed and unclothed bodies of Aztlán's inhabitants.

This is all meant to galvanize a few salient moments when Aztlán has been felt or actively ignored in Marfa, and to allow us to begin building tools to read any work produced in Marfa as also produced in Aztlán. It aims to be, in the end, the vehicle by which Marfa's claims to Aztlán can circulate. This vehicle, appropriately, might take the form of many Chicanxs' ride of choice: a lowrider (figure 2.10). "In her *Bodywork* project, Liz Cohen converts a utilitarian East German Trabant automobile into a Chevy El Camino lowrider. She engineers it so that it can convert itself back and forth repeatedly once activated. To accomplish this feat of hydraulic engineering, Cohen spent eight years learning the necessary mechanical skills at a local body shop. Simulta-

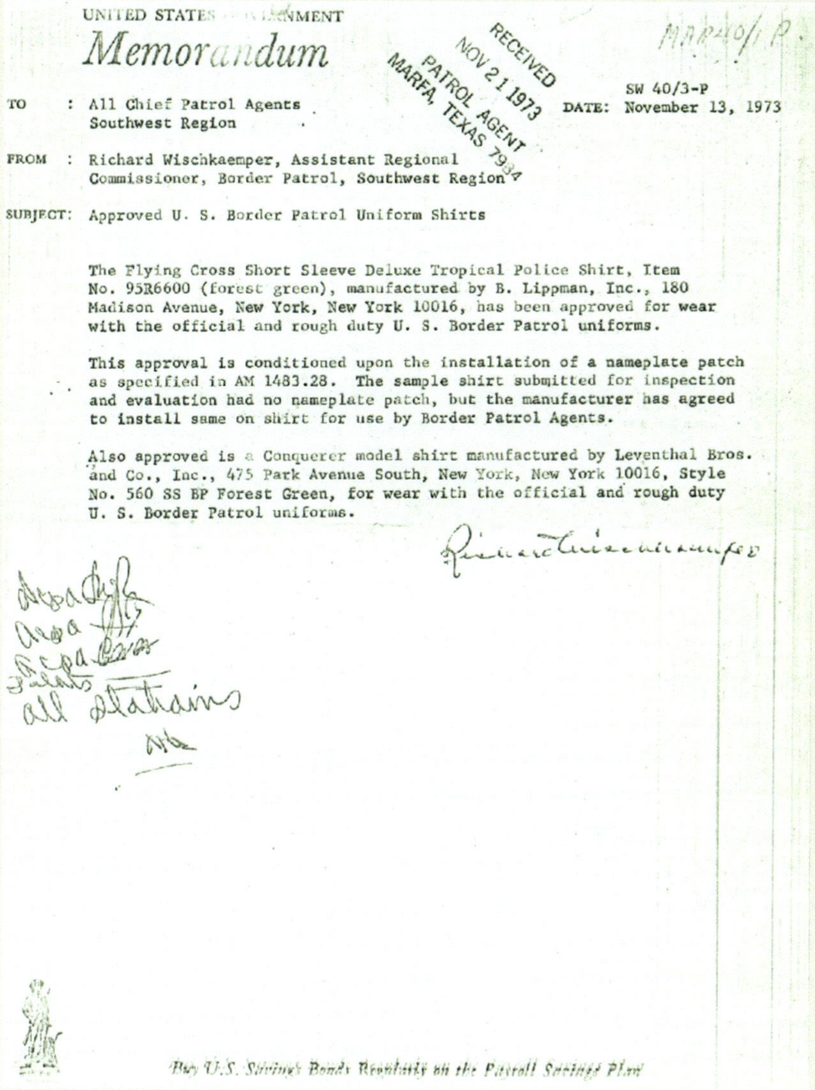

UNITED STATES GOVERNMENT

Memorandum

RECEIVED
NOV 21 1973
PATROL AGENT
MARFA, TEXAS 79843

MAR 40/1 P.

SW 40/3-P

TO : All Chief Patrol Agents
Southwest Region

DATE: November 13, 1973

FROM : Richard Wischkaemper, Assistant Regional Commissioner, Border Patrol, Southwest Region

SUBJECT: Approved U. S. Border Patrol Uniform Shirts

The Flying Cross Short Sleeve Deluxe Tropical Police Shirt, Item No. 95R6600 (forest green), manufactured by B. Lippman, Inc., 180 Madison Avenue, New York, New York 10016, has been approved for wear with the official and rough duty U. S. Border Patrol uniforms.

This approval is conditioned upon the installation of a nameplate patch as specified in AM 1483.28. The sample shirt submitted for inspection and evaluation had no nameplate patch, but the manufacturer has agreed to install same on shirt for use by Border Patrol Agents.

Also approved is a Conquerer model shirt manufactured by Leventhal Bros. and Co., Inc., 475 Park Avenue South, New York, New York 10016, Style No. 560 SS BP Forest Green, for wear with the official and rough duty U. S. Border Patrol uniforms.

Richard Wischkaemper

all stations

Buy U.S. Savings Bonds Regularly on the Payroll Savings Plan

FIGURE 2.9 United States Government memorandum from Richard Wischkaemper, assistant regional commissioner, Border Patrol, Southwest Region, to Marfa Border Patrol headquarters, approving an order of shirts. Junior Historian Files, Marfa Public Library, Marfa, Texas.

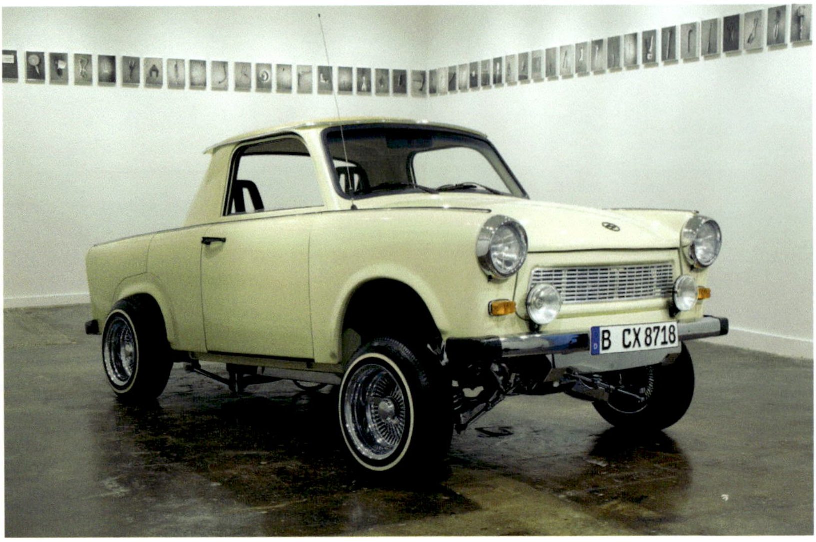

FIGURE 2.10 Liz Cohen, *Bodywork*, 2001–10.

neously, she converted herself into a car-show bikini model, and transformed the future of lowriding."[26]

From September 2011 to February 2012, *Bodywork* was exhibited at Ballroom Marfa as part of the group show *Autobody*. So, Marfa is already familiar terrain, and Cohen's work may be the perfect ride for cruising through town as a strip of drag in Aztlán. As Pérez writes, "In practice, Chicana/o discourse strips parts from 'nation,' 'nationalism,' and 'identity' *as if they were unattended vehicles on the street*. Components are recycled, transformed, and recirculated through the crevices of the symbolic and social order."[27] Clearly, I am not cruising alone in the counter-co-optation of images into unstable networks of Chicanx art, the ragged-edged field of vision called Marfa, Aztlán.

Making, Aesthesis

3

Decoloniality is at once the unveiling of the wound and the possibility of healing. It makes the wound visible, tangible; it voices the scream. And at the same time decolonial aestheSis moves towards the healing, the recognition, the dignity of those aesthetic practices that have been written out of the canon of modern aestheTics.

—Walter Mignolo and Rolando Vázquez, *Decolonial AestheSis*

I want to think of making, instead, as a process of growth. This is to place the maker from the outset as a participant in amongst a world of active materials.

—Tim Ingold, *Making: Anthropology, Archaeology, Art and Architecture*

On the second floor of 101 Spring Street, visitors first encounter a table of Judd's design. Its dimensions are cued by the measurements of the heritage glass windows running the length of the south and west walls.[1] A variety of stains and drinking glass rings mark the pinewood surface in an all-over disorder, indexing the familial and social function of this space. Located on the same floor as the building's kitchen, the table was a site of family dining. The second floor is also remembered as the location of many rambunctious social gatherings during Judd's lifetime, with the table at the center of some remarkable vignettes. Cracks spanning several of the beams that make up the tabletop lend further texture and index age. The table's legs are not precisely flush to the tabletop at their points of contact.[2] All these imperfections endeared the object to the artist, it seems, rather than constituting a reason for its replacement, as was often the case with his art.

Peter Ballantine, who fabricated the bed installed on the fifth floor at 101 Spring Street, recalls that Judd was at some point directly asked about this second-floor centerpiece: Why did he not have the table remade with a much lower tolerance for error than the existing one (i.e., the level of tolerance for measurements, joints, and seams displayed in his art)? Ballantine does not recall the artist's exact words but, according to him, Judd was unflinching in his approval and defense of this piece.[3] The family dining table was built by Celedonio "Chango" Mediano, assisted by his brother Alfredo. These two Marfa residents were employed by Judd for almost the entirety of his Marfa residence. While Judd brought so-called Minimalism to West Texas, the Medianos quietly coyoted rasquachismo into SoHo. More appropriately than *rustic* or its cognates, it is *rasquache* that accurately captures the attitude toward materials, construction, and use embedded in the table, if the Medianos' lives and the broader context of West Texas near the Mexican border are folded seriously into its evaluation.

Just a few feet from the table stands a daybed also designed by Judd. It was fabricated in Douglas fir by the Manhattan-based firm Cooper/Kato (Jim Cooper and Ichiro Kato) and entered the building between 1985 and 1989.[4] It embodies the consistent surface, finished polish, flush panels, and concealed joints typically associated with Judd's work and peak Minimalism generally. The daybed fulfills many common preconceptions of the artist's living space, while the dining table often disturbs them. The table's rasquachismo, both in the formal qualities described earlier and the attitude inflecting its construction, resists its cousin, defying these expectations. With Judd's conscientiousness toward his living and working spaces undergirding it, it also utterly belongs. This table travels worlds.

DECOLONIAL AESTHETICS (aestheSis/aestheTics)

Imagine we are seated around the Medianos' rasquache work at 101 Spring Street. The time has come to question directly that which has haunted this book so far: "decolonial aesthetics." To do so in the context of Marfa is the primary aim of this chapter. Some background is necessary. In 2007 I attended the Decolonial Summer Institute held in Binghamton, New York, organized around the works of María Lugones and Catherine Walsh. My participation continued from 2008 to 2015 primarily through the Center for Interdisciplinary Research in Philosophy, Interpretation, and Culture at Binghamton University and attendance at two Decolonial Summer School courses held in the Netherlands (2012 and 2014). Of the many ongoing projects within the group, Walter Mignolo and Rolando Vázquez write,

> We can say that these trajectories are all marked by their contact with the general frame of the project identified as modernity/coloniality/decoloniality. For short, we write "modernity/(de)coloniality" and we understand this to be a single concept not three different ones. If you are used to the relations between "words and things," you may have difficulties understanding to what "thing" these three words, united and separated by the slash "/" and the brackets "()," may "represent." They do not in fact "represent" anything. They are a signpost of conflicting enunciations: the rhetoric of "modernity," and its continuing promises of salvation; and the logic of "coloniality," the continuing hidden process of expropriation, exploitation, pollution, and corruption that underlies the narrative of modernity, as promoted by institutions and actors belonging to corporations, industrialized nation-states, museums, and research institutions. "Decoloniality" appears in between modernity/coloniality as an opening, as a possibility of overcoming their completeness. Decoloniality refers to the variegated enunciations springing from global-local histories entangled with the local imperial history of Euro-American modernity, postmodernity, and altermodernity.[5]

My consideration of Minimalism and rasquachismo encapsulates one of the "variegated enunciations" springing from the global-local history of Marfa. One of the differentials that this passage helps to clarify resides between Judd's anti-Eurocentrism and the anti-Eurocentrism implicit in rasquache styles and attitudes, through which many components of Marfa's visual, sculptural, and overall aesthetic field are composed. What Judd often called "the European tradition," the modernity/(de)coloniality group considers "an aspect of the colonial matrix of power, of the imperial structure of control that began to be put in place in the sixteenth century with the emergence of the Atlantic commercial circuit and the colonization of the New World, and that was transformed and expanded through the eighteenth and nineteenth centuries, and up to this day."[6]

There is a clear difference of power on the ground, but the dominant story, that of Judd, should not be understood as Eurocentric. His practice and rasquachismo have this in common. Both endeavors eat away at a modernity constructed in Europe and its attempt to universalize through colonization, if from strikingly different positions (which, again, have their own distinct power relationship). To put it succinctly in the terms offered by Mignolo and Vázquez, Minimalism enacts one "postmodern" approach while rasquachismo can be understood as one among many "altermodernities."

Mignolo and Vázquez's dossier, while providing this convenient snapshot of the larger group's history by way of introduction, gives most attention to delimiting the stakes of a particular subset of questions, questions about the roles of art and aesthetics in modernity/(de)coloniality. Over time, this subset has come to be identified as "decolonial aestheSis/aestheTics." Mignolo and Vázquez cite 2012 as the year when a specific set of concerns began to crystalize around questions of art and aesthetics, though the term *decolonial aesthetics* had been circulating in the group for almost a decade. It was also at the 2012 gathering that I first presented the case of Marfa to the group. What was novel that year, what crystalized, was the usefulness and relevance of distinguishing between "aesthetics" and "aesthesis." This distinction continues to generate an anti-disciplinary field in which, for my purposes, the possibilities of Judd's works in the Marfan landscape making meaning correspondent with—not merely alongside—an altar statue of the Virgin of Guadalupe can be located. Mignolo and Vázquez demonstrate the play between the terms:

> Decolonial aestheSis starts from the consciousness that the modern/colonial project has implied not only control of the economy, the political, and knowledge, but also control over the senses and perception. Modern aestheTics have played a key role in configuring a canon, a normativity that enabled the disdain and the rejection of other forms of aesthetic practices, or, more precisely, other forms of aestheSis, of sensing and perceiving. Decolonial aestheSis is an option that delivers a radical critique to modern, postmodern, and altermodern aestheTics and, simultaneously, contributes to making visible decolonial subjectivities at the confluence of popular practices of re-existence, artistic installations, theatrical and musical performances, literature and poetry, sculpture and other visual arts.[7]

In the context of this book, this distinction raises the question of what this framework means for revising, and in some cases overturning, present widespread conceptions of Marfa and the modes it inhabits. Decolonial aestheSis/aestheTics offer a generative set of questions and language for thinking about Marfa as it aims to capture "the confluence of popular practices of re-existence, artistic installations, theatrical and musical performances, literature and poetry, sculpture and other visual arts." The flowing together of Minimalism and rasquachismo are two streams feeding into the "decolonial subjectivities" becoming through Marfa (whether they reside there or not).

TIM INGOLD: BETWEEN DECOLONIAL AESTHETICS AND ART HISTORY

The other key voice in this chapter is that of anthropologist Tim Ingold, whose work enables me to think generatively about objects like the Mediano-made table in New York alongside the becoming of subjectivities and things in Marfa. Studying his work has clarified that my concerns are distinct from other significant projects that consider the making of work such as Judd's. Those projects brought the complicated evidence of postwar art's becoming—the actual constructing and circulating of objects, performances, and other required labor—out of archives, interviews, factory records, and staging areas into broader view in order to rectify the unbalanced mythos accruing to key artists through glossy publications and the gallery system. Through a variety of mechanisms, these myths tended to separate these artists from the many hands who helped to produce the works ultimately credited to their singular names over the years. Thankfully, art history has come increasingly to understand that works of art are not simply individual endeavors. This recognition has also made abundantly clear the ineluctable role of the market and flows of capital in the production of art. Two exemplary projects in this lineage are Michelle Kuo's article "Industrial Revolution: The History of Fabrication" and the films of Amie Siegel, in particular, *Provenance*.

Donald Judd is one of many artists anecdotally mentioned in Kuo's essay. She writes, "Contrary to near-mythical accounts of artists employing industrial manufacturing at arm's length—the (largely false) story of Donald Judd blindly ordering boxes from Bernstein Brothers is only the most famous example—the disconnect between conception and realization has rarely been total, never so archly aloof as it might first appear."[8] The essay more than succeeds in disillusioning the reader (if the reader held any illusions to begin with) about the rampant and multifarious evolution of delegated and industrially fabricated art "that stretches to unexpected artists, so widespread as to be invisible."[9] One effect of the essay is to bring these "unexpected artists" into the open, though Kuo's primary aims are much more subtle. She concludes by casting the evidence she offers us in the context of fabricators Carlson & Co. (especially their working relationship with the artist Jeff Koons) as one set of instances in a "perpetually deferred" fantasy of a made-to-order world possible in technocratic regimes such as ours.[10] While my aims are shades different, I understand thinking about Marfa as a response to a timely call sounded by Kuo: "But there are lesser-known scenes of the crime that bear scrutiny, and if we are to understand the full implications of fabrication and its uncanny persistence, we must trace the activity that has transpired there, charting a minor history of these sites."[11] This writing may perform such instances of exposure as well, but again, my primary stakes are different and become clear through terms offered by Ingold.

As a signal of shifted epistemological stakes in the telling of the "minor history" of Marfa, I choose to accompany the modernity/(de)coloniality group and Ingold, rather than the venerable lineage with which Kuo works (though they remain in my mind). As Kuo states, "Attention to the history of these mutinous 'post-studio' conditions is hardly new—from Caroline A. Jones's pioneering study of Stella, Warhol, and Smithson to the critical research of Benjamin H. D. Buchloch, James Meyer, and Helen Molesworth."[12] New topics afford us the opportunity to try out new methods, even as we often begin from similar or identical questions. (Who *makes* art?) With this choice, I take to Marfa as an opportunity to think beyond technocracy, industrial fabrication, and even art history to a more porous realm of human and nonhuman making applicable to art, yes, but also to all the materials and beings with which art shares and coproduces space and place.

As Kuo notes, attention to these concerns is hardly new, and they seem to have only proliferated further since the 2007 publication of her essay. A quietly spectacular example is Amie Siegel's 2013 film *Provenance*. The main presences in this video are "the silent pieces of furniture conceived by Le Corbusier and Pierre Jeanneret in the 1950s for their utopic, modernist city Chandigarh in northern India."[13] "Silent" here is fraught with meaning. It may be rather that the language of the film is not human, making us voyeurs struggling to interpret it. Who is in conversation then? If one experiences *Provenance* in a theater setting, as I did, it is possible to sense that the intended audience is the theater seats themselves. It is from a perspective like theirs that most of the exquisite slow pans of the film take place. Humans are mumbling, fidgety presences pictured only by their bottom halves and felt as interruptions in otherwise staid rooms—that is, until we become mauling hands and abusive users, accidentally bumping and scraping or deliberately stripping and deconstructing the starring characters. More disturbing than their objectness (it is not so strange to witness the act of upholstering and fabricating in general) is the art world's apparently unwavering reverence for their status. This aspect is documented in Siegel's filming of photo shoots in which the furniture is carefully lit and staged for auction house publications. They are readied for sale across the planet, following their bureaucratic life in Chandigarh. However, any disturbance of their desirability in luxury markets incurred by viewing them laid bare in a preparatory workroom is clearly temporary. The pieces sell for high prices and to competitive audiences. To drive this point home, Siegel created *Lot 248*, a six-minute film capturing the sale of *Provenance* itself as an art object. She has shown these two works together, cheekily confirming the paradoxical relationship—the psychic distance and perverse closeness—of exposing material labor and inciting market desirability.

And so, if I were setting out on such a project here, I would prioritize and make much more of, for instance, the fact that the Mediano brothers grew up near my grandfather in Marfa, in similar conditions to those that required the latter to end his formal education in the eighth grade and make a living alongside his family as a farmworker and, later, in a tire plant. These conditions are thrown into striking relief when one notes that chairs of Mediano's fabrication and Judd's design circulate in venues like Sotheby's. One was sold for $60,000 in 2003. Another, apparently unsold, was assigned an estimated value of $70,000–$90,000 in 2006.[14] But in this instance, such a project also seems unnecessary. Judd was clear and forthright about the aid he received from the Mediano brothers.[15] If any occlusion of these particular laborers occurs, the responsibility lies with us, the experiencers of the work, more than with the artist. What Ingold made clear to me is that my interests lie less in production and labor in these terms, and more in an investigation of correspondent human and nonhuman acts of making, as he approaches this verb. To put it rather dramatically (but it makes my point): I am interested in an art history of West Texas that includes the Jumano and Lipan Apache petroglyphs populating the area, the work of the auto body repair shop in town, landscape painters of the West like Tom Lea, Judd, the cooks in Marfa's handful of restaurants, and the current and future artists and makers who follow the call or are born to be there. Of course, a glaring challenge of such a vast scope is to avoid the flattening performed by, for example, "postmodernism" in the 1970s as identified by Rosalind Krauss and discussed in chapter 1.

The bulk of this project remains in the future, but I hint at it here to clarify what would not be captured by the scopes and methodologies deployed by, for example, Kuo or Siegel. However, configuring a Guadalupan statue and Judd's Marfa-sited works—produced within little more than a decade of one another—in a field in which they are both seen and felt stands as a first step. And it is precisely in response to this challenge that I enter Ingold into the decolonial aestheSis/aestheTics conversation, at a crux where Mignolo and Vázquez write:

> It is important to distinguish two currents of what has come to be called "decolonial aesthetics" (now "decolonial AestheSis"). One is aestheSis, which has been denied validity under the modern aestheTics hegemony, and which precedes any naming of the "decolonial." We can find this in what has been called popular culture and popular arts. . . .
>
> The other current, which is of course in communication with the first, is decolonial aestheSis, seen as a critical intervention within the world of the contemporary arts. This practice runs parallel to the decolonial epistemic critique being made in the realms of philosophy and academic thought. It circulates not so much around the question of the re-existence of practices and forms of sensing that remain present in everyday life, but more around biennales and curatorial projects. It stands as a confrontation with modern aestheTics within its own field. This dossier is centered around this second current of decolonial aestheSis-as-critical intervention, the one in which the artist and the curator are struggling to challenge the hegemonic normativity of modern aestheTics.[16]

Alongside the artist and the curator, I would add the art historian to this final line.

The relationship between the two currents—aestheSis preceding and continuing through modernity/(de)coloniality and "decolonial aestheSis," which originated and works from within modern and contemporary art—might seem familiar. It is structurally analogous to the inspired graduation of rasquachismo into first, second, and third degrees by Gaspar de Alba discussed in chapter 1. The distinction is useful insofar as it makes a palimpsest vision of Marfa possible; with it, one can stand between the Guadalupe of Marfa and Judd's *15 untitled works in concrete* and sense possibilities of a conversation. One no longer has to comply with blindness to one for the sake of the other. One encounters the option to do other than comply with the "hushing of the manyness," to reinvoke María Lugones's phrasing. As in chapter 1, this distinction lays the ground for a possible rich conversation among the registers.

MAKING MARFA

Together, the interdisciplinary practices of Ingold and the anti-disciplinarity of the modernity/(de)coloniality group facilitate this shift from an industrial production view of art to a lens of correspondent human and nonhuman making. All things, minimalist or rasquache, artistic or vernacular, even human or nonhuman, are made. Ingold writes:

> We are accustomed to thinking of making as a project. This is to start with an idea in mind, of what we want to achieve, and with a supply of the raw material needed to achieve it. And it is to finish at the moment when the material has taken on the intended form. . . . In the literature, the theory is known as hylomorphism, from the Greek *hyle* (matter) and *morphe* (form). . . . I want to think of making, instead, as a process of growth. This is to place the maker from the outset as a participant in amongst a world of active materials.[17]

"The literature" includes a wide array of thinkers such as Gilbert Simondon, Luce Irigaray, Félix Guattari, and Gilles Deleuze, but also, to Ingold's point, more than hints at encompassing thought produced through "the art of inquiry" demonstrated by craftspeople who "allow knowledge to grow from the crucible of our practical and observational engagements with the beings and things around us."[18] This nonhierarchical approach to academic theory and knowledge generated by engagement with materials resonates with the dissolution of the line between craft and fine art inherent in decolonial aestheSis/aestheTics projects. Ingold then recounts how he is spurred to undertake such arts along with his students, a practice sustained for years, beginning with the act of weaving baskets in the sand in northeast Scotland. This produces a shift: "To read making longitudinally, as a confluence of forces and materials, rather than laterally, as a transposition from image to object, is to regard it as such a form-generating—or *morphogenetic*—process. This is to soften any distinction we might draw between organism and artefact. For if organisms grow, so too do artefacts."[19] I make this shift here, seeing Marfa as a made organism in an ever-moving morphogenetic

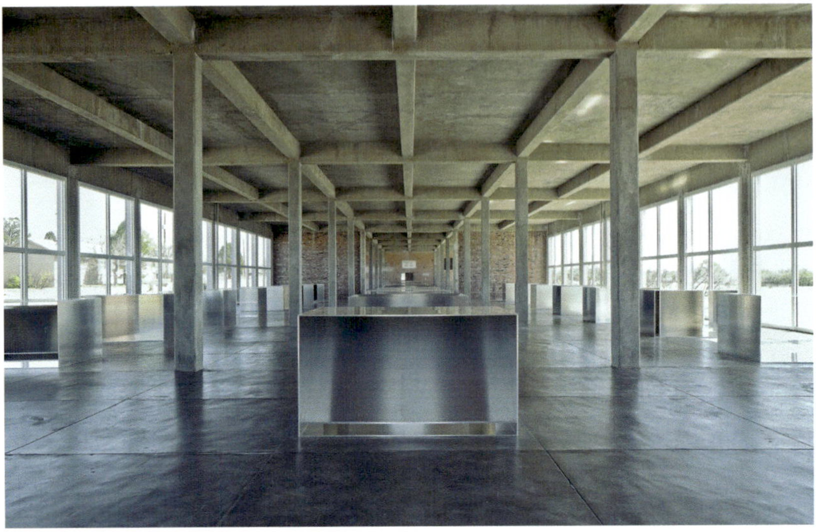

FIGURE 3.1 Donald Judd, *100 untitled works in mill aluminum*, 1982–86. Photo: Florian Holzherr and Douglas Tuck. Donald Judd Art © 2025 Judd Foundation/Artists Rights Society (ARS), New York.

process of becoming, and not a collection of unchanging artifacts, artistic or social, merely available for easy consumption.

Evidence from serious consideration of fabrication and conservation goes against a reading of Judd's works as stably hylomorphic. For one, their morphogenetic nature is audible. Judd's *100 untitled works in mill aluminum* sound off on their made-ness most mornings and evenings, for which they pay a tangible cost (figure 3.1). Temperatures shift rapidly in the desert as the sun appears and recedes; inside the artillery sheds, the quadrangular units can be heard crackling and popping as their constitutive panels contract and expand against one another in response to the quickly rising and ebbing temperatures.[20] For conservators, this provokes anxiety. For visitors, it's a surprising and spectacular behavior the works perform. With this chorus of fragility and mutability in their ears, artists and designers who access Minimalism as a staid visual referent (an image correlating directly with that held in the artist's mind at the outset) might complicate their understanding of art as made. Hylomorphic views of art cannot account for such complications beyond a discourse of conservation and damage. This is but one example.

"Made in Marfa" is now a popular tag across product types from soap and cowboy boots to sculpture, video, and photography. (One high-profile instance of the latter, Mario Sorrenti's campaign for *W Magazine*, was discussed in chapter 2.) Accompanied by Ingold's work, the meaning of this tag will take on much more weight than a mere marketing device. From here, I set out to understand Marfa as a site *for* making and as a site *in the making*. And *making* means something different than *producing* in twentieth-century industrial terms. This may very well go against the grain of Judd's own self-conception as a Marfa-sited maker, if we take at face value an observation of Judd's feelings around making offered by Flavin Judd: "Don did not like to work with his hands. He hated fussing with wood, tools or mechanical aids. His art was about seeing and feeling, not about the making, not about splashing paint on precious canvas or carving ruts in wood slabs."[21] This certainly resonates with the description of hylomorphism offered earlier. Yet the modernity/(de)coloniality articulation of decolonial aestheSis and Ingold's work both provide frameworks for seeing how Judd, as one case, also demonstrated an acute morphogenetic sensibility, one that included but decentered his own human intent. This sensibility shows up in choices made for the publication of the first Chinati Foundation catalogue.

Unintentional affinities occurring in Marfa—the borderlands, Aztlán—emerge as a major theme of this book. The 1987 catalogue for the Chinati Foundation/La Fundación Chinati is one, wrapping questions of primacy, history, and theorizing within a single binding (figure 3.2). Time to bring it in from the cold. I imagine the cold of a West Texas night. Air in the desert crisps as soon as the sun falls out of view. A picture of this solar departure fronts the catalogue, assuming the photographer aimed toward the Chinati Mountains from the Marfa side, oriented south and west. If they crossed the range and took the photo facing east, then what we see is sun*rise*, on the precipice of the day's heat but still cool. Either way, the mountain is suggested as a silhouette, a monochromatic and continuous mound settled across roughly the bottom third of our view. My measurement here, done with my fingers, is as rough as the upper edge of the dark mass. Three additional boundaries are leveled by and exist only in this given picture plane. Its roughness is made rougher by the phenomenal results of mechanical reproduction. The clarity of the line produced by the position of the sun in relation to the camera and the mountain itself is contrasted by the dissolution occurring in its printed image. Look closely. The space between half-tone dots expands in-

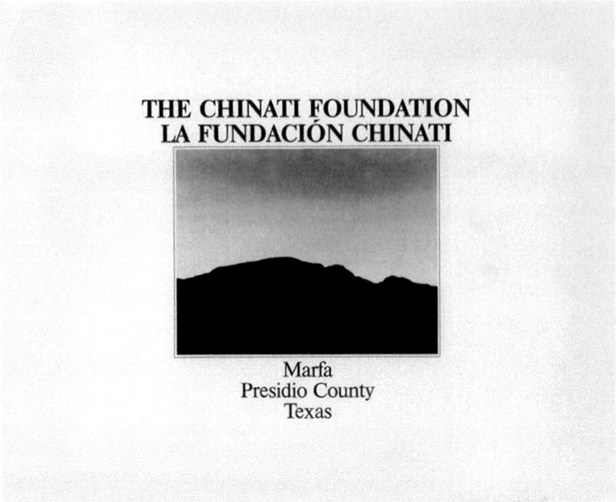

FIGURE 3.2 The Chinati Foundation/La Fundación Chinati catalog cover. Marfa: Chinati Foundation/La Fundación Chinati, 1987.

stantaneously where the sky abruptly takes over the upper two-thirds of the frame. The shift jars me into realization that this "mountain" and this "sky" are one more example of photography's failure to bring into existence that which it pictures. I have in front of me not air and dirt but ink on paper. And it is the air and dirt with which I am concerned, though the making of this image is of some interest.

How did this image come to be here? It is remarkable that neither the cover nor the first image-laden page (the same shot of Sierra Chinati as on the cover) point immediately to Judd's active object-making and architectural interventions. After all, is it not for these reasons that certain pilgrims flow continuously to the renovated army base? In sixty-nine pages of documentation around the production of the catalogue extant in the Judd Foundation's archives, consideration of the images and their order arises a handful of times. One letter from "Ellie" addressed to "Willie" contains seven questions, of which the question of the cover image is listed first.[22] Judd's own handwritten consideration appears in a brief two lines: "Put Chinati photo first / Spanish? Cerro?" Here the only question seems to be how to describe the looming mound of dirt, rock, and vegetation and in which language to do so. *Cerro*—"hill"—makes clear that Judd is signifying the mound and not

"Chinati," the museum. This muddies the situation substantially, opening up the possibility that Judd's conception of the latter was continuous with the former.

To be perturbed by Judd's choice to introduce his public collection of art with the image of their namesake landscape feature rather than a work of art may betray an imagination premised on a hylomorphic model of agency and objecthood. However, if one approaches the instance of the mountain as the cover image from a morphogenetic understanding, the relationship between the mountains and the artworks is abundantly clear: both are *made* and ever in the process of making. Ingold opens a chapter titled "Round Mound and Earth Sky" with this observation: "If you heap stuff up over a period of time, always adding to the top of the pile and allowing it to settle of its own accord, it will generally form a mound, roughly circular in plan and conical or bell-shaped in elevation. . . . From molehills to ants' nests, mounds are among the commonest forms in nature. They often result from human activities too."[23] Implied by the relationship between Judd's works and the landscape in the first Chinati Foundation catalogue, one might begin to see Marfa as a mound, as a conglomeration of materials falling due to gravity in fits and starts, the falling sometimes intervened by human hands. Judd intended his installations in Marfa to be permanent, but *permanent* is a constantly shifting term, managed and debated by the many parties invested in the future of Marfa: institutional directors, conservators, townspeople, service industry workers, transient interns, longtime staff . . . all can offer a different perspective on what *permanent installation* might mean. Weather conditions and the roiling negotiation of natural resources between themselves and among humans in the area also take part in this ongoing conversation. Shifting from hylomorphic to morphogenetic interpretations stands to change this conversation yet again. For example, is the conservator's task to maintain a work's original conditions, or to more subtly manage its inevitable "deterioration"?

Considering Marfa as a dynamic mound challenges even basic art-historical conventions such as the dating of works (yet one more modern convention to be challenged in a process of decolonizing aestheSis/aestheTics). Ingold ponders,

> What then, of the mound? Can we say how old it is? Apparently more artificial than a mountain, but more natural than a monument, the mound seems to lie halfway between the two. Yet this very distinction between the natural and the artificial, and with it the question of antiq-

uity, rests on the axiom of the hylomorphic model of making, namely that it is the imposition of pure form that raises naturally given raw material to an artificial state. The phenomenon of the mound obliges us, however, to reject this axiom.[24]

Can we interpret Judd's choices in the production of the Chinati catalogue to be one act of "reject[ing] this axiom"? This would call into question the dates assigned to his works in the landscape, like the fifteen concrete works. It would figure them, rather, as current configurations of rock paste recipes that appear to human eyes to be quite still, but whose flow is as active as that of a handful of loose dirt being poured into a pile over the span of mere seconds. To pin down the beginning and end of this flow along a string of years on a human calendar is the task of a discipline, of art history, and not of the materials themselves. Marfa-as-mound illuminates the lacunae between disciplining historical work and the art historian's other arguably more significant task: due diligence to the nature of materials before us. As Ingold puts it, "Why should we date a monument from the moment it was built? Is this not just one, relatively arbitrary point in the life of a thing, and of its constituent materials? . . . Do we not rather have to conclude of things made or built, as much as of things grown, that they are originating all the time?"[25] A morphogenetic consideration of Marfa takes one beyond typical temporal limits in art history. Such a view also takes us beyond the spatial delineation of Marfa's city limits. This is one methodological affinity with projects centered on elaborating the industrial fabrication of art. Natural phenomena like the mountains around Marfa may be outside the scope of Kuo, Siegel, and others, but a large, industrial metal shop certainly is not.

Odessa, Texas, is a two-and-a-half-hour drive from Marfa. The oil industry is foundational to the economy of this boom-and-bust town. The population is significantly larger than Marfa's, around one hundred thousand (though a major boom at the time of this writing has currently raised this number). For Marfans, it offers major medical services, shopping, occasional work, higher education institutions, and other services and opportunities not available in Far West Texas. For the Marfan Donald Judd, Odessa was the nearest location where some fabrication needs could potentially be met. In New York City, the artist worked closely with nearby fabricators Lippincott Inc. and Bernstein Brothers. Lippincott Inc., founded in 1966, specifically catered to artistic, rather than industrial, making. The Lippincott Inc. mission statement includes this description: "Known for understanding the concerns and methods of artists and for working to the highest standards, Lippincott Inc. has produced numerous iconic works since its inception."[26] Barnett Newman, Ellsworth Kelly, Robert Indiana, Claes Oldenburg, and many others called upon Lippincott Inc. for their work. But the production of large-scale works in concrete and aluminum to be permanently installed in Marfa compelled Judd to seek out fabricators closer to the site in at least one instance of interest here.

In the introduction to an interview with Lawrence Voytek and Peter Ballantine (assistant to Robert Rauschenberg and fabricator for Donald Judd, respectively), Madeleine Schwartz writes, "Artists have always had assistants—Greek sculpture was carved in workshops, and Rembrandt painted with aides whose anonymity continues to cause curatorial headaches. But the figure of the 'fabricator' is a relative newcomer in the history of art production. The fabricator was born only a half a century ago, when a push toward the use of modern materials and bigger, more complex projects meant that the art waiting to be created was unrealizable without a trained hand."[27]

These "trained hand[s]" can be understood as demonstrating a highly honed aesthesis, "an unelaborated elementary awareness of stimulation; 'a sense of touch,'" and as practiced "followers of the cut."[28] This participant in art-making is engaged in a "correspondence between mindful attention and lively materials conducted by skilled hands 'at the trowel's edge.'"[29] Some, like Lippincott Inc., took to this role to such a degree that they can now be considered archetypical of this relatively young art-world figure: the industrial fabricator. From its inception, this company understood the restructuring of the relationship between artist and maker that took place in the twentieth century and set itself up to be an indelible part of art history from that point on. Others, however, became implicated in this ongoing history with less awareness of the field they were entering by taking on artists' commissions. For companies set up to serve the West Texas oil industry—to create and repair parts of oil derricks, pumps, and other industry-specific equipment—entry into this history was not so intentional or frictionless. In one case, looking at the different venues in which images of made artifacts circulate more clearly evinces the distance between multiple entries to the town as a field of making—the distance between hylomorphic and morphogenetic modes of reception and consumption.

A Magazine Curated by . . . is a selectively curated publication headquartered in Antwerp, Belgium. Each edition is given over to a different designer

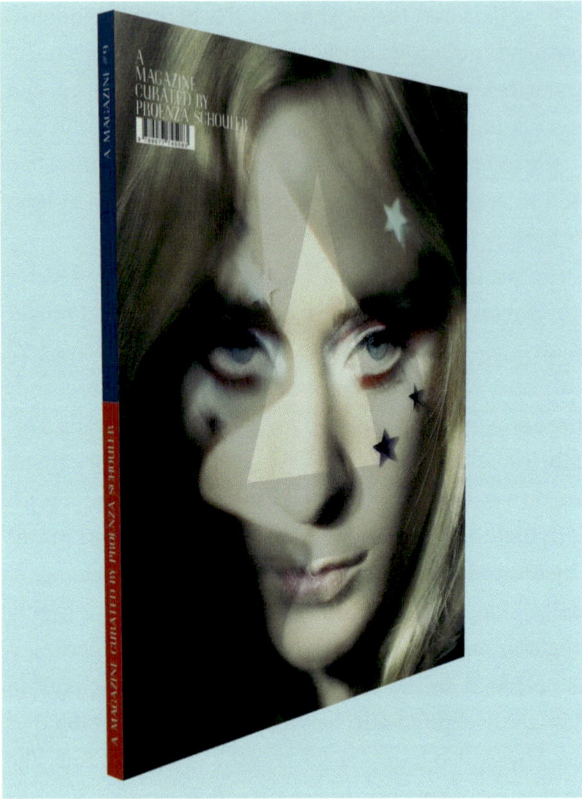

FIGURE 3.3 Cover of *A Magazine Curated by Proenza Schouler*.

to do with as they please. Fashion duo Proenza Schouler's issue includes photographer Josie Miner's *8 untitled works*, shot in Marfa in 2009 (figure 3.3). In the series, readers encounter Judd's aluminum and concrete works in front of Miner's lens, a position they now share with fashion models. Images of Judd's pieces from the same group of *100 untitled works in mill aluminum* exist in another set of bound images I encountered during research, a scrapbook belonging to Jerry "Pepper" Parsons, of Metal Fab Products Inc. in Odessa, Texas. Parsons now owns the shop, but when he was an employee there in the 1990s, he was closely involved in developing the techniques necessitated by Judd's designs in Cor-Ten and aluminum using machinery usually reserved for fabricating standardized oil industry parts.

Considering this sleek publication and the workaday record of a metal fabrication shop alongside one another demonstrates the tensions between multiple Marfas and multiple modes of engagement with Judd's and other so-called Minimalists' works. Miner's refined artwork is located in a luxe, niche culture magazine designed for a high-end market (figure 3.4). In contrast, the prosaic snapshots collected in Parsons's generic three-ring binder were taken as documentation during one of a few scouting trips to gain a first-hand understanding of the installation space intended for particular works (figure 3.5). Metal Fab Products Inc. did not produce the one hundred works in aluminum, but according to Parsons, Judd requested that he engage with this space to exemplify his understanding of architecture and artwork before starting on commissions of Cor-Ten wall-mounted pieces. If these books side by side are not enough to convince one of the distances between the legacy of Minimalism in art and design and the less celebrated histories of the actual making of canonical Minimalist works, a story might do so: On the particular trip when Parsons procured the images shown here, he ended up in a contentious encounter with a docent. There was a strict "no photography" rule at Chinati, and the dutiful attendant confronted Parsons. When Parsons's explanation of himself and his insistence that he had direct instructions from Judd to take these photographs failed to persuade the docent, the artist himself eventually had to be called in to settle the dispute. This particular maker's voice had no authority on its own in the space of art.[30]

Judd's scrupulous final examination of works often resulted in rejected trial pieces. At least one of these unrealized works remained in Metal Fab Products' storage spaces when I visited, nestled in padded crates and packed at the back of a storage warehouse since the early 1990s. As someone accustomed to encountering them in the relative austerity of galleries, museums, and collectors' homes, I found it jarring to encounter these pieces in this environment and state. This setting highlights the morphogenetic nature of the materials composing Judd's works. However, the aura of the studio—irrevocably romanticized throughout the 1960s, the inceptive moment of Judd's most recognizable artistic production—seems amoebic in its reach, easily extending to encompass the factory after my initial shock. As initially disturbing as the sight of incomplete and "mishandled" works was, telling this story and sharing my snapshots of the objects with friends and colleagues in the arts has made something clear: Ascription and expansion of aura can

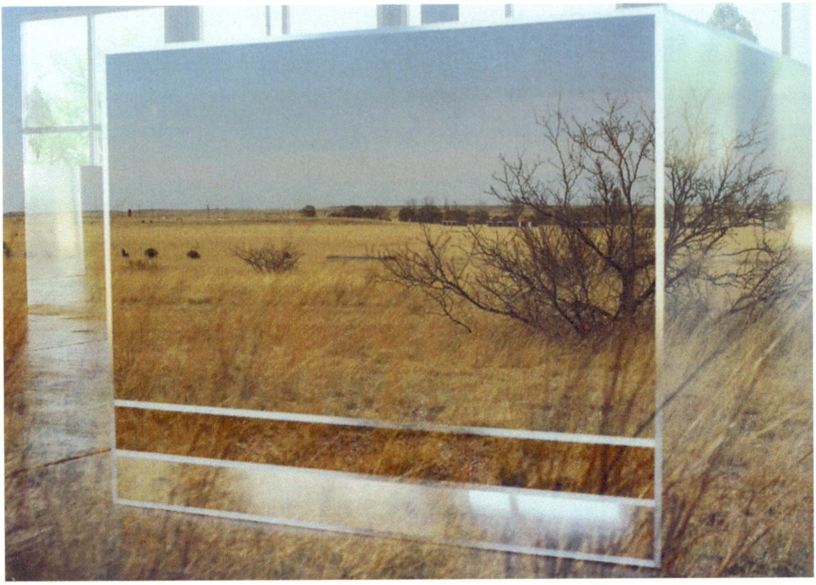

FIGURE 3.4 Josie Miner, *8 untitled works* (detail), 2009.

and does happen through means that initially seem antithetical to its construction. Encountering the work-adjacent objects nude and inchoate—set haphazardly on a dusty, workroom table by gloveless hands—is shocking at first, but eventually this feeling seems to give way and in fact bolster interest in their finished kin.

While many artists and critics took an anti-aura stance in the 1960s, manifest largely in the uptake of industrial modes of production, "As it turned out, auratic traditions would be recuperated endlessly by the market and mass culture, where the construction of authorship is crucial to commodity exchange."[31] Will Judd's authorship be challenged by the voices invoked in this writing? That is hardly expected or desired. The aim is to break down the *construction* of that authorship into a multitude of sites for making and for interpretive models. The challenge then is to persist in attempting to pierce that "inevitable" aura, while also acknowledging its function as one interpretive mechanism. Conservation offers us yet another.

In a 2011 interview, Eleanora Nagy, a conservator of Judd's works in metal, testifies against the notion that these works are in any way invincible or sta-

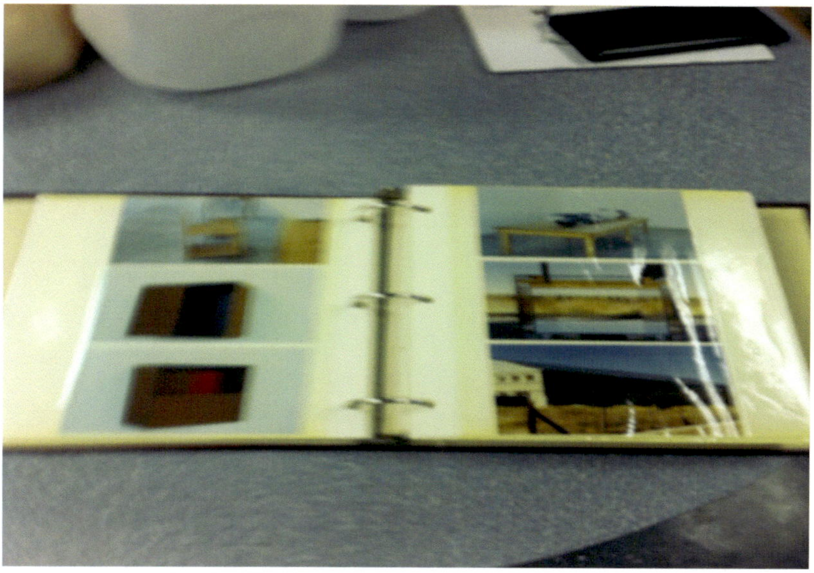

FIGURE 3.5 Pepper Parsons, two-page spread from an album of fabrication research photos, Chinati Foundation, Marfa, Texas.

ble.[32] Like other conservators and fabricators of Judd's works, she finds the opposite to be true. To understand these works as tough, imperturbable, implies a hylomorphic imagination in which works appear in the gallery immaculately, when in actuality the risky process of construction and installation led on numerous occasions to Judd's dismantling or disassociating these easily damaged artworks. In developing new methods of conservation and surface treatments in particular, Nagy has had many conversations with Judd's fabricators.[33] She reports that "they describe in detail how many sets of tests and trials they had to do because Judd demanded something that was technically very difficult to produce.... They did their very best for him."[34] And so it was with Parsons. On our walk through Metal Fab Products' massive machine rooms, he described how various bending, cutting, and shaping machines had to be retooled in unfamiliar ways solely for Judd's commissions (figure 3.6). Parsons also explained that the skills those operators needed in order to reinvent usage of these machines are now lost; in a brief twenty-odd years, the computerization of metal fabrication has rendered those skills obsolete. A whole mode of making disappeared. In Parsons's estimation, Judd's

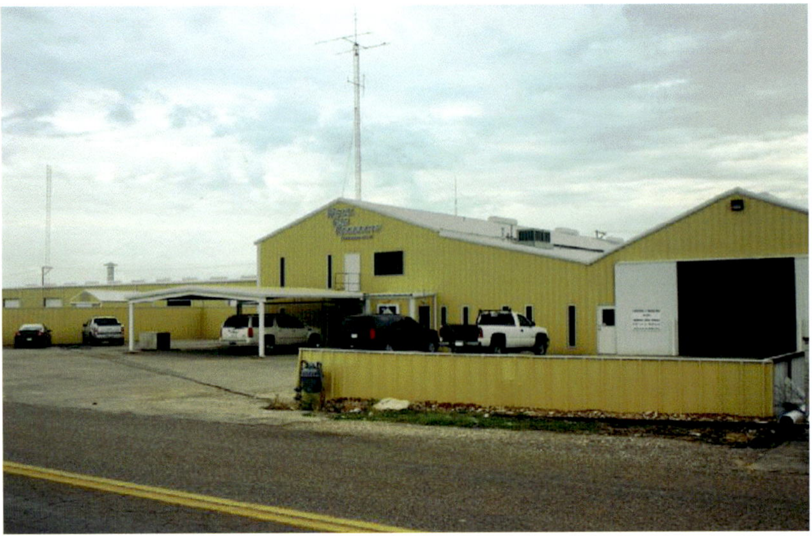

FIGURE 3.6 Exterior of Metal Fab Products, Odessa, Texas.

machine-made and therefore ostensibly infinitely reproducible works can actually never be made again.

FROM IN/VISIBILITY TO "CORRESPONDENCE"

For one long weekend every October, Marfa is inundated with pilgrims. The central event drawing them is Chinati Weekend, Chinati Foundation's annual open house. Attendees celebrate the collection itself, located throughout the grounds of the renovated army base. Regarding this site, Judd wrote, "Most art is fragile and some should be placed and never moved again. Somewhere a portion of contemporary art has to exist as an example of what the art and its context were meant to be. Somewhere, just as the platinum-iridium meter guarantees the tape measure, a strict measure must exist for the art of this time and place."[35] After Judd's passing in 1994, the Chinati Foundation and the Judd Foundation—which maintains and preserves Judd's other substantial holdings in and around Marfa and New York City—have continued Judd's experiments in permanent installation. Simultaneously, institutional efforts to make visible the interconnectivity of Judd's work with local Marfa communities have grown through various programming and artistic endeavors.

Speaking about the 2006 open house, filmmaker and Judd Foundation President Rainer Judd said that they had wanted this event, "our first major participation in years—to be more about the local community than about the international visitors. We wanted to celebrate Marfa and give recognition to the 'hidden people.'"[36] Besides shaping the nature of Judd Foundation programming that weekend, this desire also led Rainer Judd to launch the Oral History Project. This ongoing filmic oral history began to document those in Marfa who worked closely with Judd but who are "hidden" to contingents like the international visitors Judd contrasts to the locals she includes in her account. This initially includes local newspaper staff from the *Big Bend Sentinel*, a West Texas publication; figures who worked with Judd to care for his multiple properties, build furniture, and manage studio spaces, including Alfredo Mediano; and local West Texas historians. But as much work was going on in New York City as in Marfa due to Judd's extensive practice, so Rainer Judd also decided to bring in voices from New York: gallery owners, artists, and SoHo residents and friends of Judd's. All are present in the first versions of the film entitled *Marfa Voices*, a compilation of interviews set in a variety of spaces from Marfa homes to New York City art spaces, the interviewees questioned by Rainer Judd, off camera. *Marfa Voices* and the Oral History Project demonstrated how much the making of so many people besides the artist congeals in Donald Judd's works and the spaces they occupy.

In 2013, the Chinati Foundation purged some of its used furniture and various display structures through a fine art version of a yard sale. Ester Sanchez joined many locals trekking up the low hill and returned home with a shelving unit and a plinth originally intended for sculptural display. Now, the former stands in a corner of the Sanchezes' kitchen, serving a typically domestic purpose as one can see, while the latter is relegated to the outdoors, a few feet from Guadalupe, as the base for floral displays (figures 3.7 and 3.8). The dissolution of the pedestal, and how to articulate this dissolution, loomed large in the second half of twentieth-century art history. Its fate was wrapped up in the radically disrupted status of art in relation to other objects. Its "disappearance" threw into crisis the relationship of the viewer to the art: Where to stand and view it from? Where to stop the reaching hand? Where does the art begin and the pedestal's presence end?

Here I propose that, at least in Marfa though I suspect elsewhere as well, the pedestal did not disappear or dissolve but was rasquachified in one more style and attitude of making perceivable through a decolonial and morpho-

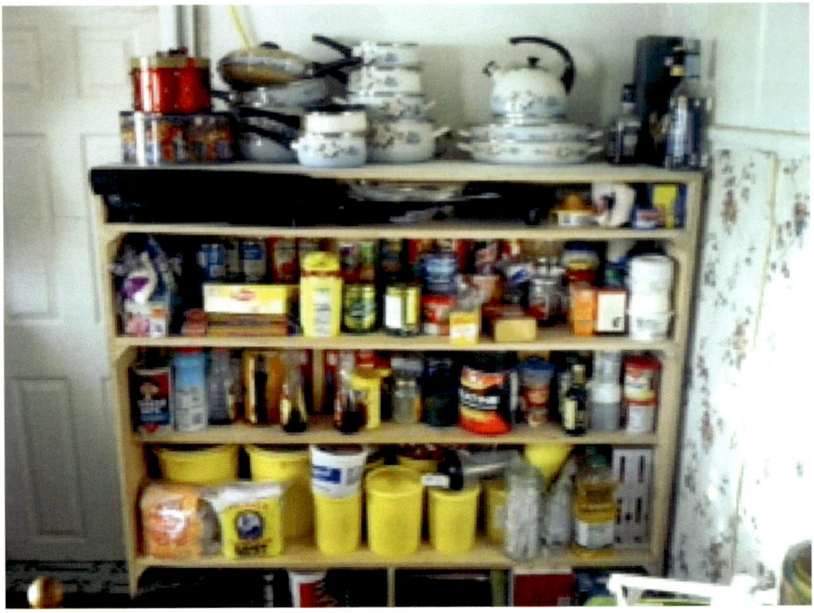

FIGURE 3.7 Ester Sanchez, repurposed shelving from the Chinati Foundation in the Sanchez family kitchen.

genetic perspective. Ester Sanchez's repurposing of the art-historically loaded plinth from her neighbor, Chinati, is just one example. The willing art historian shifts into different, decolonial modes of looking and sensing to approach them. To close, I return to tables. Both are in Marfa, always far from and close to their cousin in New York City introduced at the beginning of the chapter.

One of Judd's assistants, Jamie Dearing, tells a remarkable story when asked about the relationship between Judd and the US Border Patrol, another dominant presence in Marfa. One night, Judd invited two Border Patrol agents to dinner. As one might imagine, the topic of their career and its relationship to often-incendiary political issues arose. The agents articulated a politics of closed borders and violent control diametrically opposed to Dearing's own beliefs. At one point, enraged by the conversation, Dearing stood up to leave. Judd arrested his exit with one line: "No one has the right to leave the table."[37] In order to claim that seeing through difficult conversations is an interpersonal and human obligation, Judd invoked the object around which these conversations occur. Whereas the "disfiguring patterns" encountered by

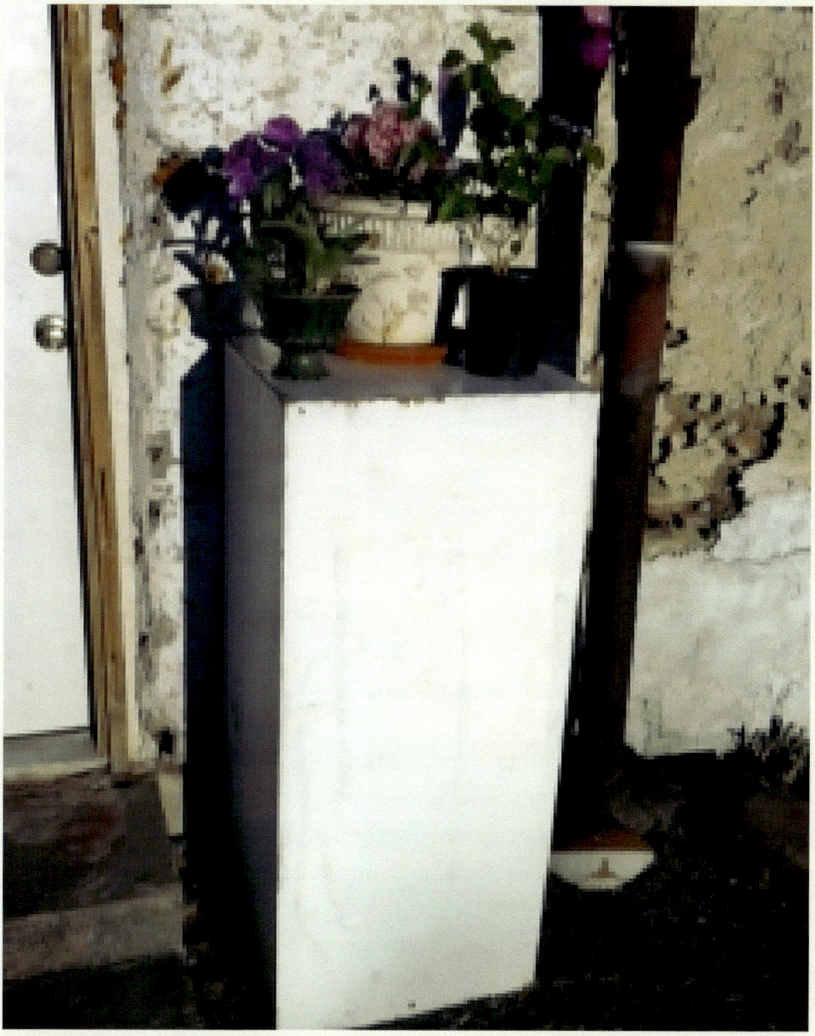

FIGURE 3.8 Ester Sanchez, rasquachified plinth from the Chinati Foundation in the Sanchez backyard.

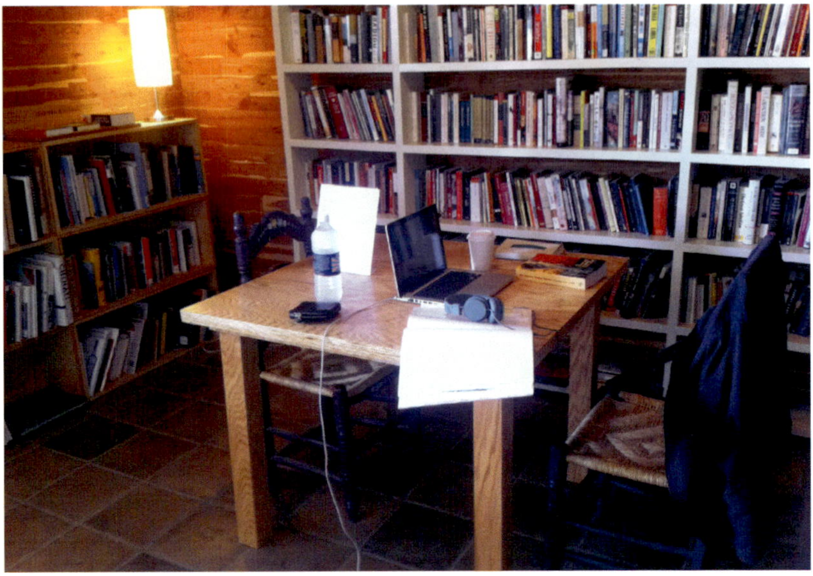

FIGURE 3.9 Table built by Caitlin Murray, in the Reading Room, El Cosmico, Marfa, Texas. Chapter 1 of this book is in progress.

Nagy and her conservation team are marks to be treated (disappeared), the signs of use marking this table's surface—both in the wood and in the knotty social encounters for which it serves as substrate—are marks to be left prominent and closely examined for social meaning in the context of art and a town fundamentally transformed by art throughout the last half century. Furthermore, difficult conversations around tables reverberate, in this instance, with the far-reaching concerns over who acts and how in the US-Mexico borderlands. The reverb in this case makes its way to those concerns through the act of Dearing's hands pushing against and away from the wooden surface of a dining table. Judd's vocal cessation of that act waves next. Then are the unknown echoes in the daily lives of those Border Patrol agents (perhaps the gesture of reaching for a weapon was altered, perhaps not), then, after many other "thens," come the manual acts involved in this writing... The table was "first" in a series of what Ingold identifies as "transducers."

Transducers "convert the *ductus*—the kinetic quality of the gesture, its flow or movement—from one register of bodily kinesthesia, to another, of material flux."[38] The table at which the bulk of chapter 1 of this book was drafted is another (figure 3.9). It was *made in Marfa* by the able hands of the Judd Foundation archivist and Marfa resident Caitlin Murray (now executive director of Chinati). Because the table was located in the Reading Room at El Cosmico, an eclectic campground, I can write that chapter 1 was also *made in Marfa*. Murray's hands are as able with transducers like saws and hammers as with the archival documents we trade in as archivist and researcher.

I invoke this final table to consider a term lifted from Ingold and invoked a few times already: *correspondence*. He writes,

> This is a word to which I have also had recourse at a number of points in my argument, and I would like to conclude this chapter by explaining more fully what I meant by it. The case of letter writing highlights two aspects that I take to be central to correspondence: first, that it is a movement in real time; and second, that this movement is sentient. . . . A correspondence is rather like a relay, in which each participant takes it in turns to pick up the baton and carry it forward, while others remain temporarily quiescent, awaiting their turn.[39]

Perhaps Murray awaits the temporary results of my early acts of writing, facilitated by her table as transducer. To correspond furthers a decolonizing of Marfa by posing questions to Murray's table and my book simultaneously, by taking everything in Marfa as always in the process of making and all making as significant. Murray's capacity to knowingly "follow the cut" of wood enabled me to take up research materials and, through scribing by hand and keystroke, animate materials into a momentary pause called a book. More importantly, remembering that a colleague's handiwork in part made possible my own is to remember, as a decolonizing act, that Marfa's history—expansive as the idea of it now is (big as the West Texas sky and the international art market)—comprises the "history . . . of me and you, life history in the flesh, moods, tendencies, and dispositions to live big or small, to tame and trash someone's spirit or to live side by side in the task of overcoming incomprehension—all levels of the political."[40]

Like tables, yards are another element of everyday life in Marfa that have come to profoundly shape the art-historical approach enacted in this book. In the conclusion, I move into this liminal space nearly a decade after the preceding chapters were written. This was necessary, as the significance of the yard required this time to emerge.

Conclusion

Love, Yard (Hanging Out in Marfa)

We are fully dependent on each other for the possibility of being understood and without this understanding we are not intelligible, we do not make sense, we are not solid, visible, integrated; we are lacking. So traveling to each other's "worlds" would enable us to be through loving each other.

—María Lugones, *Pilgrimages/Peregrinajes*

I wish there were more models, more of these artists who are interested in the narrative landscape, whose concepts of place and history include people . . .

—Lucy R. Lippard, "Land Art in the Rearview Mirror"

Scholar Colleen J. Sheehy writes in the conclusion of *The Flamingo in the Garden: American Yard Art and the Vernacular Landscape*, "Yard art in general is a testimony of Americans' love affair with material things. . . . Yet they are not frivolous things. They are objects that people need to create some kind of beauty where they live or to make some kind of statement about who they are or simply to communicate that they are there, alive and healthy."[1] This concluding chapter reexamines yards and yard-adjacent sites in Marfa through the lens offered by Sheehy to argue that, in addition to statements of beauty and presence, forms of love are expressed at these sites through "not frivolous" material things. As part of this revision, I consider Donald Judd as not only an internationally known artist, but also as another West Texan who worked

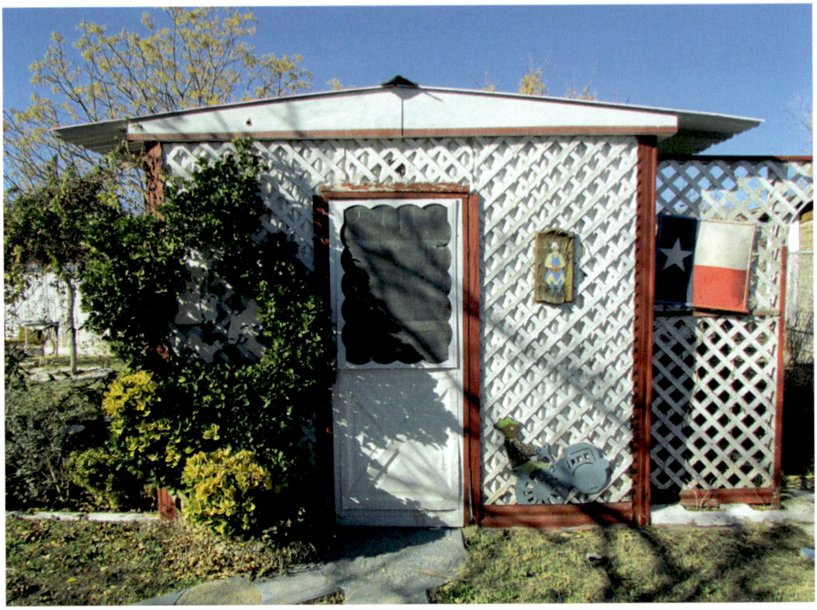

FIGURE C.1 Shed in Hipolito "Polé" Hernandez's yard, Odessa, Texas, ca. 1990–2015.

creatively in his yards. I also investigate how love can fuel an art historian's practice of long, place-conscious looking.

"A SPACE OF LOVE"

Yards have become primary sites of thinking for me in the years since the preceding chapters of this book were written.[2] Yards, it turns out, are fertile grounds for art-historical practice.[3] Marfa comprises many yards that can be variously described as domestic, institutional, semipublic, inviting, spectacular, concealed, ornamental, exclusive, inviting, and more. And while the population and physical footprint of the one-traffic-light town are small, the range of people attracted to it is as wide as the West Texas horizon. This variety creates opportunities to practice love as a methodology, to be empathetic and curious, always endeavoring to "world-travel" as conceived by philosopher María Lugones, whose writings are central to my thinking about Marfa,

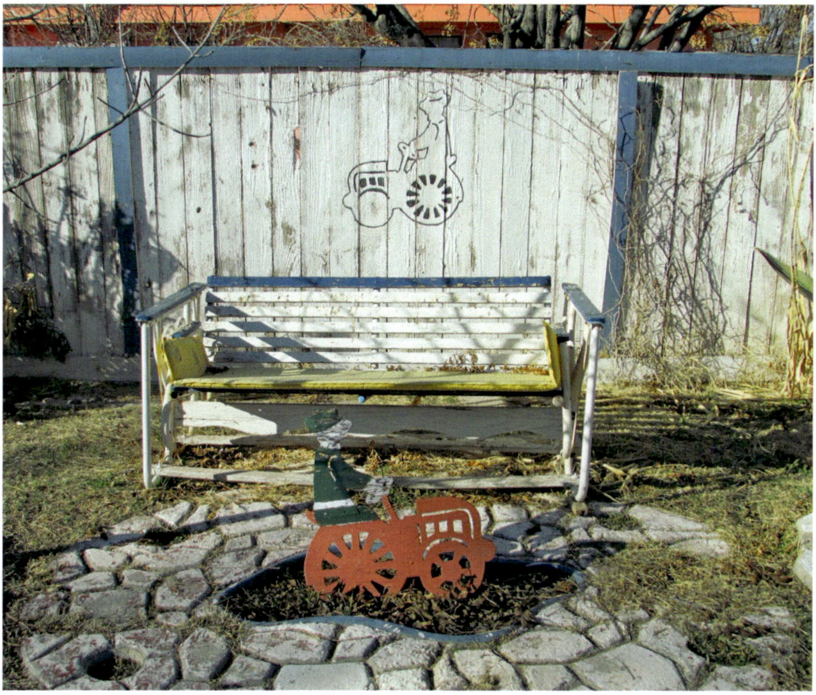

FIGURE C.2 Bench arrangement in Hipolito "Polé" Hernandez's yard, Odessa, Texas, ca. 1990–2015.

art, and the world generally.[4] How does one "world-travel"—that is, how does one love—among the yards of Marfa?

I remember learning love in a yard. In this particular yard, sculptures—perhaps specific objects but more accurately rasquache constructions—emerged continually out of a network of three small sheds that served as workshops. These pieces were then attached to fences or planted in cement or directly in the dirt by the artist, our grandfather, Hipolito "Polé" Hernandez (figures C.1, C.2, and C.3). He was not alone in his creative practice. Throughout the twentieth century, Mexican and Mexican American men of a certain generation, including my grandfather and many others, quietly transformed the region into an open-air site of art making and display. Humbler but much more colorful than spiral jetties (or cosmically arranged concrete tubes and gouged cliffsides and giant penetrative metal rods and renovated volcanoes and unpopulated cities), yards across the South and Southwest bear the fruits

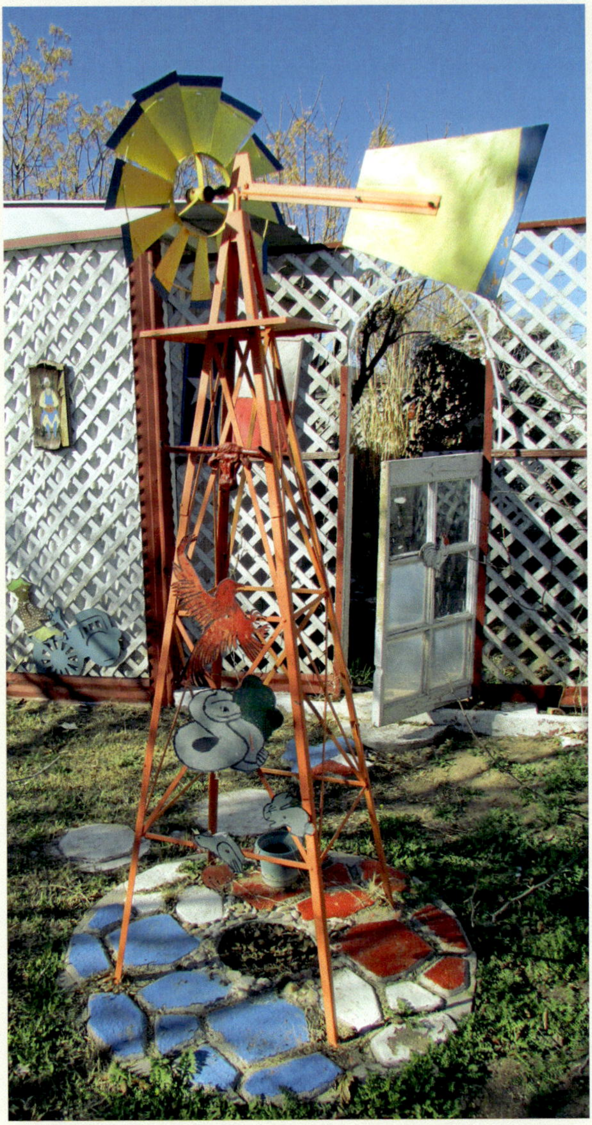

FIGURE C.3 Windmill in Hipolito "Polé" Hernandez's yard, Odessa, Texas, ca. 1990–2015.

of these artists' labor: tractor tires turned planters, outmoded playground equipment salvaged and whimsically repainted, unending varieties of poured concrete shapes, cheeky simulacra of rural architecture and farm equipment, elaborate altars, ornamented windmills . . . an endless creative variation. In this environment, my brothers, cousins, and I witnessed our grandfather's creative practice and nurtured our own. In his funeral book, our grandmother entered simply "Adorning the yard" in the section for listing his hobbies. His yard is where I learned to look and to love my family. For me, the two cannot be separated. Nor can his story and artistic practice be separated from that of the town of Marfa, Texas, where he was raised.[5]

The last time I saw my grandfather's body, lying in the coffin, I discovered something new about it and him. For the first time, I took note of the letters L–O–V–E tattooed on the four fingers of his left hand. It was almost certainly stick-and-poke like the other markings on his arm I had asked about as a curious child. If his hands had been positioned with the right one on top, I may never have learned of this one. This might give the impression that I didn't know my grandfather well or spend much time with him. That's not the case. It's just that he was muy prieto, very dark, a direct visual complement to our fair-skinned grandmother.[6] His face and arms were especially dark, a testament to Indigenous American ancestry compounded by countless hours spent working and creating outdoors.

I cannot cleave my deepest and earliest feelings of familial love from the place where I learned my earliest lessons in looking. The yard came before the dimmed classrooms, the galleries and museums, the archives, and the historic sites and homes preserved at great expense where I would later become an art historian. The yard was my first art world. Interwoven among experiences in my grandfather's Odessa yard, where I grew up, and the yard where he grew up in Marfa, where Guadalupe chose to show herself, are now years of experience in other spaces, not least of all those made by Judd. This includes the yards of his own domestic spaces and, in focus here, the grounds of Chinati, which I will consider here as yet one more yard.

Where else is love? I first found it in yards, but I discovered love again in my studies. Scholar and storyteller Tomás Ybarra-Frausto recognized the powerful relationship between sacred figures, making space, and love. In his oral history for the Archives of American Art, he describes a strategy of the Chicano Movement: "You know, [César] Chávez capitalized on this religious iconography, the Virgen de Guadalupe, which was carried on all the pilgrimages. . . . So the struggle was not only a struggle that was political and of this world, but it was also almost [spiritual], it had a deeper meaning, it had a religious meaning of brotherhood and of creating a space of nonviolence, creating a space of love."[7] A "space of love" is what I aim to construct within the ever-growing art history of Marfa. That space for me manifests in the yard rather than the activist procession. Guadalupe presides in both.

LOVE AS METHOD

Guadalupe also figures repeatedly among artists' practices discussed in scholar and curator Laura E. Pérez's book *Eros Ideologies: Writings on Art, Spirituality, and the Decolonial*, further demonstrating Guadalupe's function as a catalyst for community-making and critical practices of love. Pérez characterizes "eros ideologies" as "politically and socially relevant ideologies that we can recraft and fine-tune to our personal, local, communal, and global lives."[8] Since the Virgin's visitation in 1997, the Guadalupe of Marfa has provided a local anchor for practices of love.[9] While unfamiliar to most people outside of town, she, and the Sanchez family who care for her, are beloved among their neighbors. I am ever grateful that this wonderful family inhabits the place where my grandfather spent his childhood, and I cherish my friendship with them and especially my ongoing dialogue with Ester Sanchez about Guadalupe, Chinati (her neighbor), and Marfa.

Pérez, in her discussion of artist Liliana Wilson's practice, writes that "spectral, omnipresent danger is insistently met by inviolate eros, the life energy of love and interdependence: the human spirit's endurance, vitality, and beauty in the face of the suppression of empathy, love, and care for the other."[10] In Marfa, the omnipresent danger often takes the forms of exploitive art tourism and real estate practices that make it challenging for longtime multigenerational residents, such as my own relatives and the Sanchezes, to remain in their homes.[11] Yet, there is also a deep recognition of love and interdependence among many residents from both old and new populations.

In a snapshot from a recent trip home, my parents, Toby and Frances Franco, are seated at a table with Marfa residents Caitlin Murray and Tim Johnson, who I am fortunate to count as friends for more than a decade now (figure C.4). Murray was director of programs at the Judd Foundation for many years, then was named executive director of Chinati in 2023, a much-celebrated appointment.[12] Johnson, a poet and organizer, operates Marfa

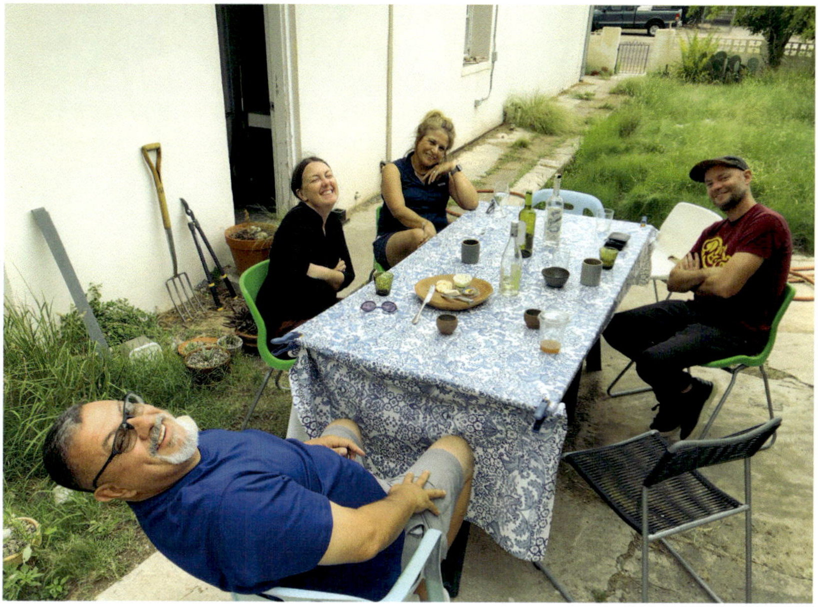

FIGURE C.4 *Clockwise from foreground:* Toby Franco, Caitlin Murray, Frances Franco, and Tim Johnson in the Johnson/Murray backyard, Marfa, Texas, August 19, 2022.

Book Co., a bookstore, gallery, and vital community space. While I took this photo for no reason other than to make a memory that day, I now realize how powerful it is in the context of this writing: The daughter and grandson of a Marfa resident who attended the segregated Blackwell School for nonwhite children in Marfa in the 1940s are happily communing with the director of the Chinati Foundation and her partner in their lovely yard.[13]

Consider this photo alongside a still from a video shot just a few blocks away, at the Sanchez home (figure C.5). In the video, Ester Sanchez tends to the altar, undertaking her annual preparations for December 12, Guadalupe's feast day. The altar, freshly painted, has been lovingly adorned with flowers and candles by Ester, her daughter, grandson, and a family friend. These images together give me hope that, despite rampant, ongoing, and facile cultural consumption of Marfa experienced largely through social media and large corporate publications, many of the town's residents and institutions simultaneously work toward a more loving and convivial future.

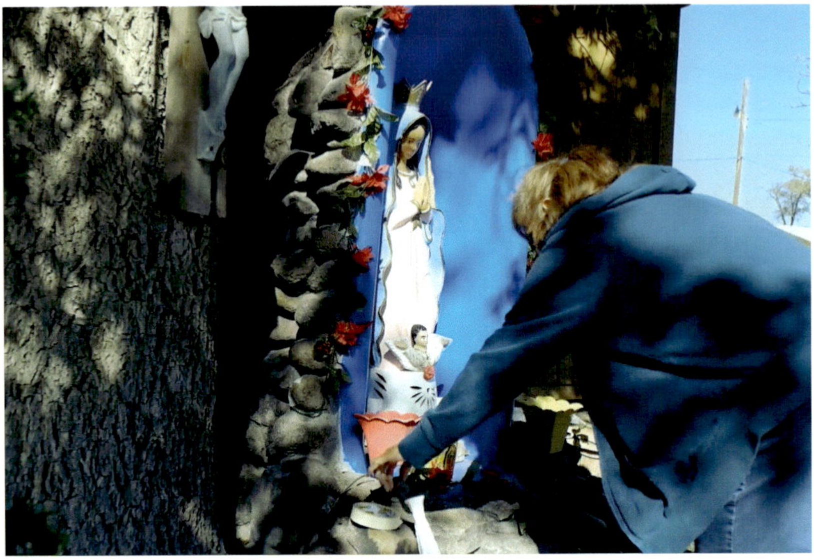

FIGURE C.5 Ester Sanchez preparing her Virgen de Guadalupe altar for the feast day, Marfa, Texas. Video still, December 3, 2023. Videographer: Sarah M. Vasquez.

In a talk delivered at Chinati as part of a panel titled "Art in the Landscape," writer Lucy Lippard voiced a desire for "more models, more of these artists who are interested in the narrative landscape, whose concepts of place and history include people."[14] This is the kind of narrative I hope to achieve here: an exploration of yards as peopled sites for building a loving art-historical methodology. In addition to Lippard's motivating call, I also look to Lugones's conception of hanging out as a model and a method. Hanging out is the practice of a figure she calls the "streetwalker theorist." I am a streetwalker art historian, ambling between places like the Johnson/Murray, Sanchez, and Chinati yards in Marfa. Lugones writes: "The streetwalker theorist cultivates a multiplicity and depth of perception and connection and 'hangs out' even in well-defined institutional spaces, troubling and subverting their logics, their intent. As resistant, contestatory negotiations make sense within and give life to different frameworks of sense, different logics, and different world(s) of sense that are not countenanced by institutionalized, dominant, 'official' sense, the streetwalker theorist cultivates an ear and a tongue for multiple lines of meaning. Her knowing is necessarily dialogical."[15]

In addition to cultivating language—"an ear and a tongue"—the streetwalker art historian cultivates their vision, their eye, through hanging out. This vision sees people and art as contiguous and interwoven elements of a landscape. It enables a dialogical art history of Marfa that includes people to counter some existing art histories that operate as if Far West Texas was an empty receptacle awaiting activation by Judd or other contemporary artists from elsewhere. Those art histories enable continued acts of colonial violence in the Texas-Mexico border region through never accounting for people and thereby dehumanizing them. In an uncanny note, Lugones offers further elaboration relevant to Marfa: "It is important to note that in this description hanging out cannot be assimilated to the various nomadisms that rehearse the romance of travel, where privileged visitors destabilize other peoples' spaces without attention to the power relations that construe the spatial occupation."[16] Before dwelling further on hanging out in Marfa, I turn to another set of experiences in and with yards that inspired this writing.

LEARNING FROM THE "YARD SHOW"

Urban planner and activist James T. Rojas writes of las yardas—the yards of Mexican American homes in East Los Angeles—that they are "such a dominant element that [they have] altered the physical character of entire neighborhoods as well as residents' behavior patterns."[17] This is also true not only of the Sanchez yard, which generated a new pilgrimage site in Marfa, but of the neighboring Chinati Foundation, which plays a significant role in Marfa's infrastructure and global notoriety. The Sanchez yard, though located in West Texas and not Los Angeles, operates in the same spirit as the yards in Rojas's study. Chinati is logically associated with other contemporary sculpture grounds such as Storm King Art Center in New York State and Glenstone Museum in suburban Maryland. Based on experiences over the past few years, however, I am compelled to introduce the field of African American yard art practices, which offer extensive lessons to those curious about American art and creativity in yards.

In April 2022, curator Hallie Ringle invited me to accompany her to Joe Minter's African Village in America in Birmingham, Alabama (figures C.6 and C.7).[18] Like the Guadalupe of Marfa, much of the content across African Americans' yards such as Minter's site expresses the maker's relationship

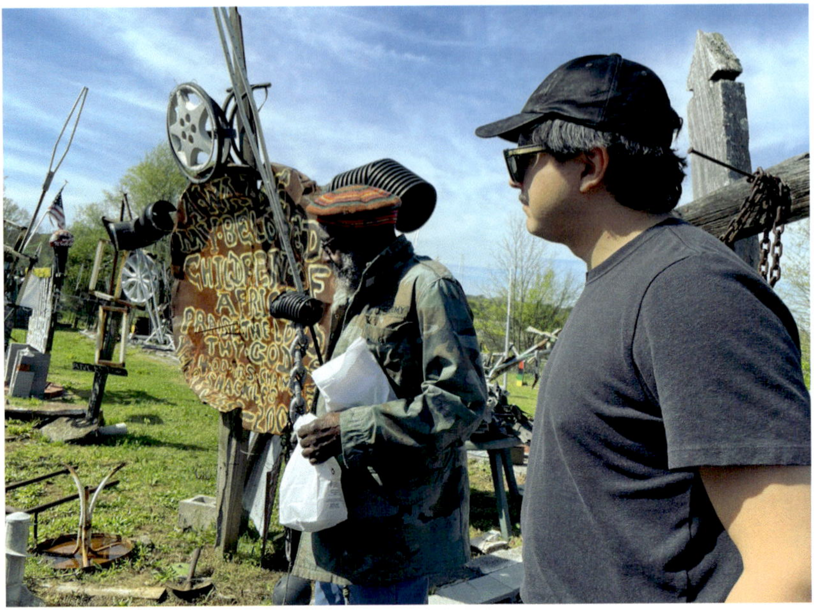

FIGURE C.6 Josh T Franco with Joe Minter (*left*) at African Village in America, Birmingham, Alabama, April 4, 2022. Photographer: Hallie Ringle.

to the sacred and spiritual. At African Village, this is clear in the number of hand-lettered signs bearing Bible verses, for instance.[19] While highly idiosyncratic, this site is also part of a network of sites whose makers often know one another. In the catalogue for the exhibition *Outliers and American Vanguard Art,* curator Katherine Jentleson notes of this site and others: "From the Dial-Lockett clan to Lonnie Holley to Joe Minter, there has been a critical mass of great artists working around the Birmingham-Bessemer area in the same decades, creating found-object assemblage sculptures, sharing ideas and practices with each other. As Bernard Herman has proposed, isn't that its own kind of school, or its own kind of art movement?"[20] Following my visit, I have concluded that it is; I have learned invaluable lessons from these artists and places that have been in communication with one another for decades. One of these lessons is that there is a "liturgy of yard work" often unacknowledged in contemporary art discourse, when it pays attention to this field at all. The inclusion of Bible verses in Minter's yard and the presence of the Virgin in the Sanchezes' demonstrate a function recognized by artist Judith McWillie and anthropologist Grey Gundaker: "that these works are,

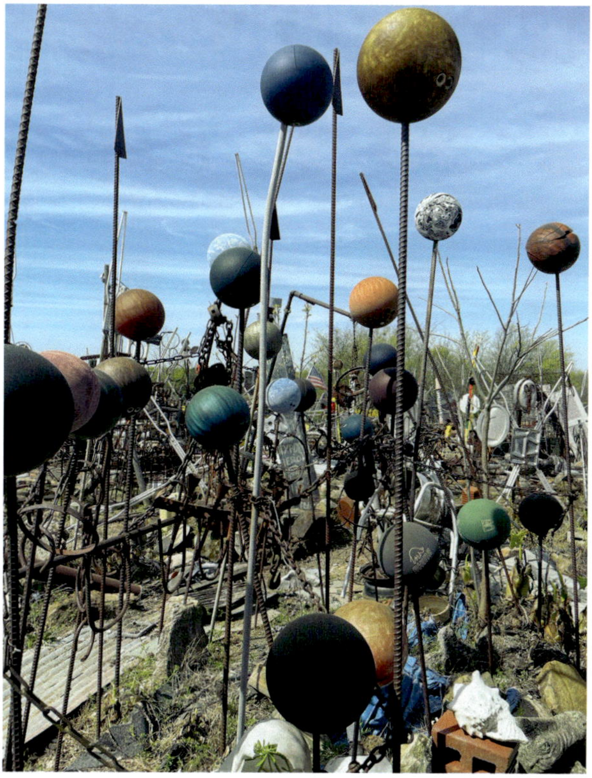

FIGURE C.7 Detail of Joe Minter's African Village in America, Birmingham, Alabama, April 4, 2022. Photographer: Hallie Ringle.

above all, directives for living that also aim a forceful critique at whoever has eyes to see."[21] This is what is so powerful about Guadalupe's siting in Marfa: The international art-loving audience coming to Chinati must always pass through her line of sight to enter the foundation's grounds and, perhaps, will contemplate the directives for living that her figure invokes. I argue that one of these directives is to love your neighbor.

In Minter's portable book version of his fantastic environment, *To You Through Me: The Beginning of a Link of a Journey of 400 Years*, the word *love* appears at least fifty-six times. Love, a simultaneously slippery and sure concept, takes a central role in aesthetic expressions taking place in yards throughout America. I take this as evidence that love is required to practice art making in the face of repression. In her own writing for the *Outliers* catalogue, curator Lynne Cooke describes the practices of artists in the exhibition, including traditions like the African American yard show, as "repressed vernacular legacies."[22] This characterization resonates with Ybarra-Frausto's description of rasquachismo: "To be rasquache is to be down but not out—*fregado pero no jodido*."[23] Both respond to repressive forces, suggesting that there is a coalition to be built between Chicanx material culture as it manifests in yards and the practices of Black artists who have also elaborated and embellished this liminal space. The resonances continue; regarding the (rasquache-codable) practice of using materials at hand, artist John Outterbridge describes his father's creativity, which informed his own engagement with assemblage: "My father was a man who found aesthetics *in his backyard*. . . . I think that was a beginning for assemblage for me, though it was not called assemblage. . . . Many of the aesthetics existed all around me, done by people who didn't find it important to put a signature on anything. They just made it."[24] It is important to note that through the work of many, such as Cooke and other curator-scholars cited here alongside the artists themselves, their status is less and less "repressed" as their place in the wider consciousness of the art world grows year to year.

Unlike artists of his generation who also turned to the American West (particularly land artists such as Robert Smithson, Walter De Maria, Nancy Holt, and Michael Heizer), Judd situated himself and his lifelong projects squarely in a town full of people, another reason to consider yard artists his peers and to reread his sites alongside the yard-sited works of "outlier" artists like Hernandez, Holley, Minter, the senior Outterbridge, and the dozens of artists included in Gundaker and McWillie's study. What Judd did in Marfa that turns out to feel most radical, if unintentional, was creating proximity between the New York–centric, museum- and gallery-based fine art world and the network of West Texas yards, a world and school unto themselves. As Lugones writes, "We are fully dependent on each other for the possibility of being understood and without this understanding we are not intelligible, we do not make sense, we are not solid, visible, integrated; we are lacking. So traveling to each other's 'worlds' would enable us to *be* through loving each other."[25] In such a concentrated social order as the small, isolated town of Marfa, intelligibility to one another is vital for the continued life of the town. Toward this end, yard art "find[s] in materials and actions the ingredients of a metalanguage not reducible to speech or writing with which to comment on the human condition and take responsibility for directing its course."[26]

ART OF THE HANGOUT

To begin closing, I propose that one can "hang out," in Lugones's sense, with artworks as well as people. In Marfa, art is often the reason for hanging out, whether in the yard prepping an altar or in a white cube for an opening. One is also often hanging out with art; for instance, Judd's works in concrete can orient and anchor solitary strolls or social ones with friends. To walk alongside them, responding to their sitedness, is a regularly occurring social act. As an experiment in deepening and extending my own hanging out with the concrete works, I turned to watercolor study, a classic and—importantly as part of a practice of hanging out—time-intensive art-historical method of active observation.[27] Watercolor painting takes time, whereas snapping a smartphone photo does not. Making, in general, is a great way to prolong the time one looks at art. I desire an art history that values hanging out with art as one might do in a familial or friendly yard, a situation where time often goes unmeasured. Before discussing this experiment further, I offer some reflection on a similar one undertaken more than a decade prior.

During the 2010–11 academic year, my typical graduate student days were split between two campus locations: the group TA office and the metalworking and sculpture shop. They were at opposite ends of the same building, a convenient setup for simultaneously being immersed in coursework upstairs and object-making downstairs. The objects were miniature reproductions of Judd's *100 untitled works in mill aluminum*, 1982–86 (figures C.8 and C.9).

These would eventually form part of my contribution to the environmental and collaborative performance work *MARFITA* (discussed in chapter 2). This sustained period of cutting and assembling small aluminum panels according to Judd's configurations informs this project alongside archival research and hours of reading. I consider it all study. The diagrams of Judd's aluminum works had conveniently been published in October 2010. It is noted prominently in a brief description that they are presented "in the sequence they were designed," which can also be said of the watercolor studies I share here.[28] The diagram-bearing pages in my copy of the catalogue bear the marks of my process: corners ticked off in pencil as the hundred miniatures were completed one by one. An act of study by way of nontextual, material-specific making, the experience preceded any inkling that my considerations about Marfa would eventually take book form. Now that they will, it seems appropriate again to suspend language temporarily as the conventional schol-

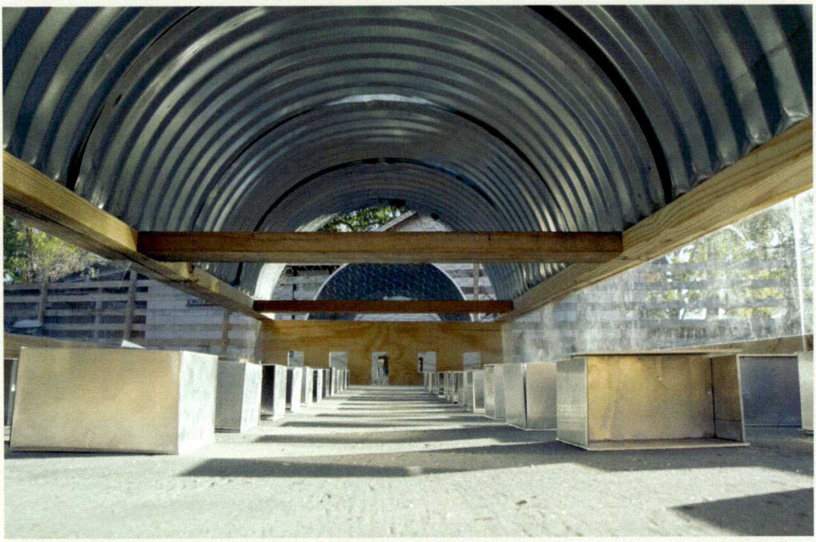

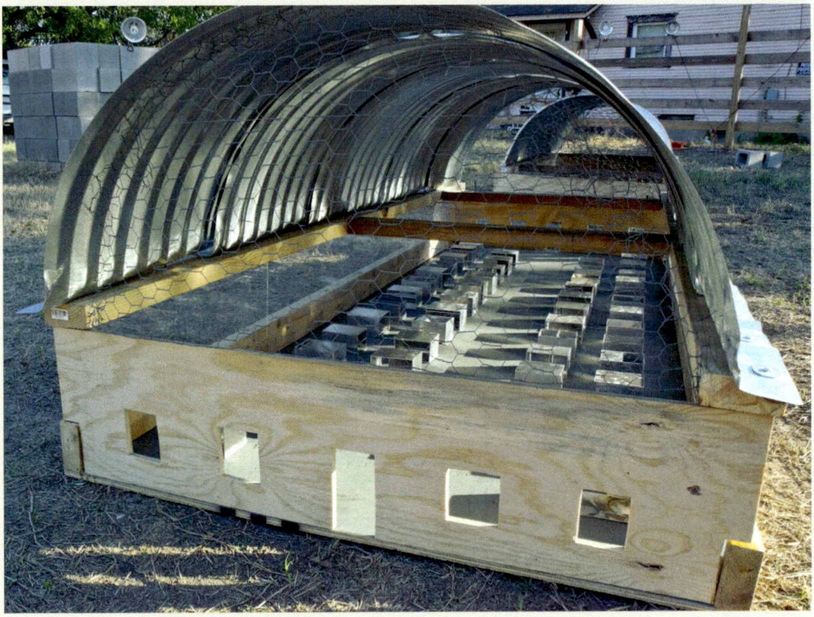

FIGURES C.8 AND C.9 Josh T Franco, interior and exterior views of a miniature replica of Donald Judd's *100 untitled works in mill aluminum*, from MARFITA, 2011.

arly method for reflection, this time in study of the other large-scale group Judd created at Chinati. While the aluminum works are sheltered, I now turn my attention to Judd's works that reside outdoors in what I am reconceiving of here as a yard, another site of making alongside those scattered throughout town on a smaller but no less creative scale and of no less significance to the art history of Marfa.

In April 2021, I spent four afternoons making watercolor studies on the grounds of Chinati (figures C.10a–m). Each session lasted between two and three hours. My time was entirely focused on Judd's *15 untitled works in concrete*, made between 1980 and 1984.[29] Rather than a notebook where thoughts could be crafted into words, which I would typically bring, I brought my black canvas rucksack containing two pads of 8-by-8-inch Fluid watercolor paper (cold press), a twenty-four-pack of Koh-I-Noor Mondeluz Aquarell pencils, and black Sakura Pigma Micron 08 pens. It was windy most of the time, and a couple of days were overcast. My lower forearms, up to the point where my rolled sleeves ended, were sunburned and peeling for days after. Most of the time I sat cross-legged on the ground, supplies set on the earth at my side, positioned facing some view of the concrete objects. I selected this view intuitively; sometimes it took several laps around a grouping to decide, while other times the best location was apparent upon first approach. Once the view was selected, close study began. I estimate I was sitting between ten and fifteen feet away in each instance. Upon sitting, I documented each view as a digital picture on my phone before taking to my watercolor notebook. This served as a ritual of transition from the mobile, interrogative state induced by selecting a position to the more meditative stillness of sustaining attention on one chosen area. The digital picture also aided in determining the view frame of each watercolor. This cycle was repeated thirteen times. The tangible results of these sessions, the objects whose crafting is concurrent to this art historian's labor in the time and place of the yard, are thirteen 8-by-8-inch watercolor studies. These are numbered in pen on the back, making it possible to track evolving facility with the medium and visual engagement with the objects. Here ends the neatness of the situation.

None of the studies was fully completed on-site or during the fieldwork just described; most had their color fields fully laid down dry, while for a few, the real-time production amounted to a mere description of the concrete edges in pen and a scratching of watercolor pencil to ensure some chromatic

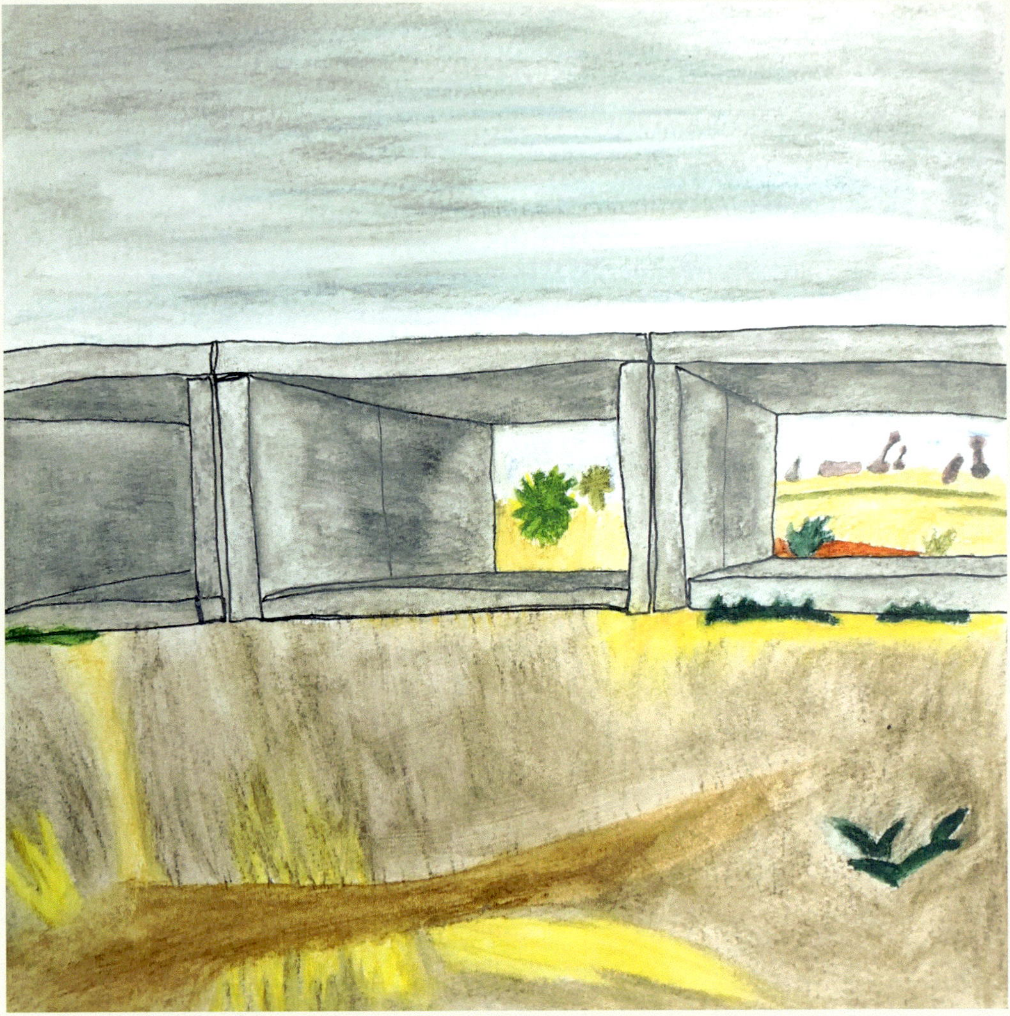

FIGURE C.10A–M Josh T Franco, details of *Watercolor Study (Donald Judd, 15 untitled works in concrete, 1980–84)*, 2021.

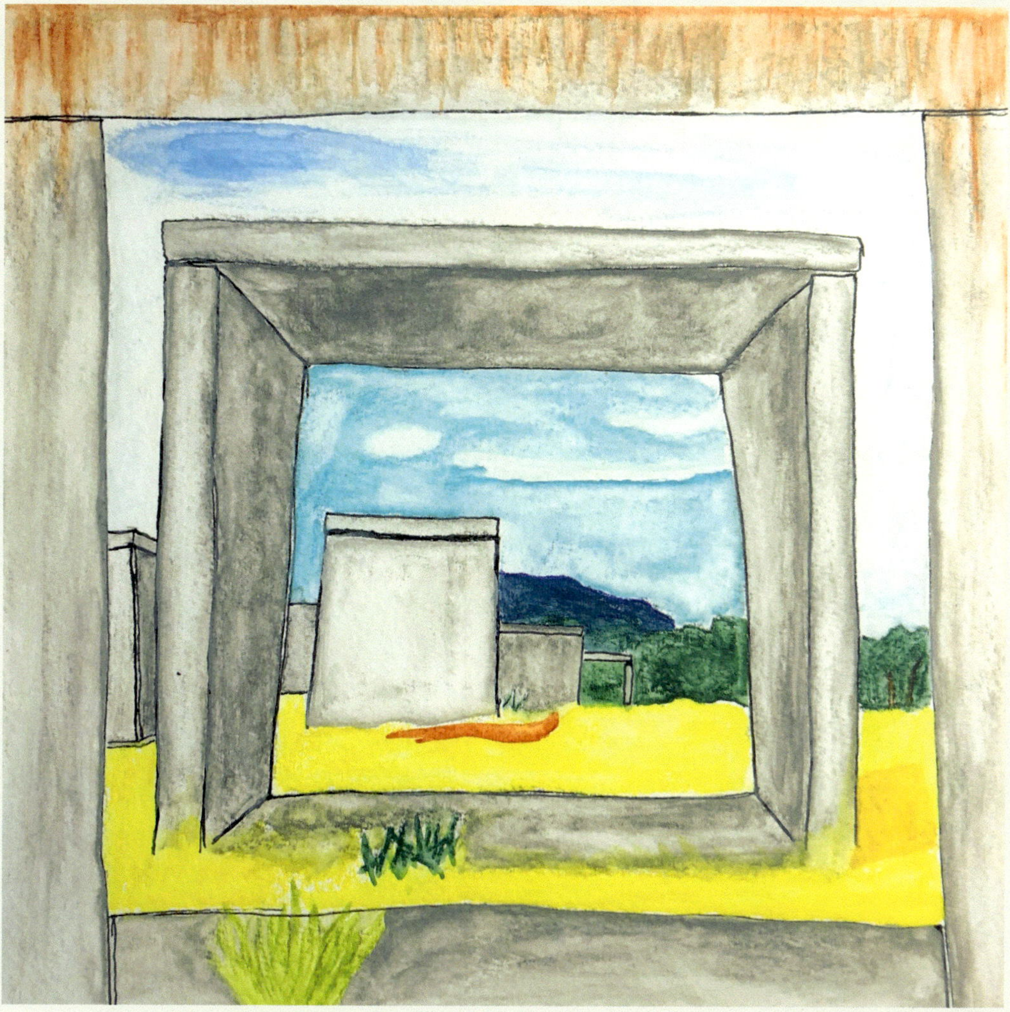

FIGURE C.10B

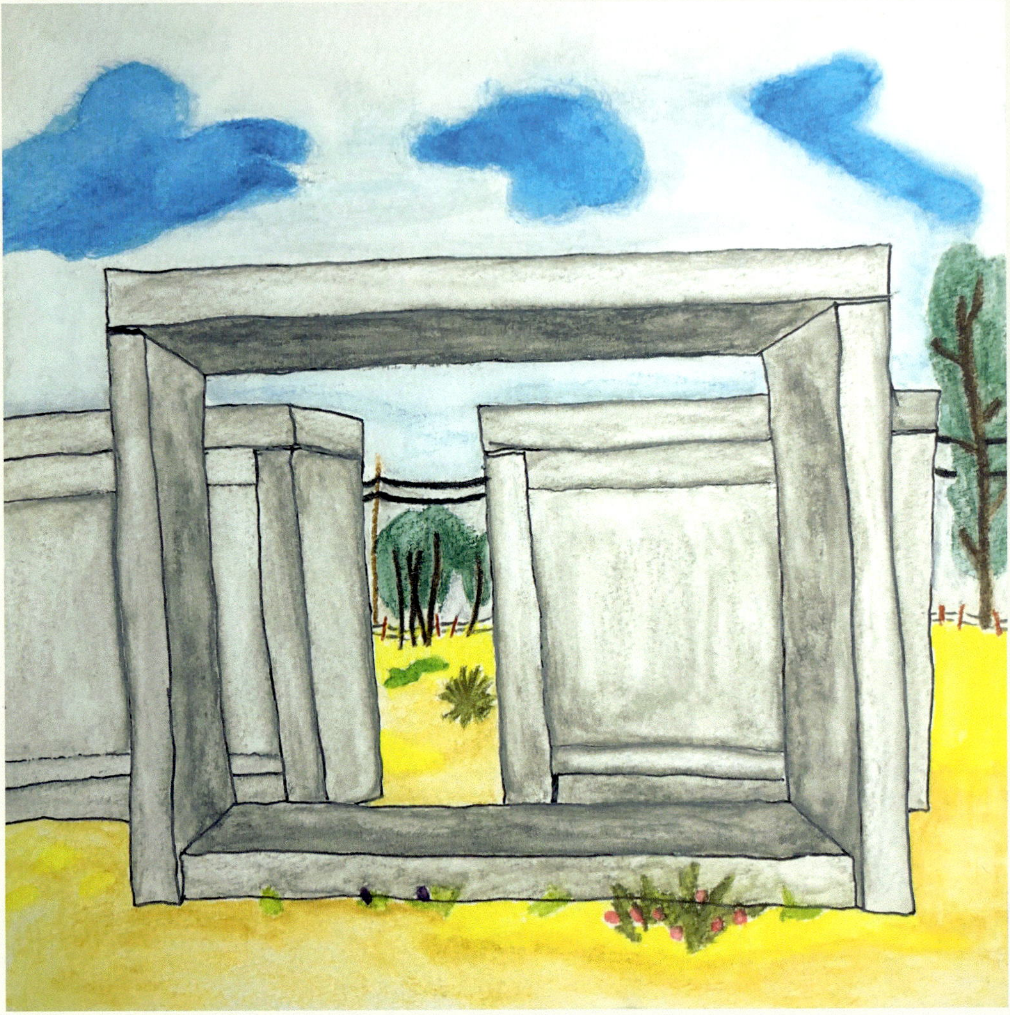

FIGURE C.10C

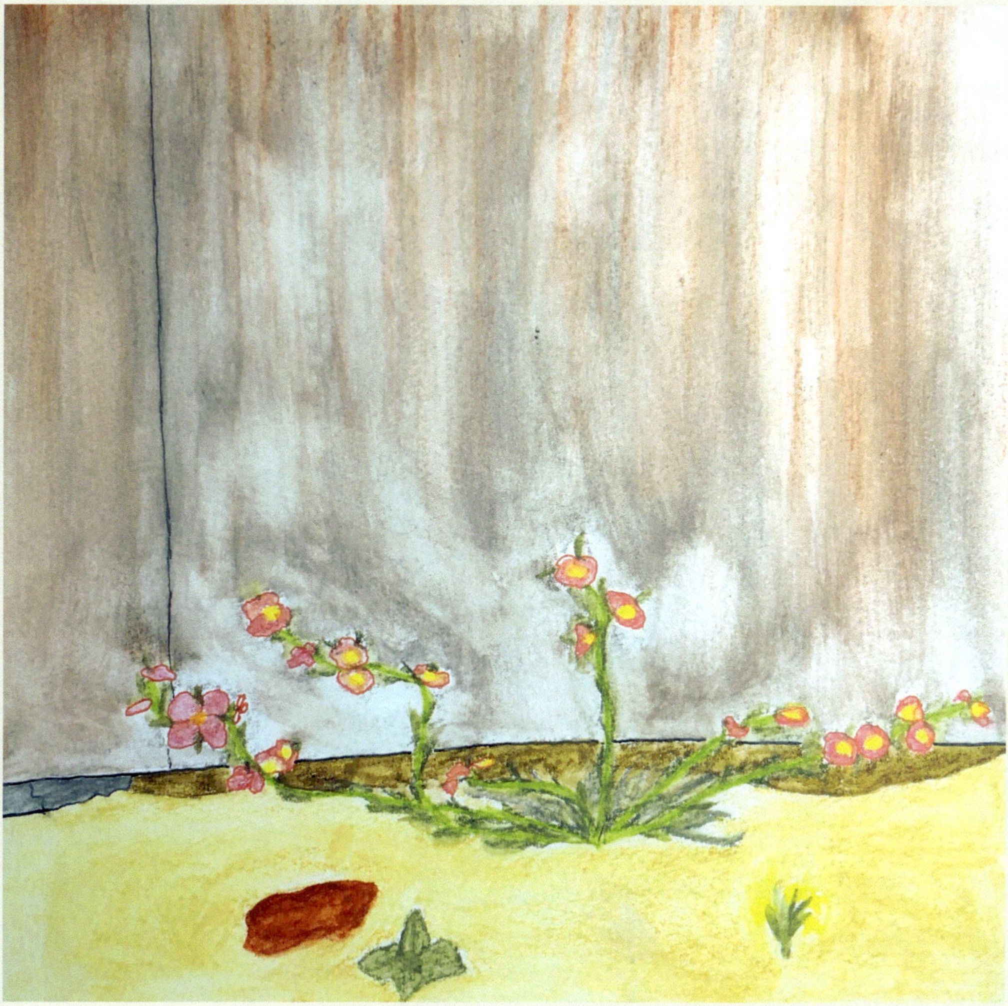

FIGURE C.10D

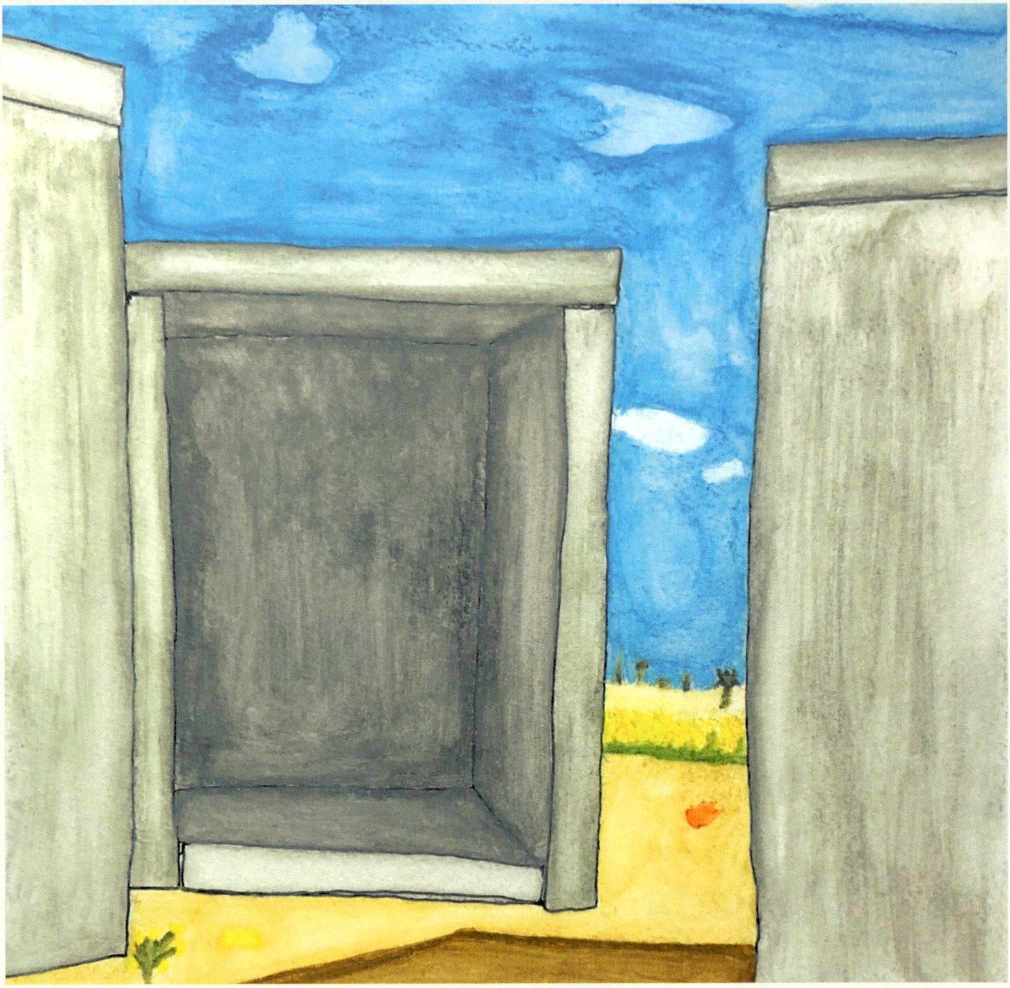

FIGURE C.10E

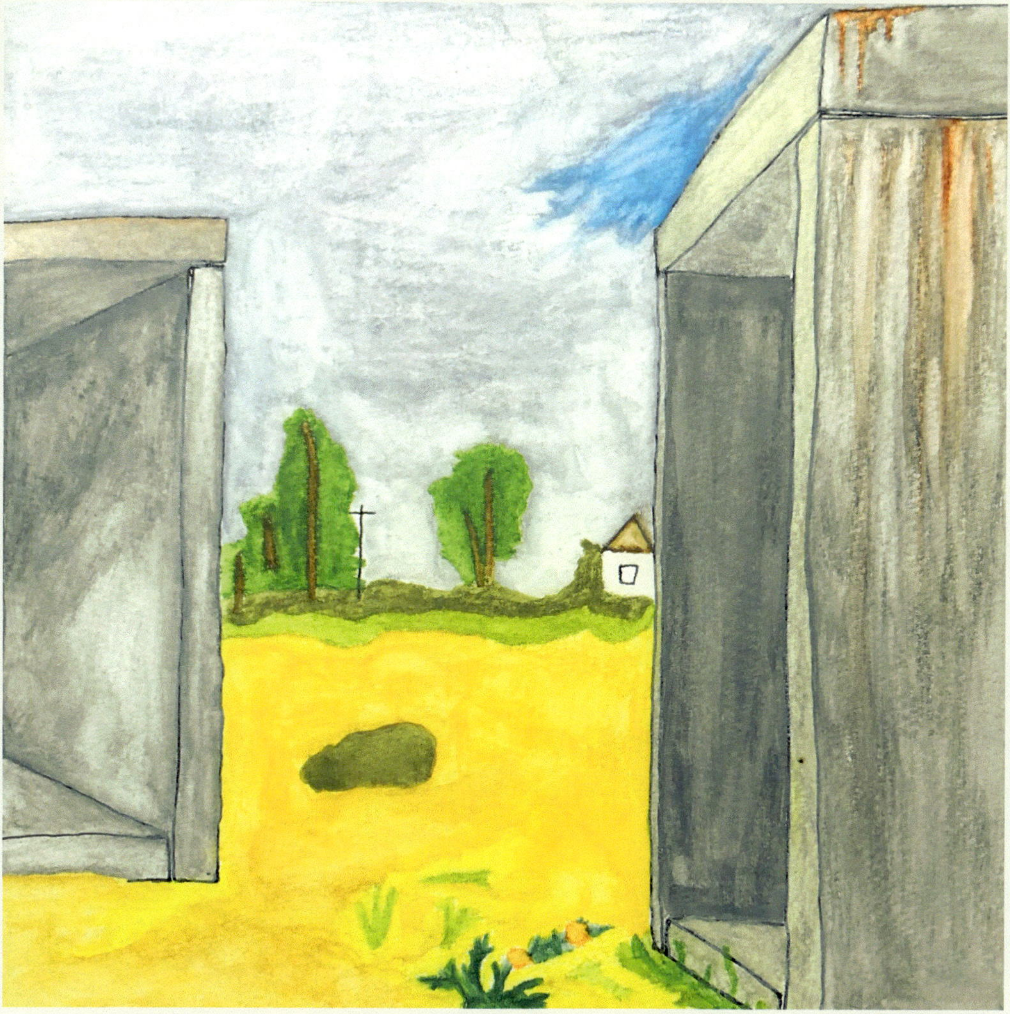

FIGURE C.10F

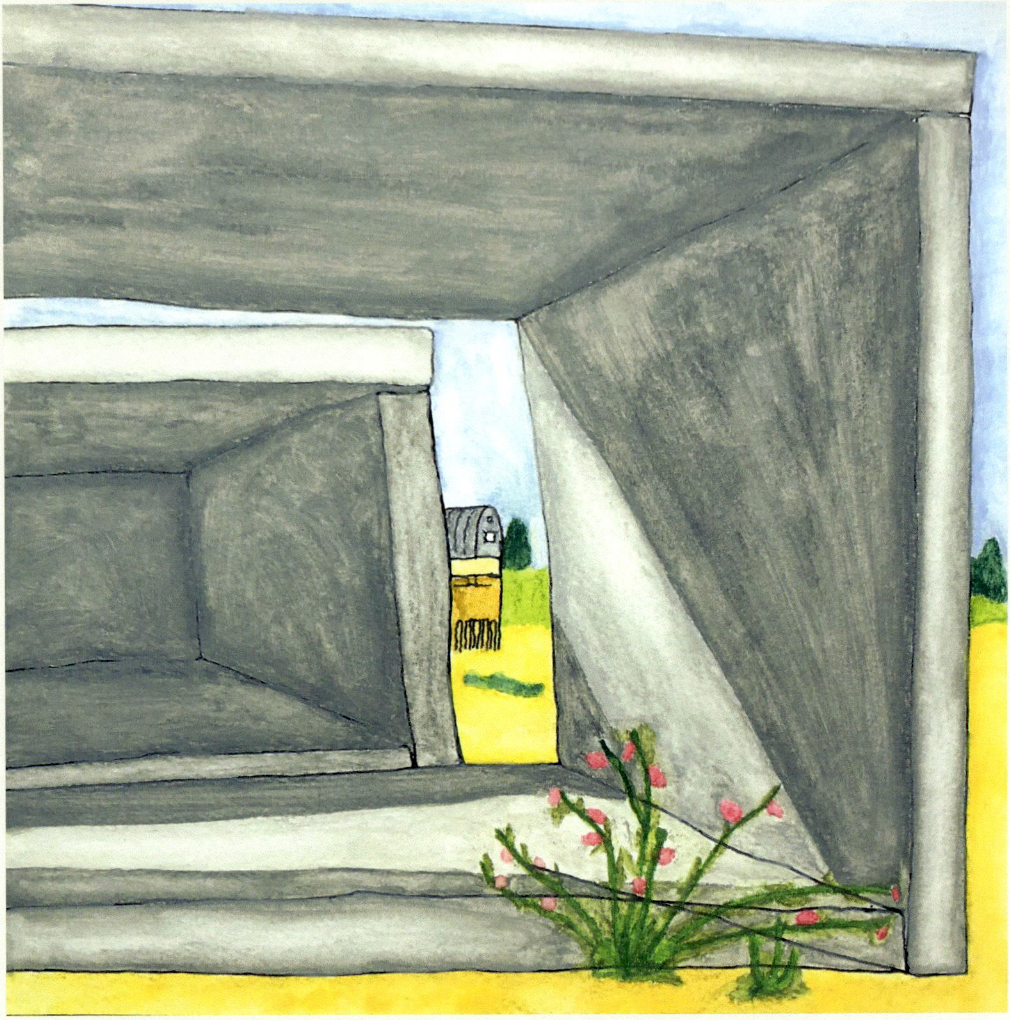

FIGURE C.10G

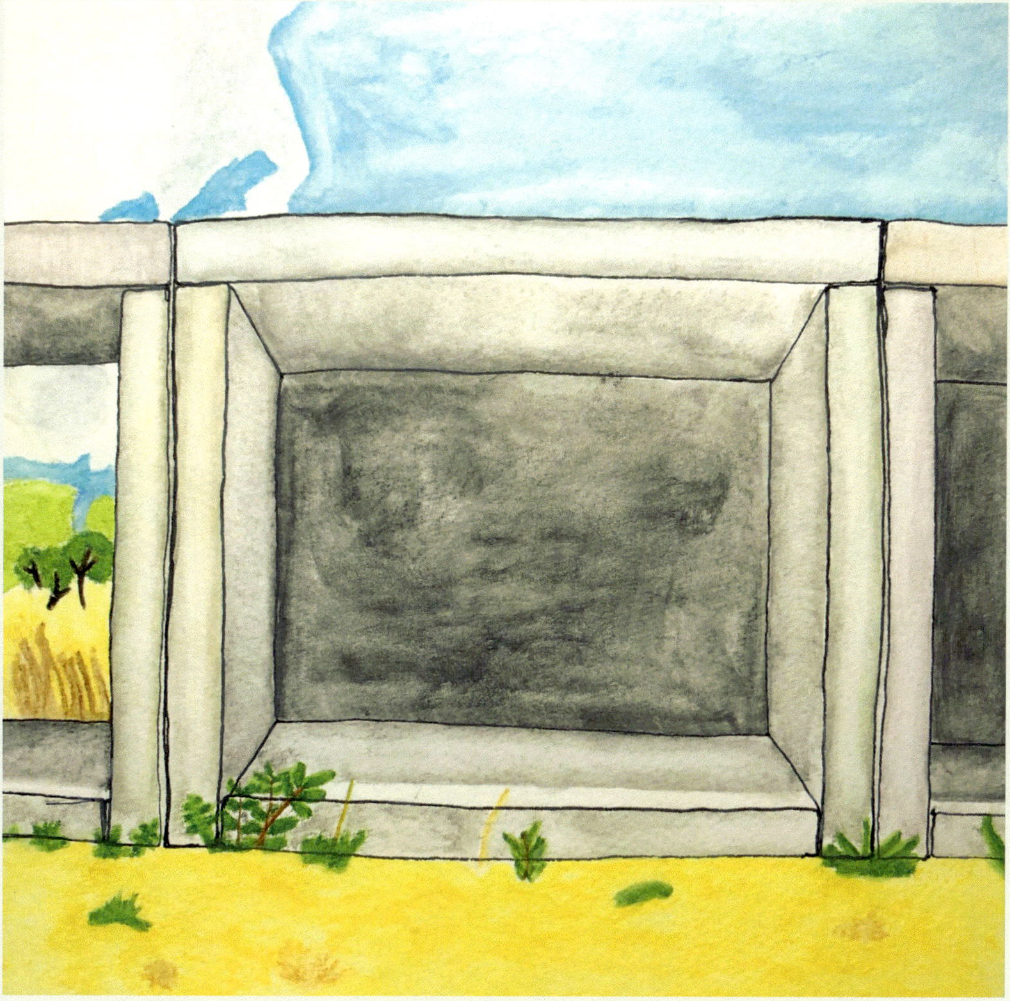

FIGURE C.10H

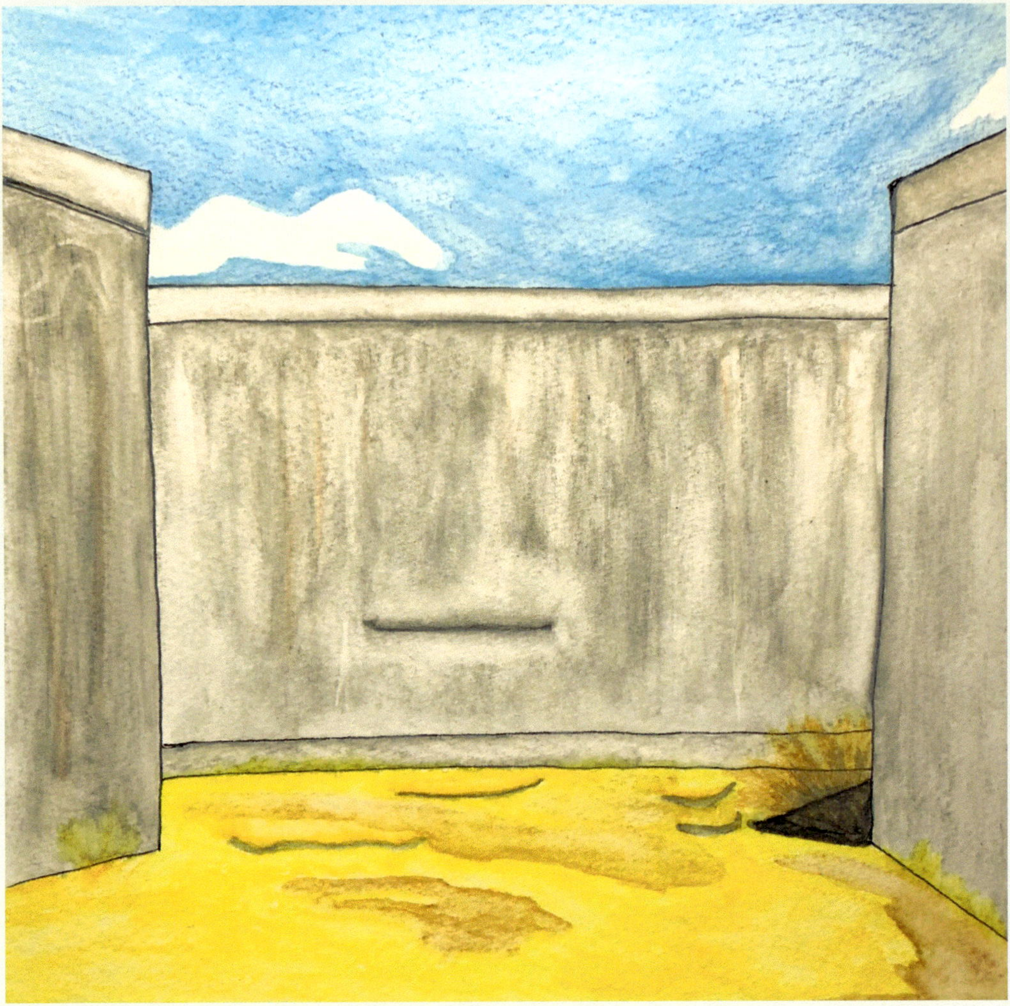

FIGURE C.101

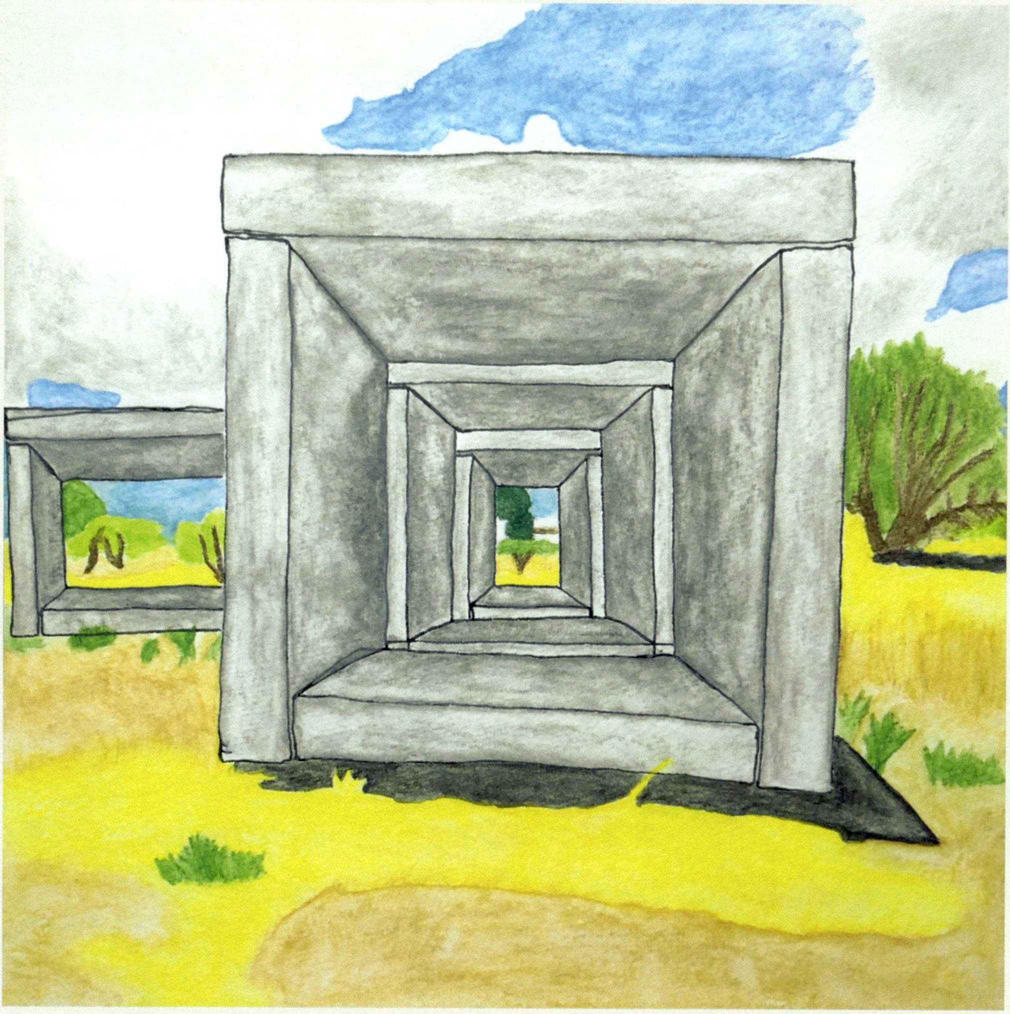

FIGURE C.10J

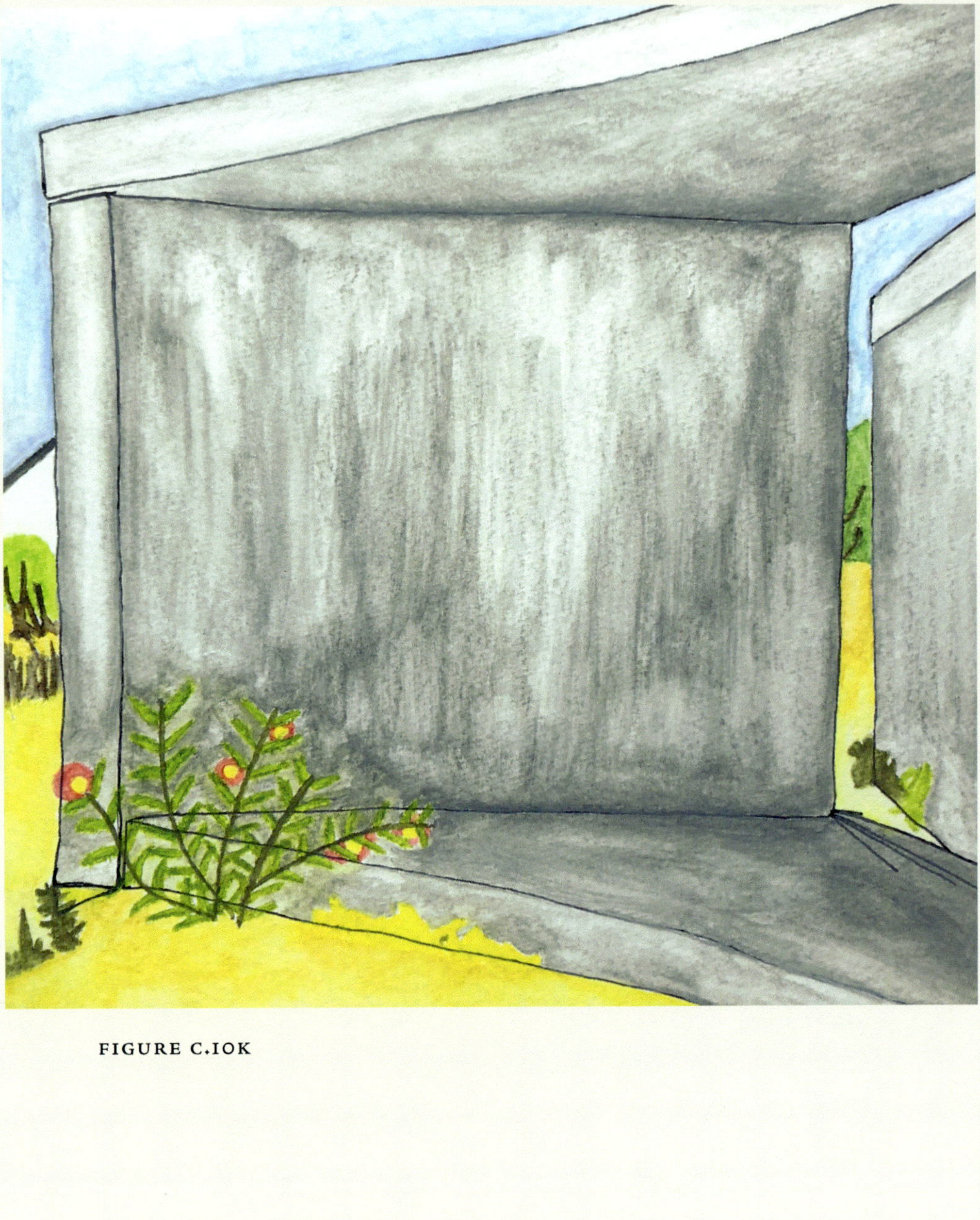

FIGURE C.10K

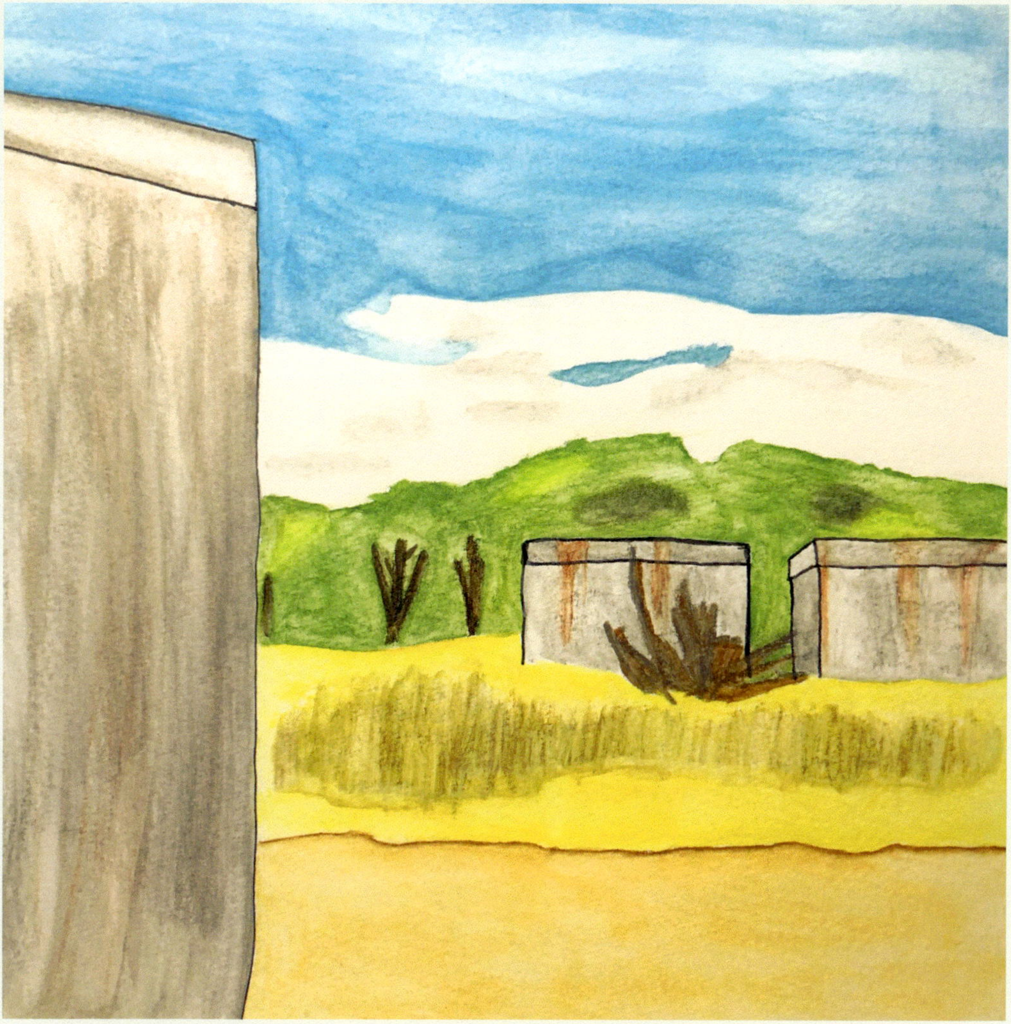

FIGURE C.IOL

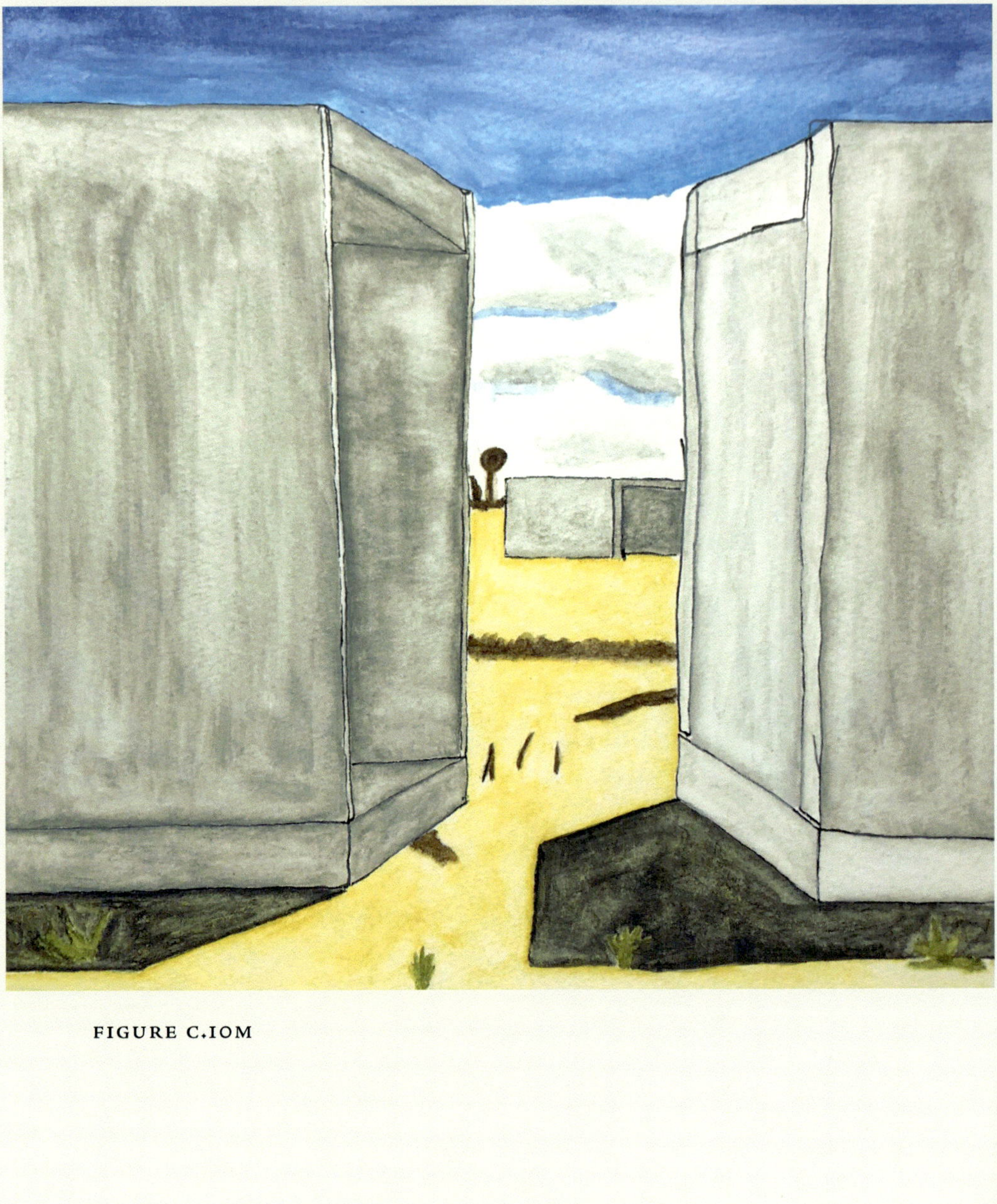

FIGURE C.10M

fidelity for later completion, away from the moments of direct observation. This created opportunities to reflect, to hang out, while engaged in the completion of a watercolor study, knowing that the act of study might never reach completion. Each morning, I made coffee, sat at the kitchen table with brushes and water, and bathed the various fields of color laid down in pencil the previous day.

I have had moments of anxiety about lavishing so much attention on an artwork and an artist who have received so much scrutiny already, particularly in the context of a book claiming to be, in part, a balance to this historically privileged visibility. There is so much more to Marfa, I have argued, but here I am returning to Judd's concrete works, whose images have been reproduced ad infinitum across scholarly venues and social media, as well as in more rarefied, luxurious venues. But rasquachismo pervades this attention, and this is not a sensibility conveyed in the prolific images of these works elsewhere. Rasquachismo here does not reside in the subject of these studies but in the subject, the art historian, who studies them. The selection of artworks is not the art-historical intervention here; rather, the critical rupture comes from foregrounding a way of looking through which these objects have not yet been closely witnessed in the art-historical record. These watercolor studies demonstrate a rasquachified art history obtained by hanging out.

HANGING OUT (A DEMONSTRATION)

Art historian Max Tolleson, who hosted me during the visit described above, would eventually rise. Max was the watercolors' first audience. Our exchanges at the kitchen table moved the watercolors to the realm of dialogue, breaking the spell of solitude around me and them up to this point. This morning-after hanging out inspired the format of the concluding section of the book: two dialogues concerning the watercolor studies and the concrete works. Each of my two interlocutors, Max and art historian Jana La Brasca, has had years of direct experience with the concrete works themselves as well as equally rich, ongoing relationships to Judd's legacy and the town of Marfa. At the heart of each conversation is their response to my request that they identify which of the thirteen watercolor studies speaks to them most. Much of the revision of art history in the past decades has hinged on breaking the notion of the single author, the single maker of an artwork. This book concludes by treating art history similarly, offering these multivocal reflections on experience with art and Marfa in lieu of the typical authorial closure. In Marfa, we hang out, we love, and we do so in yards. Join us:

★

JANA LA BRASCA IS A CALIFORNIA-BORN, TEXAS-BASED ART HISTORIAN. THE FOLLOWING HAS BEEN ADAPTED FROM A CONVERSATION RECORDED ON FEBRUARY 19, 2022.

JANA LA BRASCA: We both share an interest in miniaturization and long looking. I wonder what those have to do with how you and I have both been marinating intellectually, perceptually for years in these works.

JOSH T FRANCO: Miniaturization is definitely a topic in the Jana domain in my mind, so I'm so glad you're bringing it up right away. I made the miniatures of the one hundred works in aluminum and the sheds in 2011; you are writing and thinking so brilliantly about miniatures and scale models, many for unrealized or ephemeral projects.

JANA LA BRASCA: Right. Less so miniaturization as a quality of something, and more as part of a process of learning about something. It's something artists do. It's what Lévi-Strauss says about the work of art being this experimental field in which an artist is reducing the physical size of something, the number of senses used to perceive it, the number of dimensions it's rendered in, and actually breaking it down to see how all the parts function together.[30] In your case, you were going across the boxes in sequence and in time, trying to figure out how to actually make them in miniature.

JOSH T FRANCO: That brings something to mind that's not about miniaturization, but about that walking "across time" to perceive the blocks. This time, for the first time, I ultimately spent more time being still in front of them than walking. You know, you usually just walk and walk until you walk away. That really threw into relief how cinematic the experience of moving by them can feel, frame to frame.

JANA LA BRASCA: A friend of mine observed that even though Judd was so concerned with getting away from the illusionism of painting, the way these works sometimes appear to function as frames can give you sort of a landscape painting feeling. That makes your choice of watercolor for these studies interesting, as a way to slow down the process of looking. This really reminded me of the project that I did as part of Land Arts American West in 2013, which was about developing a looking and writing practice by select-

ing a spot at, or perhaps simply near, *Double Negative*, for instance, and determining that where I intuitively stopped was the viewpoint, and I would just describe what I saw. The results are these experimental, ekphrastic writings descriptive of the view, as if it were a picture. That was my response to Chris Taylor's simple instruction to "go work." I was this twenty-three-year-old art historian figuring out what that looked like for me. I reverted to that tool that we are taught to rely on so much, which is description. What you've done is a different type of description. I see a resonance there.
JOSH T FRANCO: I have the watercolor you chose here [figure C.10d]. In your selection, you noted this one stood out because the wildflowers stood out. The best unexpected result of these is how prominent the flowers became.
JANA LA BRASCA: What time of year was this?
JOSH T FRANCO: Late April. Can you say more about choosing this one?
JANA LA BRASCA: Where to even begin. . . . Scrolling through the options, there were so many waves of memory, of so many walks, that washed over me. There's also something about the various attitudes. The ones with closed faces, for instance, have real attitude to them. Some look like they're kiki'ing with each other. Some look like they all just got in a fight, and they've turned their backs on one another. There were a few that were giving me some trouble. I love the un-straightness of the lines.
JOSH T FRANCO: Ha, I know. What's funny about that is it echoes a moment from making the hundred aluminum miniatures, but me having a very different response. I was working on a hand-operated metal-cutting machine on borrowed time over a year. In my initial vision, the miniatures would be perfect, in the sense that ninety-degree angles would in fact be ninety-degree angles, and so on. The reality of not being able to afford professional services hit pretty quickly, and a minor freakout ensued. The great artist and friend Alison Kuo talked me down and I keep the lesson with me. It's appropriate that in doing this watercolor series a decade later, the lines wouldn't be perfectly straight either. But this time, I didn't mind in the least.
JANA LA BRASCA: Making the most out of the least. What's more Minimalist than that?
JOSH T FRANCO: Exactly! That's the DIY-ness that is so often missed. So-called Minimalism is more messy than it is shiny, if you look closely.
JANA LA BRASCA: I love that the plants growing underneath these things are a threat in preservation terms, but they are also what make the works feel present and real. They trigger the nostalgia of seasons.
JOSH T FRANCO: Speaking of seasons, this project was an opportunity to meditate on the scholarly art historian cycle of traveling to directly observe

art, then settling to research and write. Now, we snap a million pictures on our phones, but there was a time when watercolor studies filled art historians' notebooks as the document manifesting their observations. There was something very comforting about briefly inhabiting that lineage of art historians actively looking via watercolor. I love that your choice recognizes the seasonal, the temporal. This is especially present in the ones where wildflowers, which are so fleeting, are pictured.

JANA LA BRASCA: They are also a reminder that permanent installation is in itself a paradox.[31] Things want to change. Entropy exists. So, to make works of art, buildings, even landscapes stay the same, you have to introduce changes. Many of these Judd never foresaw in his lifetime. Whether or not he would have acknowledged the necessity of such changes, it's clear now that that paradox lies at the heart of the whole concept. Neither the mountains nor the Grand Canyon are permanent. Nothing is permanent. Did you read Sean Patrick Carney's *Artforum* article about visiting *Sun Tunnels?*[32]

JOSH T FRANCO: Tell me about it.

JANA LA BRASCA: He describes how land art sometimes invites you to do this horizontal scanning of the landscape—looking across, being curious, seeing what you can see on the surface. But because they often operate on a vast timescale, like *Sun Tunnels*, they also encourage us to do this vertical scanning, plumbing the space above and beneath where we stand. How long can you horizontally scan before you reach that point of wanting to expand your vision further and scan vertically?

JOSH T FRANCO: And *Sun Tunnels* invites you to do that directly, because it is oriented to the cosmos. It asks you to look up at celestial bodies and their behavior. I think my vertical impulse is to look down, to understand who is buried in the dirt beneath Marfa.

JANA LA BRASCA: Yes, looking vertically down to explore the view of los de abajo.

JOSH T FRANCO: Exactly! I'm definitely asking readers to consider whose bones the dirt of Marfa is made of, whose bones these artworks sit upon.

JANA LA BRASCA: And those are also turning into dirt.

JOSH T FRANCO: And they're supported by that dirt. And that dirt grows wildflowers! Which are what drew you to the watercolor study you chose.

★

MAX TOLLESON IS AN ART HISTORIAN BASED IN TEXAS. THE FOLLOWING HAS BEEN ADAPTED FROM A CONVERSATION RECORDED ON OCTOBER 24, 2021.

JOSH T FRANCO: Max, it's been a weird weekend. I've just been in this hotel room alone, writing and thinking really hard. You're the first person I've really talked to in a couple of days. Did you read the draft of the chapter? You're in it because that makes sense.

MAX TOLLESON: I did! Can I tell you why I chose this particular watercolor to look at [figure C.10c]? I remember when you came to stay with me in Marfa, and you explained your plan to make these watercolors of the concrete works. You were a great guest, by the way, and I was really happy to have you. [*both laugh*] So, each day you would go to Chinati, make a watercolor, come back to my house, and then you'd show me your work. I recall my very first impression of the very first one you made was complete disorientation. I couldn't figure out where you were standing, what configuration of works it was . . . I was very confused in the landscape. I thought that was funny, because I usually know where I am when moving through that landscape, and so I chose this particular watercolor because there are elements of the built environment that allow me to know where I am. The telephone pole, wires, and fence are indications that I'm looking east.

JOSH T FRANCO: I think the fence is adorable.

MAX TOLLESON: It is. I love the way it rolls up and down. It's cute, for sure.

JOSH T FRANCO: And that's the highway, right?

MAX TOLLESON: Right. But a number of the perspectives you chose for the compositions are closely cropped, which makes it difficult to identify which configuration I'm looking at. Was this something you were thinking about when you made these?

JOSH T FRANCO: I was definitely very conscious of which ones had signs of infrastructure and which ones didn't. Although I guess someone could read the cottonwood trees themselves as a sign of infrastructure, as they were planted intentionally in that pattern. You know, I don't want to impose that "nature/not nature" thing. But, yes, I was very aware of *built* things being in a picture or not. I see how the one you chose provides a clear orientation.

MAX TOLLESON: All of the watercolors also offer only partial views of each configuration. I was wondering about the history of how these works have been represented by others, either through photographs or drawings like the ones Judd made, which tended to depict the works from a bird's-eye view.

Were you responding to a history of representation of these objects and not just the objects themselves?

JOSH T FRANCO: Totally. Elsewhere in the book, I write about Josie Miner's photographic survey of the aluminum works for *A Magazine*, for instance.[33] This weekend, I was looking again at the 1987 Chinati catalogue, and it includes this series of portraits of the concretes. I was wondering how these guys chose their angles, or did Judd choose these angles?[34]

MAX TOLLESON: I've noticed that some of the photographs in the 1987 catalogue present the works at an angle so you can see multiple configurations in one view, maybe, I'm guessing, so a viewer can sense an evolution. What I like about your watercolors is how their close-cropped views create a destabilizing effect. It's true to life in the sense that when I view these works in person, I get a peculiar sensation that what I'm seeing, especially what I'm seeing through them, is not quite the whole picture, and the picture I do get has a peculiar aura. The landscape becomes image, object, and artistically charged field all at once because the concretes pull it through an aesthetic framework.

JOSH T FRANCO: I do like getting really close to them, so that almost my entire field of vision is concrete. You have to get nose-touchingly close. Do you ever do that?

MAX TOLLESON: Yeah, I've done that.

JOSH T FRANCO: The sacrifice is that you see cut-off objects.

MAX TOLLESON: But is there even an ideal position from which to view them?

JOSH T FRANCO: No, of course not, right? There's no one universal position.

MAX TOLLESON: I think you capture that aspect very well. Like, why even bother to try? Judd called this *fifteen [untitled] works in concrete* because he saw each configuration as one work. But of course, why try to capture the whole thing if it's an impossible task? These watercolors lean into that and show the partial view you actually see when you're there.

JOSH T FRANCO: There's also feeling. I was guided by the question, What looks like how I feel sitting here? You said something about landscape and the built environment that I like. I was thinking about the Hudson River School and how much industrialization was happening while they were making these pictures of, you know, "pristine" views of the land.

MAX TOLLESON: And Judd's work here is very much in dialogue with the built environment. He's not trying to disguise it. Although, you know we could talk about that; it's possible he planted those cottonwood trees precisely to block the view of the highway. At the same time, the concrete works act like conduits for viewing the space around them. I found this quote from Judd in 1977 when he was describing his first permanent installations in Marfa: "The work is not disembodied spatially, socially, temporally as in most museums."[35] It's like the Marfa works are invitations to look elsewhere.

JOSH T FRANCO: Like they pull the fabric of the rest of Marfa into view through themselves. I get that about the one you chose. For instance, the black marks composing the telephone wires are strong, and they tug the navel of this picture forward from the inside. You know, Marianne Stockebrand describes The Block as a "microcosm," and I am uncomfortable with that idea.[36]

MAX TOLLESON: She writes in *CHINATI: The Vision of Donald Judd* that entering The Block is like being transported to another world.[37]

JOSH T FRANCO: Right, and that rubs me the wrong way. And I think this one you chose is an important counter to her reading, even though she's referencing a different Judd space downtown. They are certainly related.

MAX TOLLESON: These telephone lines and highway roads comprise networks, right? And the concrete works are part of this network, part of Marfa, the rest of Texas, etc. There's a sense that these works are in a particular place, like a node. When you see them in person, you also see Marfa.

JOSH T FRANCO: I do want to read Stockebrand's characterization generously, too, and try to understand why it feels so far from our experiences. Positively, how is one "transported to another world" when entering Chinati or even The Block?

MAX TOLLESON: When you cross the threshold into Chinati, and there is a threshold, what does it feel like for you?

JOSH T FRANCO: Thresholds are strong things. And there are two thresholds really, the one at the traffic circle and the gate by the offices. For me, it feels like entering a forbidden zone, or it did for a long time anyway. That's the trope that comes to my mind. Forbidden zone and not "another world." Coming from our different entry points, Stockebrand feels permitted and happily transported entering Judd's worlds, while I feel transgressive and skeptical. That's not the only feeling, of course. When I do feel empathetic to this idea of Judd's projects in Marfa as another world, I think about proposals such as growing food at The Block—that kind of material world-making that is about sustenance and survival rather than exclusivity. I mean, Max, what is going to happen in one hundred or five hundred years? Will these grounds, Chinati, be given over to agriculture? Will they be occupied at all?

MAX TOLLESON: Well, before Judd and Dia purchased the land, it was already given over to agriculture. The land was leased by farmers, some of the buildings were occupied by tenants. It could happen again. And, of course, before that it was a military base. Layer after layer of use and occupation. There have also always been forms of sociality on Chinati's grounds. I remember living and working there as an intern and thinking, wow, am I supposed to think of this place as my backyard? I live in this apartment and I'm looking out my window at the concrete works. Do these somehow belong to me, or me to them? I felt a sense of responsibility—for these works, this land—on a scale I had never known. As a young person in my mid-twenties, it was a formative moment of personal growth. Of course, it was also strange to live inside Chinati because it could feel like a gated community. There are people who live there on a daily, nightly, basis and know the place intimately. Then there's the public who are allowed to visit for a certain number of hours during the day.

JOSH T FRANCO: And then the temporary interns, and the artist residents . . .

MAX TOLLESON: Judd started the tradition of the annual public gathering at Chinati he called the "Open House." So, there's very much a sense of a dwelling there for *someone*. Since its inception, Chinati has served as a communal living space, inhabited by people upholding the mission the founder started. Had I not had the opportunity to live and work there I'm not sure I would have developed as deep an appreciation for this place (and by place, I mean Marfa as a whole) as I have now.

JOSH T FRANCO: Max, changing topics a bit to close out; it is wild to me that you have written a dissertation about Marfa, as I did a few years ago.[38] This is a very small group of people, and it's a relief that we get along and like and respect each other.

MAX TOLLESON: I couldn't agree more. It's been wonderful to have this running dialogue with you about Marfa and Judd. And on the topic of our shared discipline, I have to say Marfa has raised for me serious moments of critical reflection. I am trained as an art historian, and a fair amount of my training has been object-oriented. But Judd's work in Marfa presents a case where the objects are inextricable from the surrounding environment and communities. Where, then, do you draw the line? That's why I chose the watercolor I chose; I like that those telephone wires and that fence take you beyond the work and into the rest of town. Your watercolor also levels up to my own experience with these works. Because I don't feel I'm in a sublime landscape when being with them. I'm in a specific place. Think about this:

A friend visited me recently here in Marfa. She knew about Chinati from her art history studies as an undergraduate, through lectures based on photographs of the concrete works and others. But until she visited, she had no idea that Chinati neighbors the Border Patrol headquarters for this area. Her class did not include the context of the town, and that's the first thing she noticed when she was actually here. My point is, the way art history has worked in the past can sometimes disguise or omit the fact that artworks exist in living, evolving contexts. I see your work, and also mine, as making visible the relationships between Judd's site-specific artworks and the communities that exist around them. Chinati, Marfa, there is so much to learn from these places.

Coda

Is your red candle still lit? It must be low. What began with an invocation of an American goddess closed with conversation and a call to curiosity, to love, to look, to travel worlds. You've been to Marfa, Marfa, Marfa . . . You've finished reading. Is your vision
rasquachified?

Time to get up. Blow out your candle. Go. Look. Love. Hang out.

I'll see you out here.

C/S

Acknowledgments

"Writing is a lonely, isolating process." How often this axiom hit my ears while I wrote the first version of this book's manuscript. Such a truth could not be further from my experience, and this persisted throughout the process of writing this book. The problem before me now lies in accounting for the debts accrued along the way in the form of lifelong connections, unexpected moments of joy, and the ceaseless, rich sense of conviviality this so-called isolating process brought me. I feel infinitely less alone now than when I began.

Daisy Hernández writes in her memoir, "Writing is how I leave my family and how I take them with me." This book is an extension of my family's story. It would not exist without them and their willingness to watch me go far away from West Texas to write it. Nor would it exist without their emotional and financial support and assistance in the research itself. How convenient to have a whole network of family willing to run down local documents or people or head to Marfa on a weekend to snap a photograph, which is much easier to do from Odessa, Texas, than from upstate New York or Washington, DC. My second cousin Ed Cobos also provided a place to stay in Marfa. Besides Ed, I will only name my grandparents and parents here, but know there are also many aunts, uncles, cousins, and second cousins who provided or sought information on my behalf. To Florentino "Tino" Franco, Esperanza Blanco Franco, Hipolito "Polé" Hernandez, Esperanza Subia Hernandez, Toby Franco, and Frances Hernandez Franco: Thank you for life from beginning to end, and for ancestral memory that extends much further.

Another family's story is intertwined with ours: the Sanchezes of Marfa. They live in my maternal grandfather's childhood home, and it was to them that the Virgin of Guadalupe showed herself in 1997. She chose her stewards well. Ester Sanchez, this book would not exist without you. You and your family provided original documents, a welcoming research site, delicious meals, and, of course, the altar sculpture that is a centerpiece of this writing. I hope my writing honors your family.

For shepherding me into the once wildly unfamiliar territory of the discipline of art history, I thank Kim Smith at Southwestern University. If I have any confidence in articulating my position in the field, it began with discussions in your classroom and in your office. It also attaches to images I still carry with me of papers substantially reddened—attempts with generous criticality to reign in my writing so that it would not leave the research behind. I hope this book shows how seriously I kept these lessons with me. In any case, I hope you are as proud of this book as I am of having been your student then, and your friend and colleague now.

I left my undergraduate career tattooed. This tattoo is shared physically by four friends and borne spiritually by a number of others with whom I shared those formative years. In the context of these deepest friendships I began in earnest to think about art and community. I was terribly elitist and formalist in those early days, and without people I consider loves of my life keeping me accountable and sharing their intellects, their faiths, their talents, their time, their general brilliance, I would have gone off in some terrible directions. Ashlee Andrews, Mary Claire Angle, Jacob Beswick, Emily Calhoun, Vicky Chang, Jason Dolloff, Meagan Elliott, Sarah Gomillion, Natalie Goodnow, Travis Jeffords, Ben Johnson, Daniel Webb, Aubrey Weeks, Patrick Wenda: I trust y'all more than I do my own gut.

Before it was ever thought of as a written document, this book began as an installation. From 2009 to 2011, artists Alison Kuo and Joshua Saunders committed to researching, creating, and exhibiting *MARFITA*, a multimedia artwork that—for the span of a few unforgettable hours and an audience of a hundred or so—successfully switched attention paid to Marfa from contemporary art to vernacular, sacred space and altar production, and from English alone to English, Spanish, and Nahuatl. The roots of our friendships were fortified in those two years, and how wildly they have grown! I am still awed by how much you gave to *MARFITA* and by the artists and people you are and are still becoming. I am forever yours. Natalie Goodnow, an already acclaimed teatrista with a legendary path before her, brought the space of the artwork (and, indeed, the whole neighborhood surrounding it) to vibrant life alongside her danzante comrades. I imagine many there on that opening night still recall the sensation of the drumbeat, the scent of the copal, and the deep call of the caracol as I do. Natalie, keep doing your work and changing the world. *MARFITA* was supported by a slew of family and friends who, following a failed Kickstarter campaign, sent direct checks and cash anyway. Y'all are amazing. Finally, to Sean Gaulager and the devoted team at Co-Lab Projects: Your incredible vision for the arts in Austin and Texas have made so much more than *MARFITA* possible. You will show up in acknowledgments for decades, I am sure. This one is but one in a long list.

The Judd Foundation has supported this project in ways conventional and unexpected. First to thank must be Rainer Judd, president, and Flavin Judd, artistic director. Years ago, following your father's untimely passing, you made a difficult decision—really, *the* difficult decision—to keep his legacy intact. There were simpler paths you could have taken. I cannot imagine what it means to have spent decades dedicated to this work, but I hope to add productively to it. This book would not be possible if the foundation were not in the world.

In January 2013, alongside nineteen strangers, I began the training program for the inaugural cohort of artist-guides at 101 Spring Street, set to open to the public in June of that year. For months, we pored over the most cumbersome binder of documents I have ever wielded and discussed among ourselves and with a host of stellar presenters, all of whom worked closely with the artist in his lifetime, everything from SoHo's prewar manufacturing history to interpretations of Donald Judd's work in Japan. Museum educator extraordinaire Miri Young designed and oversaw the inspired program with academic breadth, pedagogical ingenuity, and unmatched warmth. While years later we still debate historical minutiae, artistic interpretations, and pedagogical approaches, our admiration for Miri is one thing on which all of us artist-guides agree. Thank you, Miri! And after the inimitable experience of training and working at 101 Spring Street, those nineteen strangers are now my friends. To Clifford Allen, Lourdes Correa-Carlo, Jenn Gapetz, Fatima Haider, Charlotte Hallberg, Jessica Kaire, Rebecca Layton, Charlotte Meyer, Dominic Nurre, Alessandra Pohlmann, Leah Raintree, David Rosenberg, Stacy Seiler, Finnegan Shannon, Michael Sirianni, Susan Stainman, Anthony Viti, and Tricia Wright: I wouldn't trade our time training and working together for anything, not even a stack.

My debts to the Judd Foundation continue. For reading drafts and helping me navigate the ephemeral facts of relationships and intimate histories touched on in my work, and for all the myriad roles you play to keep the Foundation running magnificently, thank you Christopher Longfellow, director of operations. To Allison Ake, visitor services and events manager for New York: You have my deep and ongoing gratitude for keeping us artist-guides organized, informed, and, well, wrangled. I may no longer be a foundation employee, but for you I am always on call. Michele Saliola, former director of institutional advancement, is a force; she helped shape early programming at the foundation, which was a thrill to witness. Maria Quinata was catalogue raisonné researcher during my time as an artist-guide; where would I have been without my inside man? Not many researchers have a texting relationship with those most in the know. Lacking a quick fact never held up the writing longer than it took to shoot you a question and receive a reliable answer in an afternoon . . . from a friend who will take a lunch break to get their aura photographed with you in Chinatown or just go window shopping, for which I also happily thank our partner-in-crime Elizabeth Abrahamson, former programs and communications manager. To the ever cool and calm Richard Griggs, chief operating officer: Your leadership is appreciated, as are the moments you find to drop words of encouragement, often very funny ones, between demanding tasks and meetings. Finally, my thanks go to Erin Schneider, archivist, for expert fact-checking and to Andrea Walsh, senior director of content and communications, for facilitating the accurate and nuanced telling of significant stories that relate to Judd's with care, including this book.

Katy Rogers, now president and CEO of the Dedalus Foundation, was the first to welcome me into the close-knit professional world built around Donald Judd's legacy. Katy, the collegiality and friendship that we have grown in the ensuing years is now bigger than that world, and I look forward to a lifetime of meals and hangs in New York, or wherever.

A significant object discussed in this book is a table intended for everyday use. This table, located in the reading room at El Cosmico in Marfa when I used it, was crafted by Caitlin Murray. Besides being an excellent maker, Caitlin is executive director of the Chinati Foundation. When we first met, she was the Marfa-based Judd Foundation archivist, working tirelessly to organize and preserve the foundation's rich holdings. Caitlin, as noted at the close of chapter 3, I owe you thanks for access to the archives, the furniture on which the first chapter was largely written, and so much more.

Because of poet and organizer Tim Johnson, also of Marfa, there is at least one whole section of an earlier draft of this book that does not appear here. Tim, at a crucial time you provided needed critique and insight only a Marfan could offer. My writing is better thanks to your wisdom. While life has taken me far from home, it is a constant relief that daily you are present, in a deep sense of the word, in West Texas. Thank you for watching over and building up the place where my ancestors are buried and much of our family still lives.

The Center for Interdisciplinary Studies in Philosophy, Interpretation, and Culture (CPIC) at Binghamton University provided one of the most constant and vital spaces for thinking through the issues discussed in this book. Peers and mentors met through CPIC were and are invaluable interlocutors, helping to locate coloniality in Marfa in a global context. The Decolonial Summer School in Middelburg, Netherlands, operated by Walter Mignolo and Rolando Vázquez, is a significant node in the same network of activist intellectuals and artists with whom it's been my privilege to engage over the years. Thank you for the strength of your voices and your ongoing camaraderie: Walter, Rolando, Fabián Barba, Maria Chaves, Pedro Di Pietro, María Lugones, Hil Malatino, Laura E. Pérez, Gabriela Veronelli, and the many, many others committed to this now global network.

Imagining America's Publicly Active Graduate Education (PAGE) Fellowship changed everything. At its heart, PAGE is a community that permits itself to reconfigure academic pursuit as community-building. For us, stories matter as much as scholarship. It is difficult and dangerous to assert this alone, but through each other's strength it is possible and it is happening. We give each other permission to make bold claims; we work for our communities, not just our degrees; we will fundamentally shift the means of intellectual production in this country; we will change the world. Fabulous, fabulous PAGE family: Thank y'all!

The Ithaca College Predoctoral Diversity Fellowship is one of the most valuable opportunities for academics of color in the United States today. I am deeply honored to have been given the time, space, and rich intellectual environment provided by the fellowship at a true gem of a school. Being invited to stay on and teach for an additional year was a fantastic bonus and provided the means for continuing this project. Thank you to my wonderful colleagues in the art history program: Mara Baldwin, Nancy Brcak, Stephen Clancy, Jennifer Germann, Jennifer Jolly, Randi Millman-Brown, Lauren O'Connell, David Solomon, Gary Wells, Paul Wilson, and Julia Yang. It is an honor to be associated with you.

In a moment of institutional crisis as the interdisciplinary program in which I completed my master's degree was dissolving, the art history department at Binghamton University mobilized valiantly to not only bring me into the department but provide full multiyear funding through the Clifford D. Clark Fellowship. This book is a small return for an immense action and a generous gift. The years of rigorous conversation and close reading and looking I will always cherish add substantially to my debt. Karen Barzman, Kevin Hatch, Tom McDonough, Pam Smart, John Tagg, Nancy Um, and Julia Walker, I am forever grateful.

Tom McDonough challenged and grew alongside me at every turn. I witnessed his mind changing as he changed mine. To have a guide like Tom, who leads with sureness and openness simultaneously, is invaluable. Tom is an expert editor who, atypically, pored through my document, reviewing every level from the content and structure to the citations and format. I can never repay this work. Tom, thank you for this and so much more.

Pam Smart, you most of all understand my Texan heart and how modernism operates in the land that bore me and inspires this work. I learned so much from you regarding the relationship between contemporary faith practices and postwar art. How museums play their role in this would have felt like an impossibly daunting question had I not had your work as a model and your generous interlocution as constant encouragement. One of my highest hopes is that my work is seen in a context your work has created. I would consider it an honor.

When I contemplated applying to graduate school almost twenty years ago, I was guided by a single question: With whom, most of all, do I want to work? The answer: María Lugones. This decision, based on the gamble of a hypothetical working relationship, is one of the best I have made in life and has been rewarded far beyond the hypothetical. Over the years, we have had all kinds of exchanges at every register: as student and teacher, as friend to friend, as activist to artist, as travel companions, as elder and witness. There have been some tears and lots of laughter. María, I will spend a lifetime grateful and continuing to work through your lessons on coloniality, philosophy, art, anger, political organizing, and much more. You taught me how to travel worlds. All my selves thank you.

The final chapter of this book was written a decade after the others. I am indebted to Laura E. Pérez and Ken Wissoker for conspiring to get this book published with the exemplary Duke University Press. Ken and his colleagues were incredibly patient while I worked on the manuscript around a full-time job and growing studio practice. I am also grateful to the Terra Foundation for American Art for a generous publication grant that enabled beautiful design, something I consider a necessity for a truly successful publication.

The final stretch of writing this book took place at the National Gallery of Art's Center for Advanced Study in the Visual Arts. The Lauder Visiting Senior Fellowship provided the time, space, and resources to complete the concluding chapter in an invigorating collegial environment. I am forever grateful to the selection committee; the center's dean, Steven Nelson; and the wonderful staff who skillfully tend to the ongoing growth of art history from our nation's capital.

And finally, thank you, Ed Hamann, for your steady daily presence, which I could not do without.

Notes

INVOCATION

1. Castillo, introduction to *Goddess of the Americas*.
2. Here I follow Laura E. Pérez's example in activating the pun between *alter* and *altar*: "As a form of domestic religious practice outside the domain of dominant religiosities, the altar has been a site for the socially and culturally 'alter,' or other, to express, preserve, and transmit cultural and gender-based religious and political differences." Pérez, *Chicana Art*, 91.
3. Salgado Halpern, "Virgin Mary Image Appears."
4. Allen, "Donald Judd and the Marfa Objective," 1. Allen's dissertation includes the otherwise unpublished Dutch interview in which Judd discusses spirituality and states "all forms are spiritual."

INTRODUCTION. RASQUACHISMO, MINIMALISM

1. My situating Minimalism and rasquachismo cara a cara, or face-to-face, is undertaken in the vein of feminists of color. It signals that race and ethnicity's co-constitution with sex and gender plays a formative role in this writing. Along with art, they also play crucial roles in the social fabric of Marfa. As María Lugones does in her essay, in a different context, I too "am thinking about cracked mirrors that reflect us falsely because I want to lead you into the spaces where I explore racist ethnocentrism." My spaces are Marfa and the spaces of art history. Cracked mirrors abound in both. Lugones, "Hablando cara a cara," 46–54.
2. Art historian Christina Noel Robbins came across a letter from Michael Fried to Philip Leider in the Smithsonian's Archives of American Art in which Fried expounds on the "faggot sensibility" of Minimalist art. Robbins's resulting article is a profound assessment of art criticism since the publication of Fried's "Art and Objecthood" (1967). She argues that those "sensibilities" identified and demonstrated by Fried are not merely anecdotal but in fact integral for understanding art criticism. Paying due attention to anecdote and the lived world around art, as this book does, is the remedy to Fried's misguided attempts to identify "pure" Modernist art. Robbins, "Sensibility of Michael Fried," 432.
3. In the conclusion to this book, art historian Max Tolleson provocatively uses the idea of the town's fuller context being "pulled through" a watercolor picture of one of Donald Judd's works.

4. Cheech Marin, reflecting on touring West Texas as a performer, aptly described my homeland as "the place you can see your dog run away for three days." Josh T Franco, "Oral history interview with Cheech Marin, 2017 October 16–17," Archives of American Art, Smithsonian Institution.
5. These publications and the fashion industry's preoccupations with Marfa are addressed at length in Franco, "Exposed: Process, Couture, and Photography in Marfa, Texas," available on Vimeo, accessed August 28, 2025, http://vimeo.com/65853302. There is nothing new about the tight relationship between glossy magazines and Minimalism. James Meyer's assessment of such publications—including a close reading of Francesco Scavullo's portrait of Donald Judd and Julie Finch, from *Harper's Bazaar*, July 1966—offers a clear demonstration of how "just as the artists used this venue for their own purposes, so too they were used. Their presence in *Harper's Bazaar* was part of a larger marketing strategy or 'culture sell,' whereby a product's image could be 'upgraded' by associating it with the most advanced culture." This uneasy symbiosis remains active today, with esteemed destinations standing in for individual artists. Meyer, *Minimalism*, 29.
6. D. Judd, "Casa Lujan and La Catorcena," 29.
7. Neda Ulaby, "Marfa, Texas: An Unlikely Art Oasis in a Desert Town," National Public Radio, August 2, 2012, http://www.npr.org/2012/08/02/156980469/marfa-texas-an-unlikely-art-oasis-in-a-desert-town.
8. Meyer, *Minimalism*, 29.
9. This was the first time I was explicitly confronted with the notion of Chicanismo as a process rather than a fixed identity. Lyrically, Guillermo Gómez-Peña demonstrates this point in a chiasmic observation of himself and collaborator Roberto Sifuentes: "Two important borders separate Roberto and I: cultural and generational. He is a Chicano in the process of Mexicanization (which means that he is looking South) and I am a Mexican in the process of Chicanization. (Will I ever become a 'real' Chicano? Will I ever 'arrive'? Will 'they'—the border guards of identity—ever let me?)" Gómez-Peña, *Dangerous Border Crossers*, 11–12.
10. The original design included a shallow cement pool that held water; this was later filled in with more cement for ease of maintenance.
11. Salgado Halpern, "Virgin Mary Image Appears," 1, 7.
12. Many of these instances were gathered in the 2008 exhibition *Phantom Sightings: Art After the Chicano Movement* at the Los Angeles County Museum of Art. While *Modernism* was the preferred term through and against which many of the curators' catalogue essays review this group

of work, it was nevertheless clear that Minimalism in particular provides many of the gestures and forms appropriated by the artists.

13. For understanding the geographic associations of Chicanx art, it is instructive to note which states were singled out and which areas were grouped to organize the regional committees for the watershed exhibition CARA: *Chicano Art—Resistance and Affirmation, 1965–1985*: "Arizona, Northern California, Southern California, Colorado, Eastern Seaboard, Mid-West, New Mexico, Northwest, Texas." Griswold del Castillo et al., CARA, 11.
14. Although Chicanx artists have occasionally exhibited work in Marfa, there is no critical mass or institutional support that would encourage one to consider it a site of Chicanx art making. Notable exceptions all took place at Ballroom Marfa: Franco Mondini-Ruiz's installation *Giant* (2004); the group show *In Lieu of Unity/En lugar de la unidad*, which included Margarita Cabrera's soft-sculpture *cacti* (2010); rafa esparza's *Tierra. Sangre. Oro.* (2018); and *Los Encuentros*, which included Justin Favela, Ozzie Juarez, Antonio Lechuga, Narsiso Martinez, and Yvette Mayorga (2025).
15. Some Marfa-based artists who do identify as Chicanx include artist Mateo Galindo, multimedia artist Prepney, photographer Sarah M. Vasquez, and artist Rigo A. Zamarron.
16. According to DATA USA, accessed January 2, 2025, https://datausa.io/profile/geo/marfa-tx/.
17. Ybarra-Frausto, "Rasquachismo," 156.
18. As Ybarra-Frausto himself is well aware, use of the term *rasquache* dates at least to the early twentieth century. Taking it up as an intellectual concept is relatively new. My grandmother saw me give a version of this chapter as a talk in the summer of 2013; afterward, I asked her what she thought. She was "impressed" by what had been done with the word and what I was doing with it, and she explained her own lifelong understanding as follows: "When I was a little girl, if your friend invited you to get ice cream, then asked you to pay for yours and hers *after* ordering . . . that was rasquache." Esperanza Hernandez, conversation with author, July 15, 2013.
19. Ybarra-Frausto, "Rasquachismo," 155.
20. Ybarra-Frausto, "Rasquachismo," 156.
21. Ybarra-Frausto, "Rasquachismo," 159.
22. The other artists identified by individual works in the CARA exhibition are Diane Gamboa, José Montoya, Teddy Sandoval, Carlos Santistevan, Ruben Trejo, Linda Vallejo, and Larry Yañez. Ybarra-Frausto, "Rasquachismo," 162n2.

23. Ávalos references the moment of this impression in an oral history taken by Margarita Nieto for Smithsonian's Archives of American Art. He saw an exhibit that included Oldenburg's work in Stockholm while he was stationed in Europe during the Vietnam War. Margarita Nieto, "Oral History with David Ávalos, 1988 June 16–July 5," accessed June 20, 2013, https://www.aaa.si.edu/collections/interviews/oral-history-interview-david-avalos-5428.
24. For an extended analysis of the political, queer import of the ascendant lipstick, as well as a list of press and published sources where Ávalos might have encountered documentation of the work, see Williams, "Lipstick Ascending."
25. "Rasquachismo is a sensibility that is not elevated and serious, but playful and elemental. . . . It is witty and ironic, but not mean-spirited (there is no sincerity in its artifice)." Ybarra-Frausto, "Rasquachismo," 155.
26. Lee, *Chronophobia*, 44.
27. Lee notes her own awareness of the well-worn quality of this narrative, though ultimately argues for the novelty of her approach: "To revisit Fried at this moment would seem to belabor the point, a calculated redundancy: how many times must we return to this canon text? Yet as many critics and historians have noted, such attention is deserved, for no text articulates the peculiar mechanics of minimalism's reception as brilliantly as it does, in spite of its antagonism toward the work in question." Lee, *Chronophobia*, 38.
28. "Well, I hate the term 'minimalism.' There was in no way a group at all. It's a real concoction; it's a publicity thing. . . . It's just some sort of publicity thing which comes from art history, where they think everything comes from styles and groups and so forth, which is kind of doubtful anyway, if you go back and look at it." Judd and Murray, *Donald Judd Interviews*, 498.
29. Gaspar de Alba, *Chicano Art*, 12–13. There is a second-degree rasquachismo, as the reader may suspect. Second-degree rasquache works are commercially produced and proliferate flat, seductive images of otherwise complex icons. Consider images of the Virgin of Guadalupe as fashion accessories (key chains, T-shirts, embroidered jackets, etc.) divorced from the meanings and practices constitutive of her origin and role in Latin American faith practices.
30. Anzaldúa, "Speaking in Tongues," 167.
31. More recent developments in theorizing visual appropriation as a method of (dis)identification by those whose work is uneasily, and often unwillingly, located in the category of Chicanx art include a strikingly analogous distinction to the one Gaspar de Alba articulated between "identity politics" and a "politics of identity" in her survey of the 1992 ex-

hibition CARA: *Chicano Art—Resistance and Affirmation*. In a concise, dense discussion of Juan Capistran's quotations of the punk band Black Flag's logo and Frank Stella's early monochromatic stripe paintings, Rose G. Salseda writes, "These artists' engagement with the past and their commitment to expanding notions of identity ably articulate the distinction between the concept of postidentity and that of post-race. Post-race discourse altogether dismisses the legitimacy of racial identity, pointing to the falsehood of the biological concept of race or insisting that race was a 'problem' that has somehow been resolved. Postidentity discourse, by contrast, is a critical mind-set that favors nuanced understandings of identity and challenges the naturalized and policed notion of what it means to be black or Chicano, and so forth. In this sense, the term 'postidentity' constitutes a fundamental reimagination of identity politics." Salseda, "New Wave of Identity Politics," 27.

32. The emergence of the term *Chicano* was concomitant with the Chicano Movement, which emerged in the 1960s as part of the larger civil rights movement occurring throughout the United States. It was and remains closely identified with groups like the United Farm Workers, which was founded by César Chávez and Dolores Huerta in 1962 to advocate for better conditions for agricultural labor forces, which included large Mexican American populations. In the 1970s and continuing today, the same fight for fair treatment and equal rights entered other domains beyond the agricultural sector, such as higher education, museums, and galleries. The 2008 exhibition *Phantom Sightings: Art After the Chicano Movement* focused on this afterlife and the complexities of Chicanx identities when historically removed from the movement's origins (the same problem Gaspar de Alba approaches). Art was always a part of the movement, but as time passed, artists who identified as (or were identified by others as) Chicanx naturally began working in much more expansive terms. One significant problem that arose was that of audience: If the purpose of Chicanx art is no longer exclusively to build movement adherents and solidarity or confront the oppressor with powerful imagery, who is it for? Of complications generated by this shift over time, *Phantom Sightings* cocurator Rita Gonzalez writes that "discussions regarding audience and community engagement carried over into the 1980s as a number of Chicano artists landed in commercial galleries nationally, producing anxieties about the dilution of what artists and historians found was distinctly Chicano about Chicano art. In the late 1980s and throughout the 1990s, a larger conversation about art, activism, and diversity was influenced by the changing landscape of arts funding and the import of relational forms of art—from Fluxus to feminist art to what Suzanne Lacy has called 'new genre public art.'" Gonzalez et al., *Phantom Sightings*, 47.

33. Gaspar de Alba, *Chicano Art*, 12.
34. Opposite "successful" Modernism according to Fried, the literalist or Minimalist works he criticized "redirect a viewer's experience away from the contained and self-sufficient work of art and out toward the world. The redirection results in an ambiguity as to what exactly is to be included in the aesthetic experience, which becomes infinitely expandable, in both space and time, capable of including the site of display and all the atmospheric nuances therein, including the mobile body of the viewer herself." Robbins, "Sensibility of Michael Fried," 436. What Fried disdains in Minimalism is in fact exactly what I aim to accomplish in this book, attention to "all the atmospheric nuances" around and including art in Marfa.
35. See Chave, "Minimalism and the Rhetoric of Power," 116–40.
36. Mesa-Bains, "Domesticana," 157–58.
37. Mesa-Bains, "Domesticana," 159.
38. Sanchez-Tranquilino and Tagg, "Pachuco's Flayed Hide," 97.
39. Noriega, "Dissension of Other Things," 4.
40. Noriega, "Dissension of Other Things," 4.
41. Pérez, *Chicana Art*, 14.
42. González, *Subject to Display*, 133.
43. Mesa-Bains, "Domesticana," 306.
44. Mesa-Bains, "Domesticana," 307.
45. Mesa-Bains, "Domesticana," 307.
46. Mignolo, *Local Histories/Global Designs*, 34.
47. Lugones, *Pilgrimages/Peregrinajes*, 83–84.
48. Lugones, *Pilgrimages/Peregrinajes*, 84.
49. Lugones, *Pilgrimages/Peregrinajes*, 89–90.

1. PILGRIM, APPROACH

1. Judd's appreciation for the flora of the Southwest began long before his 1972 move to Marfa. I describe the collection as "beloved" based on the account of Judd's longtime assistant, Jamie Dearing, who recounts one of the earliest tasks Judd set for him: Moving the cacti collection from his and Julie Finch's Nineteenth Street apartment down to 101 Spring Street in 1968. Shortly thereafter, Dearing would again oversee the move of this highly climate-sensitive collection, this time from New York City to Marfa. Dearing, discussion, Artist-Guide Training Program, 101 Spring Street, Judd Foundation, January 28, 2013.
2. Turner, *Ritual Process*, 95.
3. For more information on MARFITA, see the documentary film by Sean Gaulager, including artist interviews, available on Vimeo, accessed August 28, 2025, http://vimeo.com/31273553.

4. Van Ryzin, "Marfa's Culture Clash," 12.
5. Turner, *Ritual Process*, 95.
6. Lugones, *Pilgrimages/Peregrinajes*, 89–90 (emphasis mine).
7. Turner, *Ritual Process*, 96.
8. Turner, *Ritual Process*, 97.
9. Lugones, *Pilgrimages/Peregrinajes*, 4.
10. Judd used this term in regard to the Chinati Foundation specifically: "Somewhere, just as the platinum-iridium meter guarantees the tape measure, a strict measure must exist for the art of this time and place. Otherwise art is only show and monkey business." D. Judd, *Complete Writings*, 111.
11. Gruzinski, *Images at War*, 104.
12. Ester Sanchez quoted in Salgado Halpern, "Virgin Mary Image Appears," 1. The debates that began in the sixteenth century in Spain and the "New World" continue today. Socorro Castañeda-Liles provides a succinct overview of the main interpretive avenues that diverged from the Guadalupe phenomenon: Catholic apparitionist (practicing Catholics who believe in a divine intent and agency behind the apparition image itself); Catholic non-apparitionist (practicing Catholics who recognize, like Ester Sanchez, natural phenomena as the cause of the apparition but understand the image as a call to devotion regardless); historical (this position disregards any divine agency in favor of the narrative in which an Indigenous painter known as "Marcos" was recruited by the Catholic Church to fabricate the Guadalupe image and install it covertly on Tepayac Hill, the sacred site where she first appeared); and Chicanx feminist (based on literature and visual art produced since the 1960s by Chicanx feminists). Near the conclusion of her broad survey of Guadalupe interpretations, from the original 1531 appearance to counter-narratives produced in the present day, Castañeda-Liles writes, "True or not, her defenders argue that [the instability of her appearance's historical credibility] does not necessarily mean that she is not from God." Castañeda-Liles, "Our Lady of Guadalupe," 174.
13. Salgado Halpern, "Virgin Mary Image Appears," 1.
14. Sanchez, log of pilgrims, n.p.
15. This "fermentation" has not ceased. If anything, it boils more raucously than ever. Laura E. Pérez recruits the work of Serge Gruzinski to show how his model for connecting the interpretive fervor of the sixteenth century to debates in visual cultures today functions specifically for Chicanx feminist artists. This also aptly describes how I understand the relationship—yet to be fully explored—between Minimalism and rasquachismo. Pérez writes, "In the United States Latina/os, along with other socially marginalized groups, are at the forefront of newer, socially

relevant, and trendsetting forms of both art making and new religiosities. Gruzinski's model of religious visual cultural warfare and mutual cultural appropriations in colonial Mexico are, in fact, as he hopes, useful for understanding urban postmodernity, particularly in the study of contemporary Chicana/o cultural practices. . . . Western high-art conventions, for example, may be seen as the language through which those Chicana/o and Mexican American popular cultural beliefs and practices that are rooted in Amerindian or other so-called pagan or Goddess cultures are rephrased. Alternately, the discourse of Western high-art conventions are interrogated through culturally different conventions of 'art,' beauty, and value that Indigenous, Mexican American, and popular urban or rural classes hold." Pérez, "Hybrid Spiritualities," 342–43.

16. Ester Sanchez, email message to author, March 2, 2013.
17. "Leo has always accepted the necessity of doing new work, usually large, expensive and unsaleable. I was very impressed when, before the show I had at the Whitney in 1968, Leo borrowed $10,000 from the bank to construct new pieces." D. Judd, *Complete Writings*, 12.
18. For Judd and many of his contemporaries, acts of making were intimately tied to articulations of political positions, though each artist would perform and interpret this intimacy differently, sometimes dramatically so. See Bryan-Wilson, *Art Workers*.
19. Following their divorce (filed in 1976, finalized in February 1979), Judd took sole direction of the ongoing renovation of 101 Spring Street until his death in 1994.
20. "In the context of Minimalism and Modern art, rasquachismo is more than an oppositional form; it is a militant praxis of resistance to hegemonic standards in the art world." Gaspar de Alba, *Chicano Art*, 12. See my introduction for related in-depth discussion.
21. Shannon, *Disappearance of Objects*, 161.
22. Judd and Murray, *Donald Judd Interviews*, 341–42.
23. Judd was certainly not alone in being drawn downtown for the large spaces. According to a 1973 City of New York designation report: "It was not until the 1960s that a new movement began to stir. This, surprisingly enough, was caused by the trend among artists to paint on larger and larger canvasses. The high-ceilinged, empty lofts of SoHo provided the large spaces that they needed for their work and the rents were very low. With the help of City agencies, the zoning laws were imaginatively amended to permit the migration of artists into the area without, at the same time, driving out the marginal industries whose employment of semi-skilled workers fills a necessary niche in the City's economy." Judd refused to take advantage of these amendments in any official capacity and remained a technically illegal resident of the building for his entire

life. Landmarks Preservation Committee, SOHO–*Cast Iron Historic District Report*, 8.

24. "In addition to my developing idea of installations and my need for a place in the Southwest, both due in part to the harsh and glib situation within art in New York and to the unpleasantness of the city, I had set a deadline for finding a place. . . . Also the new and old pottery I had bought in the Southwest was spalling in the humidity of New York, and the cacti I had collected were dying." D. Judd, *Complete Writings*, 98.
25. Judd would not, however, sell 101 Spring Street. It continued to be a site of experimentation as he developed his conception of "permanent installation" and pursued many architectural investigations. Also, it continued to serve throughout his career as a hive of studio assistant and clerical activity, as well as a studio, residence, and social gathering place for Judd and his family in New York City. However, Marfa afforded unique opportunities not possible in the crowded urban environs of the city. By 1972, Judd and his children were residing mostly in Marfa.
26. D. Judd, *Complete Writings*, 96.
27. D. Judd, *Complete Writings*, 98.
28. Stockebrand, *Making of Two Works*, 2.
29. Reading, *Marfan*, n.p.
30. D. Judd, "Oral History Project: Marfa Voices," Judd Foundation, accessed August 27, 2025, https://juddfoundation.org/archives/oral-history-project/.
31. Krauss, *Perpetual Inventory*, 91.
32. Krauss, "Sculpture in the Expanded Field," 41.
33. Krauss, "Sculpture in the Expanded Field," 38.
34. "The historian/critic simply performed a more extended sleight of hand and began to construct his genealogies out of the data of millennia rather than decades. Stonehenge, the Nazca Lines, the Toltec ballcourts, Indian burial mounds—anything at all could be hauled into court to bear witness to this work's connection to history and thereby to legitimize its status as sculpture. Of course Stonehenge and the Toltec ballcourts were just exactly *not* sculpture, and so their role as historicist precedent becomes somewhat suspect in this particular demonstration. But never mind." Krauss, "Sculpture in the Expanded Field," 33.
35. Bataille, "Extinct America," 3.
36. Hal Foster recognizes this "residual" and "tenacious" reliance on atavistic thinking in art-making (which I argue is equally present in art history), and his articulation is relevant here, further illuminating Krauss's deployment of anthropology's "othering" function: "anthropology was founded on a mythical mapping of time onto space based on two presumptions: '1. Time is immanent to, hence coextensive with, the world

(or nature, or the universe, depending on the argument); 2. Relationships between parts of the world (in the widest sense of both natural and sociocultural entities) can be understood as temporal relations. Dispersal in space reflects directly, which is not to say simply or in obvious ways, sequence in Time.' With space and time thus mapped onto one another, 'over there' became 'back then,' and the most remote (as measured from some Greenwich mean of European Civilization) became the most primitive. This mapping of the primitive was manifestly racist: in the Western white imaginary its site was always dark." With this in mind, I understand Krauss to be suggesting that the critics she is critical of write from this darkness, unaware of the extent to which those civilizations she refers to are still culturally active today, mangled and transformed by colonial encounters as they are. This is not entirely (perhaps even barely) a problem of the art historian's unwillingness to know, but a deeply rooted epistemological problem of "the West," in which Krauss herself was trained and in which she is expert, particularly about sculpture's meaning. As Foster continues, "It remains tenacious, however, because it is fundamental to narratives of history-as-development and civilization-as-hierarchy. These nineteenth-century narratives are residual in discourses like psychoanalysis and disciplines like art history." Foster, *Return of the Real*, 177.

37. "Dear Joshua, We have not answered because we wanted to ask someone about the Indigenous Indians, but I don't think anyone in our family knows. I'm sorry, son. The only thing I know, I believe, is that we Mexicans come from the Aztecs and the Spaniards." Esperanza Hernandez to author, March 23, 2010.

38. This was a lesson Judd learned through experience: "Eighteen years ago someone asked me to design a coffee table. I thought that a work of mine which was essentially a rectangular volume with the upper surface recessed could be altered. This debased the work and produced a bad table, which I later threw away. The configuration and the scale of art cannot be transposed into furniture and architecture." Judd and Murray, *Donald Judd Writings*, 586.

39. "The baseboard of the fifth floor is the same oak as that of the floor, making the floor a shallow recessed plane. There is no baseboard, there is a gap between the walls and the floor of the third floor, thus defining and separating the floor as a plane. These ideas were precedents for some small pieces and then for the 100 mill aluminum pieces in the Chinati Foundation." Judd and Murray, *Donald Judd Writings*, 586.

40. Romero Cash, *Santos*, 230.

41. Romero Cash, *Santos*, 72, 176.

42. Turner, *Beautiful Necessity*, 7.

43. Pérez, *Chicana Art*, 6.
44. González, *Subject to Display*, 124.
45. Espinoza et al., *Amalia Mesa-Bains*, 6.
46. Van Ryzin, "Marfa's Culture Clash," 14.

2. MARFA, AZTLÁN

1. Josh T Franco, "Letter to Donald Judd," September 2012, author's website, accessed November 25, 2025, https://www.joshtfranco.com/letter-to-donald-judd.
2. Gonzalez et al., *Phantom Sightings*, 76.
3. Stockebrand, *CHINATI*, 265.
4. Dobie, *Apache Gold*, 4.
5. "Marfa: The Light and the Land."
6. Chaplin, "Gypset Travel," accessed August 28, 2025, https://www.shoplatitude.com/blogs/journal/112871235-gypset-travel-marfa-texas.
7. Nafziger, Camacho, and Elrod quoted in "Marfa: The Light and the Land."
8. Andrea Claire, conversation with the author, July 23, 2013.
9. Rainer Judd, interviewed by Josh T Franco, Judd Foundation, 101 Spring Street, New York City, December 4, 2014.
10. Martínez, *Desert America*, 294. For more on this topic, see Hart, "Arts and Civic Participation."
11. Martínez, *Desert America*, 261.
12. Martínez interviews Valda Livingston, the real estate agent in Marfa "perfectly positioned" to facilitate the sales of homes to the influx of the creative class in the late 1990s and 2000s. The journalist notes her discomfort: "When I asked her about Marfa's segregated past, her cheeks reddened. 'I don't think there was any discrimination until someone put that in their heads,' she said. 'They had the same opportunities as everyone else.'" Martínez continues: "Notwithstanding Livingston's claims of equal opportunity, the town was and is neatly divided by the railroad tracks. Long past *Brown v. Board of Education*, Mexican students could only attend the Blackwell School from kindergarten through eighth grade; Marfa's movie theaters and churches were also segregated." Martínez, *Desert America*, 268. My own grandfather was a student at Blackwell.
13. The group's name derives from the Spanish word *chingados*, the "fucked ones." In an act of Chicanx Caló poeisis, the adolescent boys in the novel reappropriate and hybridize the word with English grammar, resulting in *Los Chinglers* (The fuckers). Such acts of recuperating agency first through language is widely discussed in Chicanx studies. For a foundational text, see Arteaga, *Chicano Poetics*.

14. Cano, *Other Side of the Tracks*, 162.
15. Martínez, *Desert America*, 269.
16. Alurista, "Preamble," Latinopia, accessed August 28, 2025, http://latinopia.com/latino-history/plan-de-aztlan/.
17. Maldonado-Torres, *Against War*, 3, 4.
18. Alurista, "Preamble."
19. Ballroom Marfa Programs, "Franco Mondini-Ruiz," accessed November 25, 2025, https://www.ballroommarfa.org/program/468/.
20. Cary Cordova, "Oral History Interview with Franco Mondini-Ruiz, 2004 July 7–8," Archives of American Art, Smithsonian Institution, accessed August 28, 2025, http://www.aaa.si.edu/collections/interviews/oral-history-interview-franco-mondiniruiz-12062.
21. Pérez, "El Desorden," 38–39.
22. Ballroom Marfa Programs, "In Lieu of Unity/En Lugar de la Unidad," accessed August 28, 2025, https://www.ballroommarfa.org/program/in-lieu-of-unity/.
23. Margarita Cabrera website, accessed August 28, 2025, www.margaritacabrera.com; Margarita Cabrera, interview by author, October 25, 2011, El Paso, Texas.
24. US Customs and Border Protection, "Southwest Land Encounters, accessed August 28, 2025, https://www.cbp.gov/newsroom/stats/southwest-land-border-encounters.
25. Ballroom Marfa Programs, "Prada Marfa," accessed August 28, 2025, https://www.ballroommarfa.org/prada-marfa/.
26. Gonzalez et al., *Phantom Sightings*, 231.
27. Pérez, "El Desorden," 20 (emphasis mine).

3. MAKING, AESTHESIS

1. When the table's builders asked Judd what dimensions the table should have, he pointed to the nearby window. Peter Ballantine cited this as one example of Judd using "found geometries" to both determine and harmonize design choices throughout his spaces. Ballantine, discussion, Artist-Guide Training Program, Judd Foundation, 101 Spring Street, May 14, 2014.
2. The same craftsmen who built the table also built the liquor shelving on the second-floor landing. The horizontal planes of the shelf demonstrate the same qualities, being as much as a quarter inch off from one plane to the next in some places.
3. Peter Ballantine also provided this anecdote. He did not mention who asked but was sure the question had been put to Judd. Ballantine, discussion, May 14, 2014.

4. Zukowski, *Furnishings Investigation,* 158–59.
5. Mignolo and Vázquez, "Decolonial AestheSis," pt. II, para. 2.
6. Mignolo and Vázquez, "Decolonial AestheSis," pt. II, para. 1. The nonstandard capitalizations are intended to draw attention to the distinctions being made here between modernity's aesthetics and a notion of aesthesis continuing from a time before modernity/coloniality.
7. Mignolo and Vázquez, "Decolonial AestheSis," pt. II, para. 2.
8. Kuo, "Industrial Revolution," 309.
9. Kuo, "Industrial Revolution," 309.
10. Kuo, "Industrial Revolution," 306.
11. Kuo, "Industrial Revolution," 309.
12. Kuo, "Industrial Revolution," 309.
13. Siegel, CATALOGUE, 316.
14. Sotheby's Lots, Auctions, and Exhibitions, accessed September 26, 2015, http://www.sothebys.com/en/search-results.html?keyword=celedonio+mediano.
15. "Next to the children's buildings [in the area known as The Block] is a pergola and a pool, both built by Celedonio Mediano, who has built everything. His brother, Alfredo Mediano, takes care of the art, a serious matter not sufficiently so regarded by those reputedly interested in art." Judd and Murray, *Donald Judd Writings,* 430. Mediano is also mentioned in another brief statement in the same collection: "Later, in a large place in [Marfa], I designed desks and chairs for the children using the same method of construction. More furniture developed from this beginning, now made better, but still simply, by Celedonio Mediano." F. Judd and Murray, *Donald Judd Writings,* 452. And as already mentioned, Rainer Judd—through her film and documentary work—has continued the attention to labor initiated by her father.
16. Mignolo and Vázquez, "Decolonial AeSthesis," pt. II, para. 3.
17. Ingold, *Making,* 20–21.
18. Ingold, *Making,* 6.
19. Ingold, *Making,* 22.
20. One can find these sounds incorporated into the work of sound artist Stephen Vitiello. The compacted polarity of climatic conditions producing the cracks and pops is associated with the same extremeness in Marfa's topographical and vegetal features in the *Pitchfork* review of Vitiello's album: "It's in a harsh desert clime, a vast gasp of land between mountains gone green on one side and brown on the other." From, respectively, Vitiello, *Listening to Donald Judd;* Andy Battaglia, review of *Listening to Donald Judd, Pitchfork,* 2007, accessed August 28, 2025, http://pitchfork.com/reviews/albums/10110-listening-to-donald-judd/.
21. F. Judd, introduction to *Donald Judd: Woodcuts,* n.p.

22. Ellie Meyer was Judd's assistant and, as of fall 2015, manager of the Judd Foundation's ongoing catalogue raisonné project. Willie Null, Judd's Marfa-based bookkeeper, is listed by Judd in a draft of the credits for the catalogue as "scribe." The questions, while delivered by Meyer, come from book designer GianFranco Verna.
23. Ingold, *Making*, 77.
24. Ingold, *Making*, 81.
25. Ingold, *Making*, 81.
26. "About," Lippincott Sculpture, accessed August 28, 2025, http://www.lippincottsculpture.com/about.html.
27. Madeleine Schwartz, "Notes from 21 South Street," *Harvard Advocate*, accessed August 28, 2025, https://theharvardadvocate.com/content/notes-from-21-south-street-art-in-hand-a-conversation-with-lawrence-voytek-and-peter-ballantine.
28. Mignolo and Vázquez, "Decolonial AestheSis," pt. III, "aesthesis" definition.
29. Ingold, *Making*, 11.
30. Jerry Parsons, interview with author, June 4, 2012.
31. Jones, *Machine in the Studio*, 2.
32. McCoy, "No Preservatives."
33. In 2013, Nagy and a team published an article detailing the novel challenges posed by the metal surfaces of some of Judd's works, as well as proposing innovative solutions. See Nagy et al., "Disfiguring Organic Residues."
34. McCoy, "No Preservatives."
35. D. Judd, *Chinati Foundation/La Fundación Chinati*, 1.
36. R. Judd, "Interview." With this phrasing, Judd also echoes venerated Texan and Smithsonian historian Lonn Taylor: "But there is another history of the Big Bend that I like to think of as its secret history. This is the history of the Spanish-speaking people who started coming here from Mexico at about the same time that the first Anglo ranchers arrived and whose numbers increased after the Mexican Revolution of 1910. They, too, built communities and institutions, and they often came into conflict with Anglo settlers, but their story is seldom found in the same easily accessible sources as that of the Anglo-Americans, so it has been largely omitted from even the best published histories. It remains a secret history, known only to the descendants of those who lived it." Taylor, *Texas People*, 212–13.
37. Jamie Dearing, discussion, Artist-Guide Training Program, JUDD Foundation, 101 Spring Street, January 28, 2013.
38. Ingold, *Making*, 102.

39. Ingold, *Making*, 105.
40. Lugones, *Pilgrimages/Peregrinajes*, 4.

CONCLUSION. LOVE, YARD (HANGING OUT IN MARFA)

1. Sheehy, *Flamingo in the Garden*, 177.
2. My grandfather, a yard artist, passed away in 2015, around the time I was completing my PhD. While home for the days around his death, I felt compelled to document his hand-built yard art environment in detail. This profound experience became the basis for an exhibition I guest curated at the Institute of Contemporary Art, Philadelphia, *Where I Learned to Look: Art from the Yard* (July 12–December 6, 2024). In 2025, I worked on the exhibition's related publication as a Leonard A. Lauder Visiting Senior Fellow at the Center for Advanced Studies in the Visual Arts, National Gallery of Art.
3. Artist, educator, and curator Gregg N. Blasdel argued as much as early as 1968, naming the individuals who work in yards and other non-museum, non-gallery venues "grass-roots artists." His documentary photo essay offers brief biographies of fifteen artists accompanying illustrations of their creations. He suggests the importance of expanding art research to include these figures: "Obvious but purely coincidental relationships drawn between grass-roots art and some current directions of professional art make its existence that much more poignant. The constructions of the grass-roots artist display an intuitive sense of color, form, design and space relationships. The continuous patterns, geometric shapes and symmetrical compositions are at times suggestive of the products of the hard-edge and pop schools, and the choice of objects and materials as well as the attitude of total involvement is comparable to that of contemporary artists concerned with assemblage, environments, happenings and light art." Blasdel, "Grass-Roots Artist," 25. The article's timing and patronage are meaningful too; Blasdel's research for the piece was supported in part by the Whitney Museum of American Art, where, notably, Judd's first major retrospective would take place in the same year.
4. Lugones, *Pilgrimages/Peregrinajes*. See the introduction for an extended description of "world-traveling."
5. You can still find his youthful football team photo preserved and sometimes displayed at the Blackwell School, now preserved to acknowledge the history of educational segregation in the region. In Marfa, this echoes the historic exclusion of Brown folks from certain art worlds as well.

6. Like so many Mexican and Mexican American families, ours is a ranging color study; there is no predicting the shade of brown of the next newly birthed cousin.
7. Tomás Ybarra-Frausto, "Oral History with Tomás Ybarra-Frausto, 2014 April 30–2015 May 25," interviewed by Gilberto Cardenas, Smithsonian Archives of American Art, https://www.aaa.si.edu/download_pdf_transcript/ajax?record_id=edanmdm-AAADCD_oh_379312.
8. Pérez, *Eros Ideologies*, 9.
9. Salgado Halpern, "Virgin Mary Image Appears," 1, 7.
10. Pérez, *Eros Ideologies*, 127.
11. Short-term rental properties largely marketed to tourists are one challenge. While some of these are established by nonresidents as income-generating ventures, others are generational homes that families rent out in order to keep up with rising property taxes. See Allegra Hobbs, "Chamber Leaders and Locals Urge City Council to Regulate STRs, as Some STR Owners Push Back," *Big Bend Sentinel*, April 12, 2023, https://bigbendsentinel.com/2023/04/12/chamber-leaders-and-locals-urge-city-council-to-regulate-strs-as-some-str-owners-push-back/.
12. Zachary Small, "Chinati Foundation Finds Its Next Director Close to Home," *New York Times*, March 10, 2023, https://www.nytimes.com/2023/03/10/arts/design/chinati-foundation-director-caitlin-murray.html.
13. Thanks to the work of the Blackwell School Alliance and many others, Blackwell School was designated a National Historic Site in 2024. "Many Presidio County residents of the Big Bend know pieces of the school's history: A segregated campus for Mexican American students in Marfa from 1909–1965 that finally integrated its students with Anglos 11 years after Brown v. Board of Education declared segregation unconstitutional; the requirement that students not speak Spanish, with punishment (sometimes corporal) for those who did, and forcing students to bury Spanish words on paper in a cigar-box coffin; how the Blackwell School Alliance nonprofit persisted for years in preserving and elevating the site's history." Rob D'Amico, "Blackwell School Ribbon Cutting Provides Reflection on Importance of New Park," *Big Bend Sentinel*, September 18, 2024, https://bigbendsentinel.com/2024/09/18/blackwell-school-ribbon-cutting-provides-reflection-on-importance-of-new-park/.
14. Lippard, "Land Art," 16.
15. Lugones, *Pilgrimages/Peregrinajes*, 224.
16. Lugones, *Pilgrimages/Peregrinajes*, 234n18.
17. Rojas, "Enacted Environment," 48.

18. I will forever be grateful for the invitation and the trip, which informed the exhibition we later co-organized: *Where I Learned to Look: Art from the Yard* (ICA, Philadelphia, July 12–December 6, 2024).
19. While not prevalent in Minter's yard, bottle trees are another recurring tradition that expresses spiritual belief in many African Americans' yards. "Much like swept yards, bottle trees—comprised of bottles, containers, and a variety of other spiritually meaningful elements arranged on or imitating trees—serve aesthetic and protective roles. The trees protect houses and yards from evil spirits by 'luring then inside the colored bottles, where they cannot get out again' (Welty 1971: 156)." Heath and Bennett, "'Little Spots Allow'd Them,'" 43.
20. Cooke, *Outliers*, 73.
21. Gundaker and McWillie, *No Space Hidden*, 10.
22. Cooke, *Outliers*, 4.
23. Aguilar et al., *Chicano Aesthetics*, 5.
24. Austin Considine, "Beyond Vernacular: An Interview with John Outterbridge" (my emphasis), Art in America, April 24, 2013, https://www.artnews.com/art-in-america/features/beyond-vernacular-an-interview-with-john-outterbridge-59401/.
25. Lugones, *Pilgrimages/Peregrinajes*, 86.
26. Gundaker, *No Space Hidden*, 12.
27. Members of the European aristocracy and upper classes preparing to undertake the Grand Tour—in which direct observation and documentation was a central activity—were advised to bring with them water-soluble paints supplied by Reeve's, an art supply company founded in the late eighteenth century (Hibbert, *Grand Tour*, 25). "The increased use of watercolour, in its modern connotation, came at the same period as the re-animation of man's interest in the visible world. Accordingly, one of its uses was for the quasi-scientific, quasi-artistic exploration of fact." Reynolds, *Concise History of Watercolours*, 10.
28. Stockebrand, *CHINATI*, 265.
29. While my focus here is on watercolor, another significant medium at work across yard sites in Marfa is cement. It is remarkable that cement, the key ingredient in concrete, constitutes both Judd's *15 untitled works in concrete* and the figure of the Virgin in the Sanchezes' altar as well as the altar's foundation and bathtub capilla (cement bonds large stones to the bathtub, elaborating it as architecture). Discussing cement's role in post-revolutionary Mexico, scholar Rubén Gallo writes, "For broken countries, cement emerges as the perfect social glue, promising to extend its powers of cohesion and solidity beyond the architectural realm and into the social fabric, to replace the chaos of *conflicto armado* with the order of *concreto armado*." Gallo, *Mexican Modernity*, 179. As a shared material

between Guadalupe's altar and Judd's work, I wonder if cement may, or already does, serve as "social glue" in Marfa as well. Architectural historian Adrian Forty discusses Judd's Marfa-sited *15 untitled works in concrete* as one example of a Minimalist artist turning to concrete, though the situation has its ironies: "[Judd's] main concern was for the objects to appear part of the desert landscape, and it seems that concrete was chosen as a more durable alternative to adobe, while retaining some of that material's primitive character . . . although ironically it turned out that Judd was disappointed by the poor quality of the first boxes in the series, and called in a concrete expert to bring the workmanship up to a more 'industrial' standard." Forty, *Concrete and Culture*, 220.

30. Lévi-Strauss, *Wild Thought*.
31. La Brasca, "Paradox of Permanence."
32. Sean J. Patrick Carney, "GROUND CONTROL: Sean J. Patrick Carney on Land Art and American Entropy," *Artforum*, July 19, 2021, https://www.artforum.com/columns/sean-j-patrick-carney-on-land-art-and-american-entropy-250266/.
33. Miner, "8 Untitled Works."
34. D. Judd, *Chinati Foundation/La Fundación Chinati*. The photographers were Sonny Lee and Robert Wilson.
35. Judd and Murray, *Donald Judd Writings*, 285.
36. "The Chinati Foundation project was begun by Judd in 1978–79 in Marfa, Texas, where he had lived for the past five years and where he had already turned two former aircraft hangars and the land around them into his own private residence. This property is a complete microcosm in its own right, which—like a monastery—has all of life's essentials, from an excellent library to a chicken coop." Stockebrand, *Making of Two Works*, 2.
37. Stockebrand, *CHINATI*, 46.
38. Tolleson, "Museum After Minimalism."

Bibliography

Aguilar, John L., Shifra Goldman, and Tomás Ybarra-Frausto. *Chicano Aesthetics: Rasquachismo*. Movimiento Artistico del Rio Salado, 1989.

Allen, Melissa Susan Gaido. "Donald Judd and the Marfa Objective." PhD diss., University of Iowa, 2005.

Anzaldúa, Gloria. "Speaking in Tongues: A Letter to 3rd World Women Writers." In *This Bridge Called My Back: Writings by Radical Women of Color*, edited by Cherríe Moraga and Gloria Anzaldúa. Persephone Press, 1981.

Arteaga, Alfred. *Chicano Poetics: Heterotexts and Hybridities*. Cambridge University Press, 1997.

Bataille, Georges. "Extinct America." Translated by Annette Michelson. *October* 36 (Spring 1986): 3–9.

Blasdel, Gregg N. "The Grass-Roots Artist." *Art in America* (September–October 1968): 24–41.

Bryan-Wilson, Julia. *Art Workers: Radical Practice in the Vietnam War Era*. University of California Press, 2009.

Cano, Tony. *The Other Side of the Tracks*. Reata, 2001.

Castañeda-Liles, Soccoro. "Our Lady of Guadalupe and the Politics of Cultural Interpretation." In Espinosa and García, *Mexican American Religions*.

Castillo, Ana, ed. *Goddess of the Americas: Writings on the Virgin of Guadalupe*. Riverhead Books, 1997.

Chabram-Dernersesian, Angie, ed. Special issue, *Cultural Studies: Theorizing Politics, Politicizing Theory* 13, no. 2.

Chave, Anna C. "Minimalism and the Rhetoric of Power." In *Power: Its Myths and Mores in American Art, 1961–1991*, by Anna C. Chave, Holliday T. Day, George E. Marcus, and Brian Wallis. Indiana University Press, 1991.

Cooke, Lynne. *Outliers and American Vanguard Art*. National Gallery of Art and University of Chicago Press, 2018.

Dobie, J. Frank. *Apache Gold and Yaqui Silver*. Little, Brown, 1939.

Espinosa, Gastón, and Mario T. García, eds. *Mexican American Religions: Spirituality, Activism, and Culture*. Duke University Press, 2008.

Espinoza, Alex, Amalia Mesa-Bains, and Laura Meyer. *Amalia Mesa-Bains: Geography of Memory*. Press at California State University, 2011.

Fabian, Johannes. *Time and the Other: How Anthropology Makes Its Object*. Columbia University Press, 1983.

Forty, Adrian. *Concrete and Culture: A Material History*. Reaktion Books, 2012.
Foster, Hal. *The Return of the Real*. MIT Press, 1996.
Gallo, Rubén. *Mexican Modernity: The Avant-Garde and the Technological Revolution*. MIT Press, 2004.
Gaspar de Alba, Alicia. *Chicano Art Inside/Outside the Master's House: Cultural Politics and the CARA Exhibition*. University of Texas Press, 1998.
Gómez-Peña, Guillermo. *Dangerous Border Crossers: The Artist Talks Back*. Routledge, 2000.
González, Jennifer A. *Subject to Display: Reframing Race in Contemporary Installation Art*. MIT Press, 2008.
Gonzalez, Rita, Howard N. Fox, and Chon A. Noriega. *Phantom Sightings: Art After the Chicano Movement*. Los Angeles County Museum of Art, 2008.
Griswold del Castillo, Richard, Teresa McKenna, and Yvonne Yarbro-Bejarano, eds. *CARA: Chicano Art: Resistance and Affirmation, 1965–1985*. Wight Art Gallery and University of California Press, 1991.
Gruzinski, Serge. *Images at War: Mexico from Columbus to Blade Runner (1492–2019)*. Duke University Press, 2001.
Guilbaut, Serge. *How New York Stole the Idea of Modern Art*. University of Chicago Press, 1985.
Gundaker, Grey, and Judith McWillie. *No Space Hidden: The Spirit of African American Yard Work*. University of Tennessee Press, 2005.
Hart, Alison. "The Arts and Civic Participation: A Case Study of Marfa, Texas." Master's thesis, University of Texas at Austin, 2007.
Heath, Barbara J., and Amber Bennett. "'The Little Spots Allow'd Them': The Archaeological Study of African-American Yards." *Historical Archaeology* 34, no. 2 (2000): 38–55.
Hibbert, Christopher. *The Grand Tour*. Thames Methuen, 1987.
Ingold, Tim. *Making: Anthropology, Archaeology, Art and Architecture*. Routledge, 2013.
Jones, Caroline A. *Machine in the Studio: Constructing the Postwar American Artist*. University of Chicago Press, 1996.
Judd, Donald. "Casa Lujan and La Catorcena." In *Donald Judd: Architektur* by Donald Judd, Marianne Stockebrand, Brigitte Kalthoff, and Ulrike Schubert. Westfälischen Kunstverein, 1989.
Judd, Donald. *Chinati Foundation/La Fundación Chinati*. Chinati Foundation/La Fundación Chinati, 1987.
Judd, Donald. *Donald Judd: Complete Writings, 1959–1975*. Press of the Novia Scotia College of Art and Design, 1975.
Judd, Flavin. Introduction to *Donald Judd: Woodcuts*. Paula Cooper Gallery, 2008.

Judd, Flavin, and Caitlin Murray, eds. *Donald Judd Interviews*. Judd Foundation and David Zwirner Books, 2019.

Judd, Flavin, and Caitlin Murray, eds. *Donald Judd Writings*. Judd Foundation and David Zwirner Books, 2016.

Judd, Rainer. "Interview: Rainer Judd, Artist, Actor, Filmmaker, and President of Judd Foundation." Interview by Georgia Bobley. *Guest of a Guest*, March 28, 2012. https://guestofaguest.com/interview/interview-rainer-judd-artist-actor-filmmaker-and-president-of-the-judd-foundation.

Krauss, Rosalind E. "Allusion and Illusion in Donald Judd." *Artforum* (May 1966): 24–26. https://www.artforum.com/features/allusion-and-illusion-in-donald-judd-213725/.

Krauss, Rosalind E. *Perpetual Inventory*. MIT Press, 2010.

Krauss, Rosalind E. "Sculpture in the Expanded Field." *October* 8 (1979): 30–44.

Kuo, Michelle. "Industrial Revolution: The History of Fabrication." *Artforum* (October 2007): 306–15.

La Brasca, Jana. "The Paradox of Permanence." *Public Art Dialogue* 14, no. 1 (2024): 61–83.

Landmarks Preservation Committee, Harmon H. Goldstone, Chairman. *SoHo–Cast Iron Historic District Report*. City of New York, 1973.

Lee, Pamela M. *Chronophobia: On Time in the Art of the 1960s*. MIT Press, 2006.

Lévi-Strauss, Claude. *Wild Thought*. Translated by Jeffrey Mehlman and John Leavitt. University of Chicago Press, 2021.

Lippard, Lucy R. "Land Art in the Rearview Mirror." In *Art in the Landscape*, edited by Marianne Stockebrand. Chinati Foundation/La Fundación Chinati, 2000.

Lugones, María. "Hablando cara a cara/Speaking Face to Face: An Exploration of Ethnocentric Racism." In *Making Face, Making Soul/Haciendo Caras: Creative and Critical Perspectives by Women of Color*, edited by Gloria Anzaldúa. Aunt Lute Books, 1990.

Lugones, María. *Pilgrimages/Peregrinajes: Theorizing Coalition Against Multiple Oppressions*. Rowman and Littlefield, 2003.

Maldonado-Torres, Nelson. *Against War: Views from the Underside of Modernity*. Duke University Press, 2008.

"Marfa: The Light and the Land." *Arts in Context*, Season 2, Episode 11. Austin KLRU, Public Broadcasting Service. Accessed August 28, 2025. https://www.pbs.org/video/arts-in-context-marfa-the-light-and-the-land/.

Martínez, Rubén. *Desert America: Boom and Bust in the New Old West*. Metropolitan Books, 2012.

McCoy, Richard. "No Preservatives: Preservation, Perfection, and Patina: Eleanora Nagy Discusses Conserving Judd's Art." *Art21 Magazine*, June 29, 2011. Accessed August 28, 2025. http://blog.art21.org/2011/06/29/no-preservatives-preservation-perfection-and-patina-eleanor-nagy-discusses-conserving-judds-art/#.VoLzcUvDL8E.

Mesa-Bains, Amalia. "Domesticana: The Sensibility of Chicana Rasquache." *Aztlán: A Journal of Chicano Studies* 24, no. 2 (1999): 157–67.

Meyer, James. *Minimalism: Art and Polemics in the Sixties*. Yale University Press, 2001.

Mignolo, Walter. *Local Histories/Global Designs: Coloniality, Subaltern Knowledges, and Border Thinking*. Princeton University Press, 2000.

Mignolo, Walter, and Rolando Vázquez. "Decolonial AestheSis: Colonial Wounds/Decolonial Healings." Accessed August 28, 2025. http://socialtextjournal.org/periscope_article/decolonial-aesthesis-colonial-wounds decolonial-healings/#sthash.ZZcleafY.dpuf.

Miner, Josie. "8 Untitled Works, Marfa Texas." *A Magazine Curated by Proenza Schouler* 9 (2009): 46–55.

Minter, Joe. *To You Through Me: The Beginning of a Link of a Journey of 400 Years*. Institute 193/Tinwood, 2019.

Nagy, Eleanora E., Karlis Adamsons, and Kate Moomaw. "Disfiguring Organic Residues on Industrially Produced Sheet Metal Coupons Simulating Copper and Brass Works of Art by Donald Judd: Attenuated Total Reflectance Fourier Transform Infrared Spectroscopy Analysis and Treatment Recommendations." *Studies in Conservation* 58, no. 3 (2013): 245–55.

Noriega, Chon A. "The Dissension of Other Things." In *The Chicano Studies Reader: An Anthology of Aztlán, 1970–2010*, edited by Chon A. Noriega, Eric Avila, Karen Mary Davalos, Chela Sandoval, and Rafael Pérez-Torres. UCLA Chicano Studies Research Center Press, 2010.

Pérez, Emma. *The Decolonial Imaginary: Writing Chicanas into History*. Indiana University Press, 1999.

Pérez, Laura E. *Chicana Art: The Politics of Spiritual and Aesthetic Altarities*. Duke University Press, 2007.

Pérez, Laura. "El Desorden, Nationalism, and Chicana/o Aesthetics." In *Between Woman and Nation: Nationalisms, Transnational Feminisms, and the State*, edited by Caren Kaplan, Norma Alarcón, and Minoo Moallem. Duke University Press, 1999.

Pérez, Laura E. *Eros Ideologies: Writings on Art, Spirituality, and the Decolonial*. Duke University Press, 2019.

Pérez, Laura E. "Hybrid Spiritualities and Chicana Altar-Based Art: The Work of Amalia Mesa-Bains." In Espinosa and García, *Mexican American Religions*.

Reading, Peter. *Marfan*. Cromwell Press, 2000.
Reynolds, Graham. *A Concise History of Watercolours*. Thames and Hudson, 1971.
Robbins, Christa Noel. "The Sensibility of Michael Fried." *Criticism* 60, no. 4 (2018): 429–54.
Rojas, James T. "The Enacted Environment of East Los Angeles." *Places: A Quarterly Journal of Environmental Design* 8, no. 3 (1993): 42–53.
Romero Cash, Marie. *Santos: Enduring Images of Northern New Mexican Village Churches*. University Press of Colorado, 2003.
Salgado Halpern, Rosario. "Virgin Mary Image Appears in Marfa." *Big Bend Sentinel*, November 6, 1997.
Salseda, Rose G. "The New Wave of Identity Politics: Juan Capistran's *White Minority*." *American Art* 28, no. 1 (2014): 24–31.
Sanchez-Tranquilino, Marcos, and John Tagg. "The Pachuco's Flayed Hide: The Museum, Identity, and Buenas Garras." In Griswold del Castillo et al., CARA.
Shannon, Joshua. *The Disappearance of Objects: New York and the Rise of the Postmodern City*. Yale University Press, 2009.
Sheehy, Colleen J. *The Flamingo in the Garden: American Yard Art and the Vernacular Landscape*. Garland, 1998.
Siegel, Amie. CATALOGUE. Inventory Press, 2014.
Stockebrand, Marianne. *CHINATI: The Vision of Donald Judd*. Chinati Foundation/La Fundación Chinati, 2010.
Stockebrand, Marianne. *The Making of Two Works: Donald Judd's Installations at the Chinati Foundation*. Translated by Fiona Elliott. Chinati Foundation/La Fundación Chinati, 2004.
Taylor, Lonn. *Texas People, Texas Places: More Musings of the Rambling Boy*. TCU Press, 2014.
Tolleson, Maxwell. "The Museum After Minimalism: The Chinati Foundation, 1978–Present." PhD diss., University of California, Los Angeles, 2023.
Turner, Kay. *Beautiful Necessity: The Art and Meaning of Women's Altars*. Thames and Hudson, 1999.
Turner, Victor. *The Ritual Process: Structure and Anti-Structure*. Cornell University Press, 1969.
van Ryzin, Jeanne Claire. "A Little Take on Marfa's Culture Clash." *Austin American-Statesmen*, October 20, 2011.
Venegas, Daniel. *Las aventuras de Don Chipote, o, cuando los pericos mamen*. El Heraldo de México, 1928.
Vitiello, Stephen. *Listening to Donald Judd*. Sub Rosa, 2007. CD.
Williams, Tom. "Lipstick Ascending: Claes Oldenburg in New Haven in 1969." *Grey Room* 31 (Spring 2008): 117–38.

Ybarra-Frausto, Tomás. "Rasquachismo: A Chicano Sensibility." In Griswold del Castillo, et al., CARA.
Zukowski, Karen. *Furnishings Investigation of 101 Spring Street*. Judd Foundation, 2011.

Index

Note: Page numbers in *italics* refer to figures.